MONTH
OF THE
FREEZING
MOON

MONTH
OF THE
FREEZING
MOON

The Sand Creek Massacre
November 1864

DUANE SCHULTZ

ST. MARTIN'S PRESS
New York

Design by Kathryn Parise

Library of Congress Cataloging-in-Publication Data

Schultz, Duane P.
    Month of the Freezing Moon/Duane Schultz.
        p.   cm.
    "A Thomas Dunne book."
    ISBN 0-312-04351-1
    1. Sand Creek Massacre, Colo., 1864.   I. Title.
E83.863.S38   1990
973.7—dc20   89-77673
                                                          CIP

First Edition

10   9   8   7   6   5   4   3   2   1

To Sydney Ellen

Contents

Acknowledgments   ix

1. A Glorious Victory   1

2. You Will All Die Off   11

3. A Universal Triumph   31

4. A Soldier in God's War   45

5. The Foul Conspiracy   59

6. The Indians Are Coming!   71

7. Kill and Scalp All   85

8. What Shall I Do with the *Third*?   97

9. Assurances of Safety   109

10. Take No Prisoners   125

11. All This Country Is Ruined   143

12. A Foul and Dastardly Massacre   157

13. The Deliberate Judgment of History   175

14. The Buffalo Will Not Last Forever   183

Epilogue: You and Your Whole Command
Will Be Killed   207

Chapter Notes   209

Bibliography   217

Index   221

Acknowledgments

Every book requires the cooperation and collaboration of many people to transform an idea into printed pages. Among those who helped were the archivists of the State Historical Society of Colorado and the Kansas State Historical Society. At the Clearwater (Florida) Public Library, the able staff responded to my many interlibrary loan requests with prompt and cheerful attention. I am grateful to Anita Diamant, my literary agent, for her support and advice, and to Thomas Dunne, my editor at St. Martin's Press, for his continued encouragement through six books over the last twelve years. I would also like to thank Thomas Olofson for his keen and capable attention to all the details of publication, and Doris Borowsky for her outstanding jacket design.

D.S.

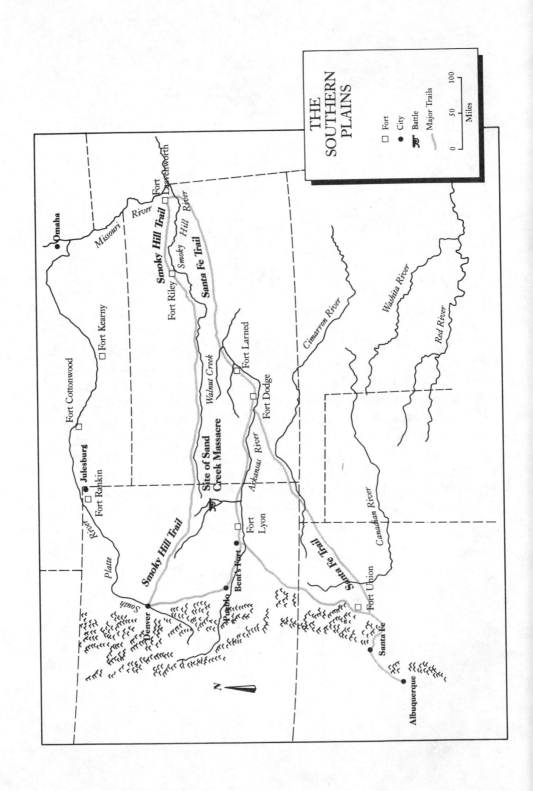

THE
SOUTHERN
PLAINS

□ Fort
● City
⚔ Battle
Major Trails

0   50   100
Miles

Omaha

Missouri River

Fort Leavenworth

Smoky Hill Trail

Smoky Hill River

Santa Fe Trail

Fort Riley

Fort Kearny

Fort Larned

Walnut Creek

Cimarron River

Washita River

Red River

Fort Cottonwood

Fort Dodge

Julesburg

Fort Rankin

Site of Sand
Creek Massacre

Arkansas River

Platte River

South

Smoky Hill Trail

Fort Lyon

Bent's Fort

Canadian River

Santa Fe Trail

Denver

Pueblo

Fort Union

Santa Fe

Albuquerque

N

1

A Glorious Victory

TESTIMONY

QUESTION: Were there any acts of barbarity perpetrated there that came under your own observation?

ANSWER: Yes, sir. I saw the bodies of those lying there cut all to pieces, worse mutilated than any I ever saw before—the women all cut to pieces.

QUESTION: How cut?

ANSWER: With knives, scalped, their brains knocked out, children two or three months old—all ages lying there.

QUESTION: Did you see it done?

ANSWER: Yes, sir. I saw them fall.

QUESTION: Fall when they were killed?

ANSWER: Yes, sir.

QUESTION: Did you see them when they were mutilated?

ANSWER: Yes, sir.

QUESTION: By whom were they mutilated?

ANSWER: By the United States troops.

The Cheyenne called it *Hikomini*, the Month of the Freezing Moon. To them, it was the time of the Hard Face, when the leaves abandoned the trees, when the cold formed ice at the edges of the rivers, when a man could see the words he spoke coming from his mouth like little white clouds. It was the month when *Hoimaha*, the Winter Man, came from the north to tell the sun to back away because he was ready to bring cold all over the land.

To the white man, it was November, the twenty-ninth day, in the year 1864. The place was a barren, desolate sector of the Colorado Territory, where a range of hills altered the course of Sand Creek a full ninety degrees. In the bend stood cottonwood and willow trees, bare and sad in winter's grip. Ice had hardened the occasional puddle left in the creek bed.

TESTIMONY

They killed everything alive in the camp they could get at.

TESTIMONY

I did not see a body of man, woman, or child but was scalped, and in many instances their bodies were mutilated in the most horrible manner—men, women, and children—privates cut out and so forth.

The killing lasted seven hours from sunrise until mid-afternoon, and the odor of cordite lingered in the cold evening air—and the smell of death, too. At four o'clock, the troops listlessly formed a hollow square and picketed their horses safely in the center. The men were exhausted. They had marched all night and fought most of the day. The excitement of the battle was dissipating. At dusk, the sergeants roused the companies from a fitful sleep and the soldiers clustered around freshly lit campfires that cast warmth, dim light, and eerie, threatening shadows over the haunted landscape.

The Indian dead were strewn all around them, but the soldiers took no notice. Scalped and mutilated bodies were common sights for the people of the Plains; and besides, these were Indians. They deserved whatever they got.

TESTIMONY

I believe that was part of the understanding, that none should be spared.
I believe it is generally the understanding that you fight Indians in that way.

Ten miles to the north, the Indian survivors, carrying their wounded and dazed, stopped to spend the night in a ravine. The temperature was below freezing and few had brought any warm clothing, the attack having roused them from their sleep. They built fires and piled grass around the injured to keep them from freezing to death. They sat around the fires howling the long, slow, mournful wail of wolves, to let other survivors know where they were, to tell their families at the Smoky Hill camp that they were coming with news.

The commander of the United States troops, John Milton Chivington, was a giant of a man. Forty-three years old, he was still in his prime, six feet four and a half inches tall. He weighed 260 pounds and very little of it was fat. He had piercing black eyes, coarse reddish-brown hair, and a deep, bellowing voice that rattled the glass in church windows. Before he became a soldier, Chivington was a preacher, the militant hellfire and brimstone scourge of sinners and backsliders. Curiously, he had once been a social activist who fought passionately and bravely against the peculiar institution of slavery.

Two years before, in a heroic battle against the Confederates, Chivington had tasted fame and adulation. The man people called the "fighting parson" was no longer content with his lot. He turned from preaching for the glory of God and eternal salvation to reaching for the glory of J. M. Chivington and high political office; from a gospel of healing, love, and tolerance to a diatribe of hatred, bigotry, and killing, often appearing in the pulpit wearing twin revolvers.

To achieve his aims, however, Chivington needed another victory in battle, and now there was a different enemy—the Indians. It did not matter which tribe, or whether they were friendly or hostile, innocent or guilty.

TESTIMONY

This village were friendly Indians.

TESTIMONY

The aforesaid Indians were recognized as friendly by all parties of this post. Colonel J. M. Chivington, on his arrival at the post of Fort Lyon, was aware of the circumstances in regard to the Indians, from the fact that different officers remonstrated with him, and stated to him how these Indians were looked upon by the entire garrison; that notwithstanding these remonstrances, and in the face of all these facts, he committed the massacre aforementioned.

*   *   *

Chivington felt only exhilaration, no hint of fatigue, as the sun set on his day of victory. And what a triumph it was! He set forth the details in a dispatch to his commanding officer, Major General Samuel R. Curtis at Fort Leavenworth, Kansas.

> Headquarters District of Colorado
> In the field, Cheyenne County,
> South Bend of Big Sandy
> November 29, 1864
> In the last 10 days my command has marched 300 miles, 100 of which the snow was two feet deep. After a march of 40 miles last night I, at daylight this morning, attacked a Cheyenne village of 130 lodges, from 900 to 1,000 warriors strong; killed Chiefs Black Kettle, White Antelope, Knock Knee, and Little Robe, and between 400 and 500 other Indians, and captured as many ponies and mules. Our loss [was] 9 killed, 38 wounded. All did nobly. Think I will catch some more of them 80 miles [away], on Smoky Hill. Found white man's scalp, not more than three days old, in one of lodges.
> J. M. Chivington
> Colonel, Commanding,
> First District of Colorado
> and First Indian Expedition

It had been a glorious achievement. To surprise an Indian camp with so large a military force was a tactical accomplishment that had eluded nearly every Indian expedition in recent memory, with even West Pointers having been unable to do it. Now a preacher leading a regiment of volunteers—civilians who had signed up for one hundred days of service—had the audacity to attack a village of more than nine hundred warriors with a smaller force of seven hundred soldiers, and then kill as many as five hundred! No wonder the colonel was elated.

TESTIMONY

QUESTION: How many warriors were estimated in Colonel Chivington's report as having been in this Indian camp?
ANSWER: About 900.
QUESTION: How many were there?
ANSWER: About 200 warriors.

TESTIMONY

I am satisfied that there were not over 125 killed. About two thirds of those were women and children.

Chivington had been defeated in his bid for a seat in the U.S. Congress, but surely he would win the next time. And after that? Who could predict how far the hero of Sand Creek could go?

TESTIMONY

He thought he had done a brilliant thing which would make him a brigadier general. I think the expression was "that he thought that would put a star on his shoulder."

TESTIMONY

QUESTION: You refer to a conversation between Colonel Chivington and others after the fight, in regard to the success of the fight. What was that conversation?
ANSWER: That the fight was the most successful thing on record, that we had achieved a glorious victory.

Chivington sought to publicize the fight, to let the residents of Denver know as quickly as possible what he had done. He wrote a dispatch to William Byers, a friend and vocal supporter who was editor of Denver's *Rocky Mountain News.*

I have not time to give you a detailed history of our engagement of today, or to mention those officers and men who distinguished themselves in one of the most bloody battles ever fought on these plains. You will find enclosed the report of my surgeon-in-chief, which will bring to many anxious friends the sad fate of loved ones, who are and have been risking everything to avenge the horrid deeds of those savages we have so severely handled.

Chivington paused, recalling the rumblings and protests from some of his officers the day before the battle. Two had even refused to participate, saying they would not be responsible for attacking Indians who were under the protection of the American flag. They were weaklings and traitors as far as Chivington was concerned, Indian-lovers unworthy of the uniform of the United States Army. Still, they might cause problems. He needed to strike first before they had a chance to say anything. He had to make people believe that the Indians at Sand Creek were hostile savages, the ones who had been murdering white settlers over the past months.

> I will state for the consideration of gentlemen who are opposed to fighting these red scoundrels, that I was shown by chief surgeon the scalp of a white man taken from lodge of one of the chiefs, which could not have been more than two or three days taken, and I could mention many more things that show how these Indians that have been drawing government rations at Fort Lyon, are and have been acting.

Editor Byers acted immediately, publishing a front-page article in the next edition of the *Rocky Mountain News* to call attention to Chivington's heroism.

> Among the brilliant feats of arms in Indian warfare, the recent campaign of our Colorado volunteers will stand in history with few rivals . . . the exploit has few if any parallels, while the utter surprise of a large Indian village is unprecedented . . . all acquitted themselves well and Colorado soldiers have again covered themselves with glory.

Believing he had covered himself with enough glory, Chivington wisely chose not to pursue the more than two thousand Cheyenne and Sioux warriors camped at Smoky Hill. Instead, he marched his troops back to Denver, arriving on December 22. His welcome was tumultuous, even greater than two years before when he had returned from his victory over the Confederates. He paraded the troops through the streets of the city, brandishing a pole with a live eagle tied to it. The shouts and cheers for Chivington and his men—now called the Bloody Third—were overwhelming. John Milton Chivington had never known such a day.

TESTIMONY

> QUESTION: Did you hear any plans suggested by officers at Fort Lyon after the battle of Sand Creek for prosecuting Colonel Chivington for the part he had taken in the battle?
> ANSWER: I don't know that I heard any plan of prosecution. They all denounced him there.
> QUESTION: Did you hear any of the officers at Fort Lyon say that they

would prosecute Colonel Chivington for the part he had taken in the battle of Sand Creek?

ANSWER: I don't know that I heard them say they would do it. I heard them say that he ought to be prosecuted; and that, when the facts got to Washington, he was liable to be, or words to that effect.

The facts were relayed to Washington, all the way to the army chief of staff, Major General Henry H. Halleck, and he acted promptly.⌐ On January 11, 1865, three weeks after Chivington's victory parade, Halleck sent a telegram to General Curtis at Fort Leavenworth. ⌐

> Statements from respectable sources have been received here that the conduct of Colonel Chivington's command towards the friendly Indians have been a series of outrages calculated to make them all hostile. You will inquire into and report on this matter.

Word of the pending inquiry reached Denver soon after, when the *Rocky Mountain News* reprinted on page two an article from a Washington, D.C., newspaper. "Letters received from high officials in Colorado say that the Indians were killed after surrendering and that a large proportion of them were women and children." The article from the Washington newspaper did not call the event a victory, or even a battle. It spoke of "the affair" near Fort Lyon, Colorado, and went on to say that it would soon be the subject of a congressional investigation.

The majority of the residents of Denver were outraged. Saloons echoed with angry talk of going after those unnamed high officials in Colorado. Incensed citizens muttered about Indian-lovers back east who were safe, who did not have to worry about their scalps being taken, who had not seen the mutilated bodies of their friends and neighbors, or been under siege for months, isolated from the rest of the country by bands of marauding Indians. "Let 'em see their wives killed," one man said, "and those bureaucrats back east would sing a different tune."

Editor Byers conducted a passionate defense of his old friend Chivington and, by extension, of all the people of Denver. "It is unquestioned and undenied," he wrote in an editorial in the *Rocky Mountain News*, "that the site of the Sand Creek Battle was the rendezvous of the thieving and marauding bands of savages who roamed over this country last summer and fall."

Elizabeth Tallman, a twenty-three-year-old pioneer from New York whose husband was a soldier at Sand Creek, recalled her own feelings many years later. "Had you been living at that time, as we were," she said, "in a constant state of fear and anxiety, almost daily seeing the bodies of friends or acquaintances that had been mutilated by the Indians, you would have found no censure in your heart for Colonel Chivington's act."

But there was no stopping the inquiry. Spurred by a wave of revulsion that swept over the people in the east, events in Washington moved forward, and with unusual speed, fueled also, perhaps, by guilt. A correspondent for the New York *Tribune* suggested:

> Perhaps the honorable congressmen are so disturbed because they feel themselves to be as guilty as are the perpetrators of the massacre. After all, did not the national government give Arapaho and Cheyenne land to the settlers? Were not the congressmen partners in depriving the proud tribes of their just rights and ancestral holdings? The mantle of guilt rests not alone upon Colonel Chivington and his men. It also falls upon the shoulders of the solons in Washington who now, no doubt, feel the need to purge themselves by probing deeply into the hideous affair at Sand Creek.

The probe began in mid-January, when the U.S. House of Representatives directed its Committee on the Conduct of the War to inquire into and report the facts on the events at Sand Creek. Only four days later, testimony and affidavits, all denouncing the attack, were collected at Fort Lyon and transmitted to Washington. In mid-March, the congressional committee took testimony in Washington from Governor John Evans of Colorado Territory, a friend of Chivington's and himself at least partly responsible for the fate of the Indians. Additional sworn statements were gathered in Denver, including one from Chivington in response to written questions from Congress.

On March 3, a second investigation opened in the capital, this one overseen by a special joint committee of both houses of Congress established originally to study the treatment of Indians throughout the western territories. A third inquiry was taking place in Denver, where a special commission of the U.S. Army held seventy-six days of hearings from February 12 to May 30. The army investigation was the most dramatic because it provided an arena for Colonel Chivington to confront his accusers. It also led to another bloody tragedy.

There would be no more days of glory for Chivington. His name would go down in history, but not as he had hoped. It would remain indelibly linked with his actions at Sand Creek in the Month of the Freezing Moon.

The pipe had been made from the shank bone of an antelope, the marrow punched out and one end filed down and made smooth. Tobacco mixed with a small amount of buffalo grease was tamped in the other end and lit with the flame of a burning stick. The pipe was passed to each chief of the Cheyenne and Sioux tribes. It was December 30, 1864, one month after the killings at Sand Creek, and the chiefs were gathered at Smoky Hill. Two of them were survivors of that massacre.

Each man observed the ritual of passing the pipe, being careful to avoid touching anything with its stem. To do so would bring bad luck. As each chief took the pipe, he pointed its stem to the sky to pay homage to their principal god, *Heammawihio,* then to the earth to the god living under the ground, *Akh tun 'o Wihio.* The stem was pointed to the east, where the sun rises; to the south, where the cold wind goes; to the west, where the sun goes over; and finally to the north, from where the cold wind comes.

Each man recited the same words as he smoked: "Spirit above, smoke. Earth, smoke. Four cardinal points, smoke." The chiefs offered their prayers, and this day the prayers were alike. Each asked that he not be killed or wounded and that he might strike many blows on his enemies. They were smoking the war pipe. It was passed to the Cheyenne chief Leg-in-the-Water. "But what do we have to live for?" he asked. The others nodded their heads as he spoke, giving voice to their own unhappy thoughts.

"The white man has taken our country, killed our game, was not satisfied with that, but killed our wives and children. Now no peace. We have now raised the battle-axe until death."

The harvest of Sand Creek was about to be reaped.

2

You Will All Die Off

He lived four lifetimes. Babies were born, grew old and died, and still this wise man lived. Every summer, he looked young, but when the grass dried up in the fall, he began to look older, and by winter, he walked with his back bent and he became a feeble old man. Yet every spring, he was young once again. The Cheyenne called him Sweet Medicine, and he foretold the doom of his people in a legend passed down from one generation to the next.* People with white skin, people no Cheyenne had ever seen, would spread misfortune and calamity.

"Listen to me carefully," said Sweet Medicine to the Cheyenne gathered in his lodge shortly before his death. "Listen to me carefully," he said four times.

"Our great-grandfather spoke thus to me, repeating it four times. He said to me that he made us, but he also made others. There are all kinds of people on earth that you will meet some day, toward the sunrise, by a big river. Some are black, but some day you will meet a people who are white—good-looking people, with light hair and white skin."

"Shall we know them when we meet them?" asked one of those seated around him.

"Yes," Sweet Medicine said, "you will know them, for they will have

<hr>

*Sweet Medicine is the best known of the Cheyenne folk heroes. There are many versions of his story. This one is drawn from the work of George Bird Grinnell, the noted anthropologist and authority on Cheyenne history and life. See Grinnell, *The Cheyenne Indians*, Vol. II, pp. 345–381.

long hair on their faces and will look differently from you. They will wear things different from you. You will talk with them. They will give you shiny things which flash the light and show you your own image, and something that looks like sand that will taste very sweet. They will wear what I have spoken of, but it will be of all colors, pretty. Perhaps they will not listen to what you say to them, but you will listen to what they say to you. They will be people who do not get tired but who will keep pushing forward. They will try always to give you things, but do not take them.

"At last I think that you will take the things that they offer you, and this will bring sickness to you. These people do not follow the way of our great-grandfather. They will travel everywhere, looking for [a certain] stone which our great-grandfather put on the earth."

The men in the lodge exchanged glances, confused and dismayed by what they heard. Sweet Medicine continued to speak in a faint, weak voice. The old man had seen many things and had much more to tell them.

"Buffalo and all animals were given you by our great-grandfather, but these people will come in and will begin to kill off these animals. They will use a different thing to kill animals from what we use, something that makes a noise and sends a little round stone to kill.

"Something [else] will be given to you, which, if you drink it, will make you crazy.

"There will be many of these people, so many that you cannot stand before them. On the rivers you will see things go up and down, and in these things will be these people, and there will be things moving over dry land in which these people will be.

"Another animal will come, but it will not be like the buffalo. It will have long heavy hair on its neck and a long heavy tail which drags on the ground. When these animals come, you will catch them, and you will get on their backs and they will carry you from place to place. You will become great travelers. If you see a place a long way off, you will want to get to it, so at last you will get on these animals. From that time you will act very foolishly. You will know nothing.

"These people will not listen to what you say. What they are going to do they will do. You people will change. In the end of your life in those days you will not get up early in the morning, you will never know when the day comes, you will lie in bed, you will have disease and will die suddenly. You will all die off.

"They will try to teach you their way of living. If you give up to them your children, those that they take away will never know anything. They will try to change you from your way of living to theirs and they will keep at what they try to do. They will work with their hands. They will tear up the earth, and at last you will do it with them. When you do, you will become crazy, and will forget all that I am now teaching you."

Sweet Medicine died, but the tale he spun, the awful prophecy he left as his legacy, was told anew to each generation until it all came true.

The Cheyenne were warriors from the earliest time, fierce, proud, and free. "Their fighting spirit was encouraged. In no way could a young man gain so much credit as by the exhibition of courage. Boys and youth were trained to feel that the most important thing in life was to be brave; that death was not a thing to be avoided; that, in fact, it was better for a man to be killed while in his full vigor rather than to wait until his prime was past, his powers were failing, and he could no longer achieve those feats which to all seemed so desirable. . . . How much better, therefore, to struggle and fight, and be brave and accomplish great things, to receive the respect and applause of everyone in the camp, and finally to die gloriously at the hands of the enemy."

Cheyenne boys were taught to fight and die gloriously, and their goal was to become the bravest of warriors. The Cheyenne focused so intently on courage in battle that they took greater risks than Indians from other nations, and, consequently, were feared by other tribes. They also lost more warriors, in proportion to their numbers.

If it was a young man's destiny to be killed, he wanted it to happen on the broad open plains, where his people could witness the act. When he died in battle, his friends would wrap him in his buffalo robe and leave him on the ground. No Cheyenne warrior wished to be buried, to be covered over with earth. It was a fine death to lie on the prairie where the animals and birds would consume the flesh and scatter the bones as far as a man might ride in a day. That was what it meant to be at one with the earth.

The Cheyenne fought for the joy of combat and to gain the approval of others. War was a game, a great hunt, and the young braves went to war with pleasure. To enjoy life fully, to feel satisfied, they needed someone to fight, and in their wanderings across the plains, it was seldom difficult to find strangers to attack. To the Cheyenne, anyone who was not of their own tribe was an enemy.

The instant a party of braves spotted a group of other Indians, they prepared for the attack, stripping off extra clothing and abandoning anything they happened to be carrying. They often threw off their saddles, as well. With much laughter and chatter, they raced in pursuit of the strangers, and if they eventually recognized them as friends, they were disappointed, as though a long-anticipated party suddenly had been canceled.

The noblest of the Cheyenne warriors belonged to the Dog Soldiers, one of six soldier bands in the tribe. Wherever the Cheyenne made camp, the Dog Soldiers established a place of their own within the larger circle of lodges. Many of them were half Sioux and sometimes were called Cheyenne Sioux. The Dog Soldiers wore a distinctive headdress: bonnets of raven feathers standing upright with tiny red down feathers glued to the tips. All the Cheyenne lived by a code of rules, but the Dog Soldiers were the most disciplined. They were also the most likely to go to war, regardless of the chance of success. It was the Dog Soldiers who would continue to make war on the whites, long after the rest of the Cheyenne accepted their fate. There had been no Dog Soldier warriors at Sand Creek.

Every Cheyenne warrior hoped for the opportunity to display his courage. Killing an enemy, however, was not a particularly noteworthy act. Although it reduced the size of the party being fought, the killing itself was not considered important. Neither was the taking of a scalp, which was looked upon as nothing more than a trophy, a way of keeping score, something to display to one's friends. Usually, a piece of scalp no larger than a silver dollar was cut out, but since the skin was fresh, it tended to stretch. Scalps were tied to war clothing—as fringe on shirts and leggings—or to bridles when riding into battle.

The greatest feat of bravery a Cheyenne could perform was to touch a foe with a stick, bow, whip, or the open palm of his hand. When a warrior touched his enemy, he shouted, "Ah haih! I am the first." The next man to touch him shouted, "I am the second," and so on. To be the first to touch an adversary immediately after killing him was a valiant deed—because the enemy might be only feigning death and waiting to strike back—but a braver deed was to touch the enemy who was unhurt and to let him live. This was the ultimate act of courage in the life of a Cheyenne warrior, to count coup on an enemy (coup being the French word for blow or strike). An Indian brave who could display no coup was considered worthless.

When two lines of warriors from opposing tribes faced one another, one brave might ride out in front and charge directly through the enemy line, touching one of his opponents, wheel around, and come back through the line to rejoin his side. In such a case, it was easy to see who had counted coup on an enemy, but in the chaos of battle, it was not always clear who had been successful. Many disputes about counting coup arose, which had to be settled around a campfire of buffalo chips. A pipe was placed on the ground next to the fire and those who claimed coups approached the fire, touched the pipe, and presented their case. If the matter could not be resolved by questioning those who had participated in the fight, the claimant could, if he chose, make a formal oath over a painted buffalo skull and four arrows. The warrior stood over the objects, raised his arms to the sky, and said, "Spiritual powers, listen to me." He laid hands on the arrows and the skull. "I touched him. If I tell I lie, I hope that I may be shot far off."

If a brave made a false claim, it was considered certain that he or a member of his family would die. No one took the oath or its consequences lightly. Claiming a coup was the highest honor a Cheyenne brave could achieve, but even for that, it was not worth tempting the spirits by telling a lie to the sacred objects.

Scalping might be just a way of keeping score, but mutilation was also practiced out of tradition and habit. It was not uncommon for a Cheyenne warrior to cut off the arms of an enemy and preserve the severed limbs as trophies. Strangers captured by the Cheyenne faced a gruesome fate. Captives were stripped and spread-eagled over anthills, their hands and feet lashed to pegs driven deep into the ground. There they were abandoned, to go blind from staring at the sun, insane from hunger and thirst, and eaten by ants and wild animals. Sometimes the Indians heaped twigs and branches atop their victims and burned them alive.

One Cheyenne brave recalled the killing of an old Shoshone man. "We cut off his hands, his feet, his head. We ripped open his breast and his belly. I stood there and looked at his heart and his liver. We tore down the lodge, built a bonfire on it and its contents and piled the remnants of the dead body upon this bonfire. We stayed there until nothing was left but ashes and coals."

A captured woman became the common property of the war party, to be raped by all until they returned to camp, where she would belong exclusively to the man who first seized her. Treated as a slave, she would often be beaten and mutilated, eventually to be killed or traded into slavery with another tribe.

Cheyenne women could be as vicious as their men. A U.S. Army captain described how after a battle Cheyenne squaws helped "scalp and torture the wounded, shooting arrows into their bodies and cutting off fingers and toes, even when they were alive."

The Cheyenne lived and fought fiercely long before the coming of the whites. Richens Lacy Wootton, a trapper and hunter known as "Uncle Dick" and popular among the Plains Indians, observed that "before there were whites to rob and plunder and steal from, the [Indians] robbed and stole from each other. Before there were white men in the country to kill, they killed each other. Before there were white women and children to scalp and mutilate and torture, the Indians scalped and mutilated and tortured the women and children of their enemies of their own race. They made slaves of each other when there were no palefaces to be captured and sold or held for ransom, and before they commenced lying in ambush along the trails of the white man to murder unwary travelers, the Indians of one tribe would set the same sort of death traps for the Indians of another tribe."

The world of the Cheyenne and of all the other Indian nations of the Plains changed when one of Sweet Medicine's predictions came true. "Another animal will come," the legend said, "but it will not be like the buffalo." It would come from the south and have long hair on its neck, and the Cheyenne would catch it, mount it, and ride it. Horses had been brought from Mexico with the expeditions of the Spanish explorers Francisco Vásquez Coronado and Hernando de Soto in the sixteenth century. Some escaped and multiplied quickly in a land with ample food and no natural predators. As early as 1680, the Pawnee tribes to the east began to capture and tame the horses, and by the latter part of the eighteenth century, so did the Indians of the Plains.

Before the arrival of horses, the Cheyenne had few possessions. They accumulated food, clothing, dogs, and weapons of stone and wood, the bare essentials of survival. They were limited to what they could carry on their backs or what the dogs could pull in travois. They could not chase the running buffalo and antelope or follow them on their seasonal migrations. The horse could carry a heavy load, however, and it gave the rider speed and the ability to travel great distances. It transformed the Cheyenne into a nomadic people, free to travel with the great buffalo herds on which they depended for so many of the necessities of life.

The horse also provided a new reason for waging war. There were two easy ways to obtain horses—capture those running wild or steal them from other tribes. Horses quickly assumed great value and became objects worth fighting for, and some Cheyenne turned to war for profit rather than for fun, for the sole purpose of acquiring horses. These warriors no longer fought for personal satisfaction or to count coup on their enemies, yet they earned honorable reputations for specializing in capturing horses. The most successful of this new breed of Cheyenne warrior was Old Yellow Wolf. He was killed at Sand Creek, on foot.

The world of the Cheyenne was transformed even more when, as Sweet Medicine foretold, they met the bearded white-skinned people. According to Cheyenne lore, the first white man arrived "long ago," when a starving traveler wandered into one of their camps. Despite the ancient prophecy, the Indians showed compassion rather than concern and took him in. He was only one man, near death. What harm could he bring to the mighty Cheyenne?

They patiently nursed him back to health and he remained with them long enough to learn their language and their ways. He said he had come in a boat and that the others with him had drowned. He came from the east, toward the sunrise, just as Sweet Medicine had known.

"Some day I will come back," he told them as he departed, "and will bring you things that will be useful to you."

One day a couple of years later, a noise like thunder resounded through the camp. The man had returned, with companions, and their long sticks had made the noise. These were the first rifles the Indians had ever seen, but they knew about them from Sweet Medicine.

The white men brought gifts—a few precious guns, steel knives, pieces of flint and sheet iron. The Cheyenne gave them pelts and furs in return, valuable goods the traders could sell in the east. The Cheyenne thought the white man's gifts were good; no harm could come of accepting them. With the flint they could start fires more quickly and easily than by rubbing sticks together. From the sheet iron they could fashion arrowheads far superior to theirs of stone and bone. The metal would penetrate a buffalo hide more deeply. The Cheyenne soon discarded their old arrowheads. They wanted more of the white man's things.

That first white man may have been a Spaniard, a Mexican, or a French Canadian. By the early 1700s, tribal histories show contact with a number of French traders and trappers. These visitors were friendly and always brought worthwhile gifts. Perhaps Sweet Medicine had been wrong. The braves refrained from attacking the traders because that might discourage others from coming with presents.

As the years passed, more whites came, bearing jewelry, sparkling glass beads, mirrors, sheet iron, and guns. They learned the Cheyenne language and customs, ate the Indians' food and smoked their pipes.

There was no fighting. They did not want the Cheyenne lands or the buffalo and they did not threaten the Indians in any way.

One early trader became as close to the Cheyenne people as any white man could, and in the process he made a fortune. He was Colonel William Bent; the title was an honorary one bestowed when he guided a U.S. Army regiment across the plains to New Mexico. The first permanent white settler in what became the Colorado Territory, Bent was a true friend to the Cheyenne.

Bent arrived in 1824 and nine years later built a trading post on the site of what is now the city of Pueblo, New Mexico. He constructed it like a fort, with adobe brick walls three feet thick and fourteen feet high. Bent's Fort, as it came to be called, had round towers at two corners that were thirty feet high and ten feet in diameter, which offered a broad field of fire for musket and cannon. A square watchtower rose over the main gate, topped by a belfry. A guard was always on duty, sweeping the horizon with a long, powerful telescope.

The fort was never attacked and the reason for that may not have been so much its defenses as the character of William Bent himself. "By his fair and open dealings, by his fearless conduct, and by his love of justice, William Bent soon won the respect and confidence of the Indians."

Two years after he built the trading post, Bent married the daughter of a Cheyenne chief and lived with her people a portion of each year, adopting their way of living. Of the several Indian tribes who traded at his post, only the Cheyenne were given free run of the buildings.

Some one hundred men worked at Bent's Fort—traders, trappers, clerks, hunters, and laborers—and it became not only a trading center for the Indians but also a hotel and way station for explorers, trappers, army units, and, in time, wagon trains of emigrants from the east. Whatever a traveler might need, Bent usually could supply it. The Indians traded buffalo robes along with beaver and other animal skins for trinkets, blankets, guns, flour, sugar, and coffee. For a couple of decades, the annual volume of trade at Bent's Fort was surpassed by only one other company—the American Fur Company of John Jacob Astor.

Every April, Bent would head east with up to thirty wagons weighted down with hides, on a three-month trek to St. Louis to sell his wares. He returned with the wagons laden with goods to stock the shelves of his trading post. At Christmas and Independence Day, he gave grand balls and dances, inviting both Indians and whites. In 1849, when the U.S. government turned down his offer to sell them the post to use as an army fortress, he blew it up and built a new one downstream, near where the Cheyenne made their winter camp.

Bent made considerable money from dealing with the Cheyenne, but he treated them honorably and fairly. The Cheyenne could safely ignore Sweet Medicine's warning with regard to William Bent, but not all traders had his scruples. Many took advantage of the Indians by offering them something Bent never had—whiskey.

In 1832, a trader named John Gannt constructed a trading post on the Arkansas River in the southern Colorado region and introduced the Plains Indians to hard liquor. "Something will be given to you, which, if you drink it, will make you crazy," Sweet Medicine had said. The Indians did not like the taste at first, so Gannt mixed the spirits with sugar, "something that looks like sand that will taste very sweet."

It worked. The Indians clamored for more, trading nearly all their possessions for the drink—valuable furs and skins, armloads of blankets, horses and weapons, even their clothing, and then their wives and children. The Reverend Moses Merrill, a missionary, was told by some traders that fully half of all the furs they obtained from the Plains Indians were paid for with whiskey, a raw alcohol watered down four parts to one. The traders also told Merrill that the Cheyenne were "wholly averse to drinking whiskey [only] five years ago; now they are a tribe of drunkards."

The settlers also brought their diseases, illnesses the Indians had never known. They had no immunity to whooping cough, measles, or even diarrhea. A cholera epidemic in 1849 killed almost half of the Cheyenne. It was just as Sweet Medicine had warned. "You will have disease and will die suddenly. You will all die off."

Some of the Cheyenne were visiting a Kiowa camp on the Canadian River in New Mexico Territory when the cholera began to spread. A Kiowa dancer collapsed. An Osage sitting on the ground watching the dance fell over dead. The Cheyenne chief rounded up his people, exhorting them to leave immediately. They fled north on horseback through the night and set up camp the next morning along the Cimarron River, believing they were safe because they had ridden so far. However, they carried the disease with them and soon began to die. Little Old Man, a Cheyenne warrior, put on his war clothes, mounted his horse, and charged through the camp with his lance at the ready.

"If I could see this thing," he shouted, "if I knew where it came from, I would go there and fight it!"

He clutched his stomach and doubled over in pain. As he fell from his horse, his wife ran to him, to cradle his head in her arms. He was dead.

The Cheyenne fled north once more in terror. All day and night they rode until they met another band of Cheyenne heading south. They, too, were fleeing the sickness. There was no escaping the white man's scourge.

Before long, there was no escaping the white man's presence. "They will keep coming," Sweet Medicine had decreed. "There will be many of these people, so many that you cannot stand before them." No longer were the Indians owners of the plains, free to roam wherever they pleased. No longer were the grass and the buffalo so plentiful. New kinds of white-skinned people invaded the prairies in great numbers.

Wagon trains of emigrants making their way west rutted deep trails across the landscape, on the Oregon Trail in the north and the Santa Fe Trail in the south. Where previously, small groups of whites had come to visit and smoke pipes and bring gifts, now thousands were crossing the land.

It began on a warm May morning in 1841, when a tiny caravan of ten wagons, their white canvas covers gleaming like sails in the sun, embarked from St. Joseph, Missouri, for Oregon and California, with sixty-nine men, women, and children. "It was a daring experiment. There was no evidence the continent could be crossed by wagon, and there was a great deal of evidence that it could not."

The journey took five months, and the travelers wrote to family and friends back east about their adventures and the bright new land they had found. Others followed. In the summer of 1843, a thousand people set out in two hundred wagons. The Indians watched them come "creeping up the North Platte valley like slow white worms eating their way along, eating up the grass and the game and the firewood, and leaving a bare, dusty track behind them." The wagons carried tools for plowing and fencing and building, tools for tearing up the earth and closing off the land.

The people in the wagons were not like the traders. "If the traders occasionally had been hard to like, these people were impossible. They were greedy and stingy both. They took the grass and wood and used the good camping places, but they gave no gifts in return. In fact, if an Indian should approach them, and make the signs for eating and smoking, they would hurry on, pretending not to see him. Or they would shame him by driving him away with shouting and guns."

In 1849, gold was discovered in California. Was this the stone Sweet Medicine said the white man would seek? The stream of emigrants became a torrent. In that one year, 77,000 forty-niners crossed the Plains territories on their way to California. The next seven years brought over a quarter of a million more. In 1858, gold was discovered at Cherry Creek in Colorado and in no more time than it took fall to turn to winter, a settlement, and then a town, sprang up. It was called Denver.

No longer were the wagons simply passing through the Cheyenne lands. Now the people from the east began to occupy them. Ranchers came and staked out huge tracts. Soldiers came and built forts. Stagecoach companies built way stations every ten to twelve miles. Huge trains of freight wagons rumbled over the grasslands, marking out the Smoky Hill Trail, a road straight through the heart of the Cheyenne and Arapaho lands.

"They will keep coming, coming," Sweet Medicine had said.

The white man not only took the land, he also spoiled it. Although the various Indian tribes had not always lived peacefully with one another, they had formed and maintained a delicate and harmonious balance with the land. They took from it only enough for their needs, without disturbing the natural order.

Wooden Leg, a Cheyenne brave who would fight Custer at the Little Big Horn, described the Indian beliefs. "It is wrong to tear loose from its place on the earth anything that may be growing there. It may be cut off, but it should not be uprooted. The trees and the grass have spirits. Whatever one of such growths may be destroyed by some good Indian, his act is done in sadness and with a prayer for forgiveness because of his necessities, the same as we were taught to do in killing animals for food or skins."

The white settlers, by contrast, shattered the region's ecological balance, felling great stands of timber, scattering the buffalo herds, fencing off the prairies, diverting rivers and streams. Horses, oxen, mules, and cattle were allowed to strip the grassy fields. Before long, no buffalo could be found within two hundred miles of the main routes west.

Uncle Dick Wootton, the trapper, recalled that just a few years before, buffalo could be counted in the millions. "I have seen the plains black with them, and it would actually look as though the prairies themselves were on the move. It never occurred to me then that I should live long enough to see all the buffalo killed off."

Thus it went—the land, food, independence, and pride, taken from the Indians in less than the span of a single lifetime. Bitterness and hatred grew apace with each new Conestoga wagon, each corral and fence post, and each wooden building added to the streets of the white man's camp at Denver.

William Bent, newly appointed government agent to the Cheyenne and Arapaho tribes, issued a warning in October 1850 to the Commissioner of Indian Affairs in Washington. "A smothered passion for revenge agitates these Indians, perpetually fomented by the failure of food, the encircling encroachments of the white population, and the exasperating sense of decay and impending extinction with which they are surrounded. A desperate war of starvation and extinction is imminent and inevitable, unless prompt measure shall prevent it."

Nothing would prevent it, however. Most Americans agreed with John L. O'Sullivan, editor of the New York *Morning News*, that it was our "manifest destiny to overspread and possess the whole continent which Providence has given us for the great experiment of liberty."

For all its expanse, the new territories were still not large enough to permit the Indians—who, as one army wife put it, were "neither Christian nor white"—to coexist with the settlers. Something had to be done. The Indians were occupying too much valuable land and their presence frightened the emigrants. They no longer could be allowed to continue their wandering but would have to be confined to designated areas. Relations needed to be formalized and documented, as if the Indians were a sovereign nation. Treaties would have to be made so that each side, particularly the Indian side, knew its place and stayed within its boundaries.

This approach was based on a false premise held by the government in Washington; namely, that the leaders of the numerous tribes of Plains Indians possessed the same kind of absolute authority over their people as European monarchs. However, the various Indian chiefs had no such authority to dictate, no power to compel, no mandate to force all the members of their tribes to conform to their wishes. The chiefs could advise, but if the Dog Soldiers or the other warrior bands chose a different path, one that violated an agreement, there was little a peace chief could do to stop them. The U.S. leaders failed to appreciate this and they relied on treaties that actually bound only the signatories—and sometimes not even them.

In July 1851, ten thousand Cheyenne, Arapaho, and Oglala and Brulé Sioux gathered at Fort Laramie for a treaty council. The Indian herds of horses were so large that they roamed for miles around the post, rapidly consuming all the available grass. It was soon obvious that the meetings would have to be moved. The new site was at the mouth of Horse Creek, thirty-five miles to the south.

On September 6, the American delegation, headed by the Superintendent of Indian Affairs, Mr. Mitchell, saw something no white man had ever witnessed. Almost one thousand Sioux warriors dressed in their finery rode four abreast in a column up to the government's tents. One carried an old American flag, said to have been given to the Sioux by William Clark during his western expedition with Meriwether Lewis, forty-five years before. A parade of Cheyenne warriors followed the Sioux. The Indians were given enormous quantities of gifts—calico, knives, blankets, copper pots, and thousands of shiny trinkets. In addition, each chief was presented with a full dress uniform of a general in the United States Army.

Two days later, soldiers fired a cannon to announce the start of the conference. The government plan was that each tribe would be given its own territory. The Cheyenne and Arapaho were assigned most of western Kansas and Colorado, an area that included the site of Denver and its goldfields, and a dry riverbed to the southeast called Sand Creek.

In return for being ceded acreage of their own—which land and more they had roamed freely for generations—and in return for agreeing not to attack whites or other Indians, the chiefs at Horse Creek granted the federal government the right to build roads and military posts, which Washington was planning to do anyway. The Indians would be paid the sum of fifty thousand dollars annually, in merchandise, over the next fifty years. Later, an adjustment was made in the treaty by the U.S. Senate. The term of fifty years was reduced to ten. No one bothered to tell the Indians.

The Treaty of Horse Creek was signed on September 17, 1851. After the ceremony, "the chiefs who had come to the council looking regal and dignified went away looking foolish and uncomfortable in their awkwardly misbuttoned uniforms with their swords flopping and banging around their legs." The American delegation left the council satisfied that they had negotiated a just and lasting peace. It may not have been just, but peace between Indians and whites did linger—for five years.

The Cheyenne continued to raid their old enemy—the Pawnee—near Fort Kearny. No words on paper or entreaties from the peace chiefs could induce the young warriors to resist the ancient call to battle. They avoided the whites, however, except to trade and to collect their annual supply of goods. Then one day in April of 1856—the details are vague—an army officer tried to arrest some Cheyenne braves who were arguing with a trader about the ownership of a horse. The trader said it belonged to him. The Indians claimed it was theirs. Soldiers opened fire and one of the braves was killed.

The Cheyenne encampment panicked. Abandoning their lodges and possessions, the Indians fled north to the Black Hills. In an incident along the way, a trapper was slain. Two months later, a war party of Cheyenne searching for Pawnee murdered a white settler near Fort Kearny and boldly approached the fort itself. They did not shoot—they may have wanted only to touch the soldiers, to count coup on them—but they looked menacing in their battle dress and the troopers opened fire. There were no casualties but word spread among the outposts that the Cheyenne were on the warpath.

In August, another group of Cheyenne looking for Pawnee tried to flag down a stagecoach, intending, according to their account, to beg for tobacco. The terrified driver, having heard the rumor that the Indians were scalping every white person they found, drew his pistol and fired several shots before racing on to Fort Kearny, an arrow protruding from his arm. A company of cavalry rode out to hunt for the marauders. They did not catch them, but they came across a Cheyenne camp of about twenty families, some eighty people. These may not have been the Indian raiders, but they would do. The soldiers attacked, killing ten and wounding ten more, and taking the horses and other goods. The Indians vowed revenge.

For more than a month, Indians attacked wagon trains, stagecoaches, and settlements, killing about a dozen people and sowing the seeds of fear as far east as St. Louis. The peace chiefs who had signed the Treaty of Horse Creek were alarmed, and they resolved to try to prevent the hostilities from spreading. They traveled to the Upper Platte River to call on the Indian agent Thomas Twiss to complain that the current troubles had been started by the soldiers. Twiss, a West Point graduate and son of an old eastern family, had abandoned his army career to live among the Indians. He agreed with the chiefs. They promised to do their best to calm the warriors. Twiss cabled the good news to Washington. It seemed to him that the fighting was about to end.

The army was not satisfied. They did not want the fighting to be over, believing that the Cheyenne had not been sufficiently punished for their outrageous and uncivilized behavior. In the spring of 1857, Jefferson Davis, the Secretary of War, authorized an expedition to discipline the Cheyenne. The man chosen to lead it was a tough frontier soldier, Colonel Edwin Sumner, known to his men as "Bull" because of the loudness of his voice—and because a musket ball had once bounced off his head without doing any apparent damage. Although a courageous and daring fighter, Sumner was not popular with his troops. "Old Sumner has had one good effect on us," an officer wrote. "He has taught some of us to pray, who have never prayed before, for we all put up daily petitions to get rid of him."

In late May, Sumner led two columns out of Fort Kearny to kill some Cheyenne. His force consisted of two companies of the First Cavalry and two of the Second Dragoons, about three hundred men in all. For two months, they searched the borders of the Cheyenne lands and discovered not a single Indian. On July 29, with his long blue columns of soldiers kicking up trails of dust deep in the heart of Cheyenne territory, Sumner found what he had been looking for, a line of three hundred mounted Cheyenne warriors patiently awaiting them.

Indians were rarely willing to fight such a large force of soldiers— too few of the Indians had guns—but this time they knew they were invincible. Their medicine man had told them that if they dipped their hands into the waters of a magic lake, the white man's bullets could not harm them.

Sumner formed his men in a line to face the Indians, and for a long moment all was silent, immobile, a tableau in a Remington painting. Then the colonel addressed his men. His words carried easily from one end of the line to the other.

"The enemy is at last in sight," he bellowed. "I don't know how many warriors the Cheyenne can bring against us, but I do know that if officers and men obey orders promptly, and all pull together, we can whip the whole tribe. Bugler, sound the advance."

The line moved forward at a measured pace. Suddenly, one of Sumner's Delaware Indian scouts charged the line of braves. He reined in midway between the two forces and fired his carbine at the Cheyenne.

"Bear witness," Sumner called to an aide. "An Indian fired the first shot."

Sumner gave another command: "Trot march," he said.

The troops picked up speed and raised their carbines to the ready. The Indians yelled and started to advance. Sumner ordered his men to stow their carbines and draw sabers instead. It was to be a cavalry charge, he decided, right out of the pages of the field manual, the stuff of drills and parades.

"Gallop march!"

"Charge!"

The cavalry thundered forward, the sun glinting on the upraised sabers. The Cheyenne faltered, turned, and fled, their confidence shattered. The magic water might protect them from bullets but not from flashing sabers. Sumner's men chased the Indians for seven miles, killing nine. Two soldiers died and eleven were wounded, including a twenty-four-year-old lieutenant, shot in the chest, who was destined for glory on other fields. His name was J. E. B. Stuart.

Two days later, Colonel Sumner left his wounded and a company of guards at a fortress hastily constructed out of sod, and led the rest of his command on the Cheyennes' trail. He found their abandoned village fifteen miles away. Burning the dwellings to the ground, he continued to scour the countryside for signs of Indians, but without success. He proceeded to Bent's Fort, in time for the annual distribution of supplies, weapons, and ammunition to the Plains Indians.

The Indian agent there, Robert Miller, was relieved to see Sumner and his men because he had received word from the Cheyenne that they would take their goods by force if the government tried to withhold them as punishment. William Bent was so concerned that he refused to allow the provisions inside his trading post. Miller had the weapons and ammunition intended for the Cheyenne dumped into the Arkansas River, and he distributed the rest of the supplies to other tribes. The Cheyenne received nothing.

Cheyenne war parties went on the rampage but were forced to stop for the winter because there would be no grass for the horses. The warriors gathered in winter camps, nursing their grievances, reflecting on how the soldiers had defeated them and how much valuable property they had lost. Through the spring and early summer, they avoided the white settlements and appeared peacefully at Bent's Fort in the late summer, hoping to receive their annual issue of gifts. Indian agent Miller wrote in his annual report that "Colonel Sumner has worked a wondrous change in their dispositions toward the whites. The [Cheyenne] said they had learned a lesson last summer in their fight with Colonel Sumner; that it was useless to contend against the white man."

For the remainder of the summer and fall of 1858, the period of the Colorado gold rush when the land was overrun with new settlers, tempting targets all, the Cheyenne kept to themselves. They watched the whites spreading across the plains, however, and saw ample evidence of how the seven-year-old Treaty of Horse Creek was being violated.

The treaty had allowed the government only a limited right of transit through the Cheyenne and Arapaho lands. Now they were taking over by sheer force of numbers, annexing fields, building towns, tilling the soil. They were gradually but firmly pushing the Cheyenne aside.

A federal commission established later to investigate the war that reached its climax at Sand Creek summed up the situation thusly:

> Before 1861 the Cheyenne and Arapaho had been driven from the mountain regions and were becoming sullen and discontented because of this violation of their rights. If the lands of the white man are taken, civilization justifies him in resisting the invader. Civilization does more than this: it brands him as a coward and a slave if he submits to the wrong. Here civilization made its contract and guaranteed the rights of the weaker party. It did not stand by the guarantee. The treaty was broken but not by the savage. If the savage resists, civilization with the Ten Commandments in one hand and the sword in the other demands his immediate extermination. These Indians saw their former homes and hunting grounds overrun by greedy populations, thirsting for gold. They saw their game driven east to the plains, and soon found themselves the object of jealousy and hatred. They must go.

Despite the provocations and broken promises, despite growing hunger from the decimation and dispersal of the buffalo herds, some Cheyenne and Arapaho tribes still hoped to live in peace. Sweet Medicine had been correct about the white man, but now there were too many for the Indians to resist. The peace chiefs realized the need to make additional concessions if their people were to survive.

In 1859, William Bent reported to Washington that the Cheyenne and Arapaho had acknowledged to him that it was useless to resist. They wanted a new treaty that would grant them a home where they would be protected from the white settlers and from hostile Indian tribes and be taught to farm so they could raise their own food. "They will tear up the earth," Sweet Medicine had said, "and at last you will do it with them."

Bent noted that the tribes "scrupulously maintain peaceful relations with the whites, notwithstanding the many causes of irritation growing out of the occupation of the gold region and the immigration to it through their hunting grounds, which are no longer reliable as a certain source of food." He warned that the only alternative to a new treaty was war.

Spurred by Bent's report, the Commissioner of Indian Affairs, A. B. Greenwood, pressed the U.S. Congress for authority to negotiate another treaty. Unless the Cheyenne and Arapaho were given protected land and food, the army would have to exterminate them in a long, bloody conflict. Congress agreed, and in September 1860, Greenwood met at Fort Wise, southeast of Denver, with two major Cheyenne peace chiefs, Black Kettle and White Antelope, plus a number of lesser chiefs of both tribes. Greenwood told them that the Great White Father in Washington was pleased with the Cheyenne and Arapaho for remaining at peace.

The chiefs replied that they wished to keep the peace and to obey the Great Father. They agreed to the tough terms Greenwood proposed: to relinquish claim to the lands they had been granted in 1851—land that was theirs to begin with—and to move to a reservation in a small, inhospitable corner of the territory, an arid tract unsuitable for most kinds of farming and almost totally lacking in game, water, and timber. There they would be dependent on the government for food and would effectively become wards of the United States.

For its part, Washington agreed to protect the Indians and to pay them the equivalent of fifteen thousand dollars a year for fifteen years. The government would give them cattle and farm implements, a sawmill, houses, interpreters, someone to teach them farming, and forty acres of land for the personal use of each brave. To encourage them to sign the treaty, and to demonstrate the government's largess, Greenwood paraded before them thirteen wagons full of blankets, clothing, scissors, knives, kettles, flour, bacon, sugar, coffee, and tobacco, all of which would be theirs once they agreed to the treaty's terms.

Black Kettle and the other chiefs signed the agreement, but some said later that they were unaware of how much they were giving up. Little Raven, an Arapaho chief, agreed that he had signed a paper but he did not know what it meant.

The younger war chiefs refused to sign a document that spelled the end of their way of life. "It was freedom of movement, the privilege of ranging far and wide seasonally that gave life meaning and dignity," wrote one military historian. "Once that freedom became threatened, his culture, his creature habits and customs, and his manner of providing for his family, all of these were imperiled. To limit him to one piece of ground that he might call his own, though it was the white man's way, must suggest to him the loss of everything that made his spirit proud. It meant living on a reservation, the very mention of which he loathed. The Indian so placed would no longer be a mounted warrior, and no longer a hunter drawing his subsistence from the migratory buffalo. Such was the stake, the forfeit for the Plains Indians that made hostilities inevitable."

*   *   *

"Listen to me carefully," Sweet Medicine had said.

The warriors listened and resolved never to live like the white man, never to sleep in a wooden shack, never to be confined behind a fence to stare out at the open plains, and never to tear up the earth like a farmer. That was the worst degradation for a warrior of the plains. That was the work of women.

"I don't want anything to do with a people who make an Indian warrior carry water on his shoulders or haul manure," said the Sioux chief Sitting Bull.

When Washakie, a Shoshone chief, heard from a delegation of whites that his people should become farmers, he stood erect and stared at them a moment, then spoke with deep feeling. "God damn a potato!" he cried.

3

A Universal Triumph

They went to Colorado to find gold, and some stayed to found a city.
It was summer, 1858, and more than one hundred men, drawn to
the Rockies by rumors of gold, panned the dry bed of Cherry Creek and
every other stream running down from the mountain peaks. They found
nothing, and by July 4, most were too discouraged to try any longer and
headed back to Kansas.

Only fourteen stubborn miners remained, led by William Green
Russell of Georgia, a man whose beard was so long, he fashioned it into
two braids and tucked them in his pants. On July 7, or maybe it was July
8, Russell and his men found their fortune at the spot where Cherry
Creek, its banks overflowing with wild-cherry trees, meets the South
Platte River. A tiny pile of gold—the stone the Indians considered
worthless because it was too soft to hammer into knives or arrowheads—
wrote the beginning of the final chapter of the Indians' dominance over
their land.

On August 26, the gold arrived in Kansas City, where wild speculation in land prices and bold plans for the future had since tumbled into a
spiral of bankruptcies and business failures. People were desperate; there
were no jobs. Within a few weeks, the news of the gold strike spread to
other towns devastated by the previous year's financial panic—to Lawrence, St. Louis, Omaha, and Leavenworth. Newspaper headlines held
dreams of salvation, the hope of instant riches.

NEW GOLD DISCOVERY
GOLD EXCITEMENT ON THE INCREASE
GOLD! GOLD!! GOLD!!! GOLD!!!!

Rumor fed rumor with tales of fifteen dollars a day to be made from mining and gold to be had by the bucket. A single nugget might weigh four pounds. Within two weeks, a thousand men were on their way and more followed in their wake. Not all of them brought picks and shovels. Some had other dreams for attaining wealth and power, men who hoped to make their fortunes not from the mines but from the miners.

One of the first to arrive was William Larimer, tall and arrogant, once a general in the Pennsylvania militia, whose self-promotion of Larimer City in Nebraska had not produced the bonanza for which he had hoped; nor had the freight service he was operating out of Leaven-worth. Larimer and his son, Will, arrived at the Cherry Creek site on November 16, and before the sun set on the following day, they had founded and staked out the town of Auraria on the creek's west bank. Five days later, they did the same on the east bank, calling the tract Denver City in honor of the governor of the Kansas Territory to which it belonged. "We are bound to have a territory, if not a state," Larimer wrote to his family, "and the capital will be Denver City with the state house near Will's and my claim."

A month earlier, two men had arrived from Crescent City, Iowa, with enough goods to open a general store for the miners. Another merchant from New Mexico arrived with a wagonload of whiskey. A farmer planted potatoes and sold one of his smaller crops for an astounding thirty thousand dollars. Eventually, he became a philanthropist and owner of 4,500 parcels of property. Someone else laid out a cemetery, and another wrote back to Kansas City for a supply of hats. William Byers, who had gone to Oregon back in 1852 and had sat in on treaty councils with the Indians in Nebraska, transported a heavy printing press over the treacherous frozen roads all the way from Omaha. His *Rocky Mountain News* sold out its first edition the following spring.

Some of the Indians joined in the excitement that sparkled brighter than the patches of ice on the Platte River that winter. Little Raven, the Arapaho chief, was a frequent visitor to the new settlements, and he had pledged his word to preserve peace with the whites. He liked the white-skinned people, he said, and was glad they had found gold, because it made them so happy. However, he reminded them that the land belonged to the Indians. He hoped the whites would not say anything insulting to his people—or stay too long.

On Christmas Day of 1858, whites and Indians held a friendly and spirited competition, wagering on horse races. A few weeks later, the miners hosted a feast of roast oxen, dried apples, bread, and coffee for five hundred Arapaho warriors and their families. The whites were amazed at how much food the Indians ate. "I have never seen men eat till now," one miner wrote. "I have heard that one man could eat an antelope at a meal, and I verily believe one Indian called Heap of Whips could eat a whole ox."

Denver City was full of optimism, hopes, and glorious dreams of a golden future—for everyone, that is, except the miners.

"We were surprised," one miner wrote home, "when we read the glowing account in the Missouri River papers of what the miners are doing out here. I pronounce them a pack of lies, written and reported back by a set of petty one-horse-town speculators." There was no more gold to be mined. Not a nugget, not a grain was found at the Cherry Creek site all winter long. Hundreds of angry, frustrated, and hungry men waited through the cold months for spring to arrive so they could make their way back east. At the same time, thousands of others waited in the towns along the Missouri, prepared to head west to the goldfields when the plains turned green with grass.

As gold fever died in the shanties along the Colorado creeks, it was reaching manic proportions in the east, fired by promoters in every gateway town. There was a lot of money to be made outfitting and equipping the miners headed for Pikes Peak, and each trumpeted itself as the best starting point for the journey. Guidebooks to the so-called new El Dorado rolled off the presses, telling of the best routes west. Seventeen such books were published that winter, one for almost every town vying to be the point of embarkation for the 750-mile trip. The Leavenworth city council bought and distributed twenty thousand copies of a handbook touting their city. Each guide outdid the next with fanciful descriptions of the easy riches to be had amidst the glories of Denver City and Auraria.

"Gold exists throughout all of this region," stated one promotional pamphlet. "It can be found anywhere—on the plains, in the mountains, and by the streams. In fact, there is no end of precious metal. Nature herself would seem to have turned into a most successful alchemist in converting the very sands of the streams into gold."

William Byers, publisher of the *Rocky Mountain News*, wrote one of those glowing treatises before he had even set foot in Colorado—*Hand Book to the Gold Fields of Nebraska and Kansas: Being a Complete*

Guide to the Gold Regions of the South Platte and Cherry Creek. It was published in Chicago and sold for a tidy fifty cents. Uncle Dick Wootton described Mr. Byers as a capable and dangerous liar. He thought the stories in Byers's book and newspaper encouraging the gold fever were ill-advised and untrue.

By February and March of 1859, thousands of would-be miners, spurred by a year of poor crops, flooded the Missouri River towns to spend more money on room, board, and supplies than most of them would ever make from mining. It cost six hundred dollars for three yoke of oxen, a wagon, and sufficient tools, tents, flour, bacon, and coffee for four men.

Enterprising businessmen slapped the Pikes Peak label on all manner of goods—hats, guns, boots, shovels—all of which could be purchased at stores with names such as Pikes Peak Outfitters. While the anxious emigrants from the states waited to leave, they could dine in the Pikes Peak Lunch Room on beef à la mode Pikes Peak. Gold fever enriched many who never set foot in the Colorado Territory, while others bet their last silver dollars on their one remaining hope—easy pickings at Pikes Peak.

The hopeful and the desperate set out from the towns along the Missouri in late April and early May. Some one hundred wagons crossed the river from each town every day, to inch across the land of the Cheyenne toward the parched portion of the eastern Colorado plains. "We seem to have reached the acme of barrenness and desolation," wrote Horace Greeley, editor of the New York *Tribune.* "Wood and water fail and we are in a desert indeed."

The trip was hellish, a nightmare of muddy trails, snowstorms, howling winds, ice, sleet, and near-starvation. Some men set out on foot, others pushed handcarts and wheelbarrows. Others rode in wagons, buggies, genteel sulkies made for city streets, and on the backs of mules. A few built wind wagons to swoop across the plains, propelled by giant puffed sails. The contraptions worked for less than ten miles. One man set out in his prairie-motor, a huge boiler powering a craft on cast-iron wheels. He did not get far, either.

On they came, in such staggering numbers that a miner could ride from the banks of the Missouri all the way to Cherry Creek and never be out of sight of other wayfarers during the day or of the beacons of their campfires at night. Some struggled, many died, others gave up and headed home, but most persevered because they had nothing to which to return. Ahead lay the promise of a life of riches.

But it was hard. "Oh, Ann," a woman wrote to her sister in

Nebraska, "you [have] no idea what I have suffered. I was taken with the ague before we [left] Columbus. Had to be carried on a bed six days, sleeping on the ground, rained on, cold, snow, besides almost starved to death. The meanest company I ever was in. Oh, the suffering that I have seen. Went a great many days without anything but a little piece of bread made of flour and oatmeal mixed together." And still they came.

Some of those who stayed behind—those who had been so busily promoting the gold rush—grew concerned that none of the miners who had wintered over at Cherry Creek had sent back any gold, let alone word of success. Then, while the wagons were still crossing the Missouri heading west, the first reports arrived. The Cherry Creek boom had gone bust. No more gold had been found. By the middle of May, those eager thousands going west met the first of the discouraged miners returning from El Dorado, some on foot, their oxen having given out.

"We met 1,000 people in one day coming back and hundreds of beggars, hundreds starved to death, 22 in one spot laid by the roadside dead on the Smoky Hill route." Those returning poured out their troubles to the newcomers, and soon hundreds of wagons turned around and crept back to the Missouri. Perhaps as many as forty thousand returned. It was a disaster for the promoters of Auraria and Denver City, whose population plummeted by two-thirds. By early June, there were no more than three thousand people in the entire Colorado goldfield region. As it turned out, they were the lucky ones.

At the same time that newspapers in the east were publishing front-page stories about what they called the great Colorado gold rush hoax, the same time when thousands of men heading west had turned around and were starting for home, a prospector rode into Denver carrying a vial containing eighty dollars' worth of gold. It was May 13, and within a day, the twin towns on either side of Cherry Creek were virtually deserted as storekeepers, carpenters, lawyers, doctors, and the local judge rushed off to the new diggings to the west and north of Denver. They needed no persuading—they could see the yellow dust with their own eyes—but it took the efforts of the country's most influential journalist, Horace Greeley, writing for the most widely read paper in the United States, the New York *Tribune,* to persuade the rest of the country that this time the Colorado gold rush was real.

Greeley did not go to Colorado to find gold but, rather, to find stories about the new American west, and so he did not turn around when he came across down-and-out miners retreating from Denver. This was part of the story he had come to write and so he kept on going. He arrived in the city on June 6 and spent the night in The Denver House, with its dirt floor, canvas roof and windows, and rooms separated by hanging sheets. Greeley called it the "Astor of the Rockies." It was really more of a saloon and gambling den than a hotel, and Greeley, whose name was widely known, was asked to favor the crowd of drinkers and gamblers with a talk. Therefore, within sight of the 130-foot bar and the bustling gaming tables, he spoke on the evils of both demon rum and the goddess of chance.

"On one side the tipplers at the bar silently sipped their grog, on the other the gamblers respectfully suspended the shuffling of cards and the counting of money from their huge piles of coin." Everyone agreed that Greeley gave a *fine* talk.

The next morning, wearing a white linen duster, Greeley headed out by mule to Gregory Gulch, forty miles away, with two other reporters, Henry Villard of the Cincinnati *Times* and Albert Richardson of the Boston *Journal*.

The miners they visited at the Gulch, shrewd fellows all, realized they had a truly golden opportunity to sell their worthless claims if these reporters wrote stories for the readers back east saying that they had found gold. So they decided to assist Greeley, to simplify their labors. They salted a mine by loading shotgun shells with gold dust and nuggets and firing them into a claim. To be on the safe—and convincing—side, they salted two other claims as well and let Greeley pan them all. Their diligence, hard work, and helpful attitude paid off.

"Gentlemen," Greeley told them, "I have washed with my own hands and seen with my own eyes, and the news of your rich discovery shall go forth all over the world as far as my newspaper can carry it."

The three journalists jointly signed a dispatch announcing to the world that a man could make as much as $494 a day—a staggering sum—from a single sluice. Two weeks later, the report reached the eastern newspapers and yet another gold rush was on.

When Greeley visited Gregory Gulch, about four thousand miners were living out in the open, scrabbling for gold. A month after his article appeared in the eastern press, men were arriving at the rate of five hundred per day, digging and destroying the landscape over an area of four square miles. It did not take long to discover that there were too few workable claims to support so many miners and that most of the gold was mixed with quartz, which would require hard-rock mining machinery to

extract. None of the miners had such equipment. The latest Colorado
gold rush looked like another bust.

Thousands of bitter men turned east again across the plains, while
others stayed and scoured every gulch and creek. Some discovered gold
that could be panned in a creek bed using a simple wood-frame sluice,
but most of the miners grew discouraged, and by the end of the summer
fewer than ten thousand remained in all the gold region, about two thousand of whom were in Denver. However, many of those who stayed were
finally striking it rich. By October, when cold weather forced the men
out of the hills, a quarter of a million dollars in gold had been found.
About five thousand miners, some of them suddenly very wealthy, spent
the winter in the city.

Denver was on the move and attracting a wild diversity of people—
visionaries, dreamers, misfits, men down to their last hope, schemers,
con men, and gamblers. Of course, they were all gamblers, willing to
risk everything, including their lives, on the chance of finding gold. But
some were professional gamblers, cardsharps, come to make their fortunes from the newly rich. In The Denver House, the gamblers kept six
tables of card games going twenty-four hours a day, the shouting of the
players and kibitzers keeping Horace Greeley awake at night.

Many of the town's founders played poker using acreage as chips,
with entire city blocks sometimes changing hands several times over the
course of an all-night game. A county judge lost thirty lots in Denver in
less than ten minutes. The sheriff pawned his pistol for twenty dollars so
he could bet on faro.

"Denver was a strange medley. There were Americans from every
quarter of the union, Mexicans, Indians, halfbreeds, trappers, speculators, gamblers, desperadoes, broken-down politicians, and even honest
men." According to one Colorado historian, they were mostly honest,
decent men. "There was the man who had traveled around the world,
and the boy who had never before left his father's farm. Doctors, lawyers, preachers, and farmers had turned to mining. Unschooled lads and
university graduates jostled each other in the narrow gulches, and attended mass meetings together to make laws for their district. The success of the day's panning, news from another gulch or from the outside
world, were usual topics of conversation; but discussions of Shakespeare,
religion, and philosophy were common. Poetry was recited in the long
quiet evenings when darkness prevented the workers from panning; and
many were the homemade verses that bubbled from the mountain
streams."

There were thieves and killers, too. Shootings, murders, and thefts occurred daily. "More brawls, more fights, more pistol shots with criminal intent in this log city of 150 dwellings than in any community of equal number on earth," Greeley wrote.

Several of the murders were committed by the most ornery varmint who ever leaned on a bar—Mountain Charley Forest. It turned out that Mountain Charley was a woman masquerading as a man and she was still the most ornery varmint who ever leaned on a bar. She had been searching throughout the west for the murderer of her husband. She killed a couple of men, but each turned out to be the wrong one. Mountain Charley finally decided to get a new husband instead and she married a bartender, to the relief of most of the men in town.

"Almost every day was enlivened by its little shooting match," observed Richardson of the Boston *Journal*. "While the great gaming saloon [The Denver House] was crowded with people, drunken ruffians sometimes fired five or six shots from their revolvers, frightening everybody pell-mell out of the room, but seldom wounding anyone. One day I heard the bartender politely ask a man lying upon a bench to remove. The recumbent replied to the request with his revolver. Indeed firing at this bartender was a common amusement among the guests. At first he bore it laughingly, but one day a shot grazed his ear, whereupon, remarking that there was such a thing as carrying a joke too far and that *this* was 'about played out,' he buckled on two revolvers and swore he would kill the next man who took aim at him. He was not troubled afterward." Most of the townspeople reacted the same way the bartender had.

The influential men of Denver soon realized that if they were to attract and keep families and responsible citizens, the lawless elements would have to be controlled. Thus, they did what they had to do. They policed their own community and organized their own system of justice. An anonymous vigilante committee known as "the stranglers" was formed, and by the time they had hanged or shot to death nine men (after each had been given a trial), Denver became a reasonably safe and respectable town.

"We never hanged on circumstantial evidence," William Byers wrote. "I have known a great many such executions, but I don't believe one of them was ever unjust. But when they were proved guilty, they were always hanged. There was no getting out of it. No, there were no appeals in those days; no writs of errors; no attorneys' fees; no pardon in six months. Punishment was swift, sure, and certain."

The founding of Denver, like the settling of dozens of other western towns, was a vital expression and demonstration of the frontier character and enterprise at work, the kind of character that was shaped by the demands of the frontier itself. It was an effective and brutal example of Social Darwinism, wherein the stronger adapted, survived, and prospered—or at least survived—while the weaker went back to the Missouri or died on some lonely hillside.

Although it was undeniably true that the miners, pioneers, trappers, settlers—even the gamblers and thieves—shaped the new wilderness, it was even more true that in the process of settling and building the west, the people themselves were changed. This was the case for those who built the Denvers of the nineteenth century and for those who had built the Bostons and the earlier settlements east of the Missouri in the previous centuries. The historian Frederick Jackson Turner observed that the colonists and the immigrant pioneers changed the wilderness, but in so doing, in the taming of that rough country, a new breed of person developed who was seen in no other part of the globe: the American, whose values, abilities, attitudes, and intellect evolved through meeting and mastering the frontier.

In describing these new Americans, he wrote, "that coarseness and strength combined with acuteness and inquisitiveness; that practical inventive turn of mind, quick to find expedients; that masterful grasp of material things lacking in the artistic, but powerful to effect great ends; that restless, nervous energy; that dominant individualism, working for good and for evil; and withal that buoyancy and exuberance which comes with freedom—these are the traits of the frontier."

Nothing could stop such a people possessing such drive and aggressiveness and perhaps, above all else, their straining, bulging, bursting belief in their own greatness and in their God-given right to dominion over all the land and everything on it. The land, the grass, the trees, the mountains, the animals, the sky above belonged to them. "I run all over town," a perceptive miner wrote that summer of 1859, "saw more gamblers and gambling than I ever saw before, and went to bed wondering what the Anglo-American race were approaching, and concluded that a universal triumph and conquest was its destiny."

Universal triumph. Universal conquest. Universal destiny. God and the miners had spoken and there was nothing that fewer than 4,000 Cheyenne and 2,400 Arapaho who lived on the plains between the Platte and the Arkansas rivers could do about it. Another civilization had come to the west.

*   *   *

Denver became a boom town. Like its people, it was bold and sassy, rich and successful, and it quickly came to look the part. In less than a year it exploded from a crude mining camp to a thriving city. In the winter of 1858–1859, Denver was a settlement of log huts and shanties with dirt floors and mud roofs. Only a few buildings had glass windows and only one had a wooden floor. By the summer of 1860, it was a prosperous business community with six thousand residents, two newspapers, thirty-five saloons, a few churches, a library, a school, civic groups, fraternal organizations, a well-attended theater, a United States Mint, banks, hotels, shops, pool halls, shooting galleries, bowling alleys, and a chess club. Little of it had been built by government aid or edict but solely by the dreams, sweat, work, cunning, and greed of ambitious men who poured $700,000 of their own money into the birth of their city.

On June 6 of that year, William Byers wrote an editorial in praise of his new home.

> Lofty buildings are rising on the business streets; solid and substantial brick edifices of which old cities might well be proud. Gorgeous saloons, with mirrors and paintings, lighted from glittering chandeliers, meet the eye of the passerby on every corner, and delicious music lures him to enter. The storehouses of our merchants groaning beneath tons and tons of goods and wares from every clime. Great trains of huge prairie freighters arrive and depart almost daily, and more than a thousand emigrant wagons arrive every week.

Both sides of Cherry Creek were called Denver by then and both were developing apace. East Denver was on a plateau, sloping down to the creek bed, and its lower streets were full of corrals, stables, warehouses, boardinghouses, saloons, and gambling dens. On the higher streets were the mint and a large general store, which, like all the shops and places of business, accepted unminted gold dust and nuggets in payment. Every store kept a set of scales for the weighing of gold. Close by, on Larimer Street, was the post office, where mail arrived from the east three days a week on the new stagecoach line from Omaha. Next to it was a bookstore and newsstand that did a thriving business, as did the large unpainted frame theater and two new hotels, Planter's House and Broadwell House.

West Denver was primarily a residential area but it also housed another hotel, Tremont House, plus the city jail, an iron foundry, and a few supply stores. In the dry bed of Cherry Creek, raised up on pilings, perched the pride of the city: the *Rocky Mountain News* building.

When the structure was completed in 1860, Byers held an open house and nearly everyone in town came to see the wood-frame building with its huge printing presses. One of those visitors was an elderly Indian who was considerably impressed by the white man's lodge, but he told Byers that he was surprised to see such a thing in the creek bed. He said that he had seen water filling up the creek and overflowing all the bottomland. The Indian raised his hands as far as he could reach over his head to show how high the water had risen, but no one paid any attention to him.

Both East and West Denver were busy day and night as more and more people arrived. The speculators, such as William Larimer, who had claimed much of the city early on, were prospering. However, by then almost everyone was doing well, and they were justifiably proud of themselves and their shining new city.

One early resident noted: "We have as sharp and sagacious merchants, as shrewd real estate speculators, as cunning and ambitious lawyers, as numerous doctors, as fine-looking young men, as handsome and stylish women, almost as can be scared up together in any single corporation this side of St. Louis or Chicago."

The city had come to be such a fine place to live that men sent for their wives and children. The families had a new high-speed way of getting to Denver in only eight days and nights on the Overland Stage Line from eastern gateways such as Omaha and Kansas City. Thousands still traveled in slow, plodding, white-topped lines of wagons, but those who could afford it traveled by coach at the amazing speed of ten miles per hour.

The Concord coaches, each costing fifteen hundred dollars and weighing two thousand pounds, had been solidly built in New Hampshire, the bodies crafted out of strong white oak braced with iron bands and slung on heavy leather braces. The windows were fitted with roll-down leather curtains to keep out the wind and rain, but on the plains nothing could offer much protection, so the passengers often rode in wet clothing. Sacks of mail and luggage went in the boot on the rear of the coach, and all valuables were locked in a strongbox kept beneath the driver's seat.

There were three seats inside, enough to hold nine passengers sitting upright, cramped shoulder to shoulder. They were the lucky ones. Up to seven extra passengers could be seated on top of the swaying, bucking coach, holding on to one another every mile of the way. The drivers were a colorful lot, dressed in broad-brimmed sombreros, corduroys trimmed with velvet, and high-heeled boots. They brandished nine-foot rawhide whips, elaborately decorated with silver trimmings.

When the drivers approached a way station, every ten or twelve miles along the route, they shouted and flicked their whips to bring the horses up to full speed. Blowing a bugle as they got closer to let the station hands know they were coming, they roared to a stop with manes flying, wheels spinning, and metal harnesses jangling. In fewer than five minutes, a fresh team of horses was harnessed and the coach raced off with the same drama with which it had arrived.

Some of the stations were equipped to serve meals to the passengers, typically jackrabbit, buffalo, or antelope stew, soda biscuits, strong black coffee, and dried apple pie, all at a cost of $1.50. Passengers were given only thirty minutes to eat because the drivers prided themselves on how fast they could get from one stop to the next. They were relieved at every second or third stop.

It was a hard way to travel. "A through ticket and 15 inches of seat," wrote one passenger, "with a fat man on one side, a poor widow on the other, a baby on your lap, a bandbox over your head makes the picture, as well as your sleeping place, for the trip."

For all its hardships, it was an improvement over the Conestoga wagon, which took at least forty days to cover the same distance, five times longer than the stagecoach. There was nothing to do on the stagecoach trip but try to doze, and there was little to look at except miles of endless prairie, long trains of wagons, and occasional herds of buffalo. There was also one other sight, something that unnerved most passengers: They saw their first Indians.

For some reason, the Cheyenne and Arapaho liked to trot alongside the stagecoaches. Perhaps they wanted to race the huge ungainly boxes that went up and down the trails the way Sweet Medicine had foretold. The Indians looked fierce and primitive and threatening to people whose only knowledge of them came from lurid newspaper accounts of gruesome massacres. Suddenly there they were, not twenty feet away, easily keeping pace with the coaches. The passengers knew there could be no outrunning the Indians if they decided to attack. They never did, not in 1860, but they scared a lot of people.

Many of the settlers remained scared when they reached Denver. If they were not frightened by the Indians, they were repulsed by them. It was common knowledge, even among people back east who had never seen an Indian, that they were dirty, thieving, shiftless, and lazy. They didn't work for a living like everyone else but depended on government handouts. They refused to farm the land the government had given them. Why did Washington have to use tax money to support them to the tune of fifteen thousand dollars a year? And why did they have to hang around Denver bothering decent white people?

There were many Indians around the city in 1860. They were intensely curious about the white man's camp and how its people lived. They came to look and to stare, sometimes turning up where—to the white man's way of thinking, with his strange notions of privacy and personal property—they had no right to be.

"Many a time in going about my household duties," wrote Susan Riley Ashley, a young bride who had come from Iowa that year, "or sitting quietly sewing or reading, an uncanny feeling took possession of me, and looking up I would discover that one or more panes of my window framed the stolid face of an Indian. On one occasion, having forgotten to lock my outer doors, I entered my front room to find three Indians in it, and others entering. With assumed bravery I cried out 'Puck-a-chee' (which I had been told was the Indian way of saying 'begone'), and I put my hands against the nearest Indian as if to push him out. They left without resistance and took their places at the windows."

The Indians meant no harm, but their ways annoyed the settlers. Mrs. Ashley also recalled hearing a strange noise from outside her home one Sunday morning. "I saw a band of Indians coming up our street, and a minute later 30 or more Cheyenne and Arapaho passed by, holding aloft on a pole five freshly taken Ute scalps. The doleful sound disturbing the Sabbath quiet was their chant of victory. That night around a campfire, built where our Union depot now stands, they celebrated their victory over a band of Ute, while many white folks looked on and felt that only fear of the white man's firearms prevented the Indians from seeking fair locks instead of those tawny scalps."

Even though there had been no attack by Cheyenne or Arapaho on any white settlers for more than a year, the threat of it, the deep-seated atavistic fear of it, was ever present, fueled by the Indians' constant presence. As a result, target practice became one of the common amusements of the people of Denver. Many women became expert shots, and no one ventured far from home unarmed.

The Indians around Denver traded with the whites, begged on the streets for food and tobacco, and stole horses, which in the white world was a hanging offense. The Indians, in their view, were achieving honor and dignity among their people by demonstrating their skill at acquiring other men's horses, something they had long done. It was not a serious offense to the Indians. It was a game, a way of life.

The Indians also got drunk in town. Whites gave them whiskey in order to gain the upper hand in trading or to take advantage of their squaws, who were molested and sometimes raped in their own lodges while their men were drunk. Heartrending stories appeared in the newspapers about intoxicated Indian warriors bartering their last buffalo robes for a bottle of whiskey and stumbling half-naked down the street in the dead of winter.

Responsible men urged temperance and compassion in dealing with the Indians. One was William Byers, who a few years later would be telling his readers that the Indians would have to be chastised "with no gentle hand." But on April 23, 1861, he expressed the hope, in the *Rocky Mountain News,* that the citizens of Denver would be prudent in promoting friendly and peaceful relations with the Indians.

> A civilized and enlightened people can well afford to remember that the tribes by which we are surrounded are our inferiors physically, morally, mentally, and that the commission of what we call crimes, assumes with them the merit of bravery and manly action. In all our dealings with these untutored barbarians, we should be governed by the greatest caution—avoiding in all cases a disposition to overreach and deceive them. They are naturally, and not without reason, suspicious of their white brethren. They feel that their rights have been invaded, their hunting grounds taken possession of, and their possessions appropriated without adequate remuneration. It should be the aim of every good citizen to conciliate the Indians, and show them by a peaceful policy, that we are not committed to an aggressive and tyrannous course.

All well and good. Noble advice and sentiments. But keep your guns loaded and ready.

4

A Soldier in God's War

On April 24, 1861, ten days after the surrender of Fort Sumter, a Confederate flag was raised over a shop on Larimer Street. Union supporters, who numbered about half the population of Denver, were outraged. City leaders appointed a committee to call on the two Southern sympathizers who owned the store. They issued an ultimatum. If the flag did not come down within one hour, then both the flag and the store would come down together. The flag was hauled down within the prescribed time. The Civil War had come to Denver.

The threat of a war between North and South had come two months earlier, in February, when the Deep South states and Texas had seceded. Suddenly, Denver and its gold mines, which produced $7 million a year for the federal government, were found to be only 250 miles from a rebel state. That threat loomed larger than the Indians camped outside of town or begging in the streets. At first, however, the consequences of secession worked to the advantage of the residents of Colorado and two other western outposts. To ensure that they remained part of the Union, the authorities in Washington quickly granted formal territorial status to Colorado, Nevada, and Dakota, and appointed a governor for each.

Relations between Union and Confederate supporters were tense that winter in Denver, and arguments split many a friendship, family, and church. The minister of the Methodist Church was a devout Union man. It was said that President Abraham Lincoln had no stronger or more vocal champion than the Reverend John Milton Chivington. Long a fighter for abolition, he never hesitated to state his views from the pulpit, even though he knew they would offend some of his parishioners. Truth and the Union were more important to him than his own popularity, or even than keeping his job.

In a Sunday sermon that winter, Chivington quoted the inflammatory words of the abolitionist Stephen A. Douglas. "Until the national authority is restored, let there be but two parties—patriots and traitors." The southern members of the church took umbrage at being called traitors and they formed a delegation to lodge a formal protest with their preacher. Chivington's response was a public one, made a few weeks later when he spoke at the funeral of a soldier who had been shot to death by a saloon keeper. He told the crowd that he refused to be silent about the greatest question of the day, the issue that threatened to divide his country. He would continue to speak his mind.

"I am a man of lawful age and full size and was an American citizen before I became a minister. If the church had required me to renounce any of my rights of manhood or American citizenship before I could become a minister, I should have very respectfully declined." No one challenged him again, and he continued to defend from the pulpit Lincoln and the Union—and to call the secessionists traitors.

When news first reached Denver that South Carolina had seceded in December of 1860, a Southern sympathizer stopped Chivington on the street to ask what he thought the federal government would do if other Southern states also withdrew. Chivington replied that such actions would be very grave indeed, and that "nothing would be left the government but to thrash them back into the Union."

The man laughed and said that would be impossible. Everyone knew that one Southerner could whip five Yankees any day. Chivington glared at the man with "a scowl that would have scared the devil himself." He drew himself up to his full six feet four and a half inches and planted his 260-pound bulk squarely in front of his questioner. He said that he was Yankee born and bred and he offered to hold a contest to find out just how many Southerners could whip how many Yankees.

"If you will go out in the town and find four others from the South," Chivington said, "I will undertake to thrash the earth with all five, and settle the matter right here on Ferry Street." The man wisely declined.

There was no meekness about the Reverend Chivington or the Gospel he preached, and he never believed that a soft answer turned away wrath. His was the fury, the righteousness, and the powerful swift sword of the Old Testament, and he lived his creed.

*   *   *

Chivington had come a long way from his birth on January 27, 1821, in rural Ohio. "As near as I can get it," he recalled, "there was no town where I was born." There was no school, either, although the local farmers had banded together to build a log house they hoped would serve as a school. They equipped it with readers, spellers, and arithmetic books but could not find a teacher willing to live in such a wilderness. Chivington, two older brothers, and a younger sister had only sporadic formal schooling, whenever itinerant teachers passed through. The travelers never stayed long, so most of the children's education was initiated by their mother, with the aid of the few books she possessed.

The four children were considered bright, particularly John, who was a quick learner. He studied diligently by the light of a hickory-bark fire in their log cabin home. His parents once went to Cincinnati to buy him a dictionary. With that, a Bible, an Episcopal prayer book, and a copy of *Paradise Lost,* the boy developed an unusually extensive vocabulary. When he was five, his father died, and the burden of rearing the family fell solely on his mother.

Each of the boys went to work in the timber business at the age of thirteen. When John was eighteen, he realized that he had persuasive gifts and took over the job of marketing the timber they were cutting. He had to spend considerable time in Cincinnati on business, and it was there he met Martha Rollason, a short, attractive, Southern-born woman two years his senior. He quickly decided that she would be his wife. "She could read and write in both English and French, was an expert seamstress, and could milk a cow and make good butter." A young man could ask for no more.

Chivington apprenticed himself to a carpenter to learn a trade so that he would be able to support a family, and he soon became a skilled craftsman. His career plans changed two years later, however, when he attended a Methodist revival meeting. Heeding the traveling preacher's call for fighters in the war for righteousness and against evil, he instantly joined the church. His newfound zeal grew and he resolved to become a preacher himself. The evangelist who recruited him said that he could be ordained without any formal study, but Chivington was too much of a perfectionist to take the easy path. If he was going to be a servant of God, he wanted to be fully prepared for the task. "I do not propose to teach the word of God in ignorance," he said. "Until I can give a reason for every particle of faith that is in me, I shall not enter the pulpit."

His goal was an admirable one, but in practical terms, he was simply too poor to attend the Methodist seminary. Fortunately, the evangelist had since become the Methodist bishop of Southern Ohio and he arranged for Chivington to begin his studies on his own. For two years, while working full time as a carpenter, he studied every night, poring over borrowed theology textbooks as well as books on history, science, and economics. He completed the same course of study required at the seminary and was ordained in 1844, a man knowledgeable not only about theology but as well educated as many college graduates of the time. It was a remarkable achievement.

The life of a small-town preacher was strenuous, and John and Martha Chivington moved the family—which now included three children—from place to place every two years. Wherever they went, Chivington always left the church solvent and the services well attended. He also took his fight for what he called "right and decency" beyond the pulpit, working to develop community schools and libraries and to root out lawless elements. He preached a gospel of social activism. It was not enough to pray for the less fortunate; he believed in actively helping them.

In 1848, while serving a parish in Quincy, Illinois, his interests broadened to include the explosive issue of slavery, a question on which the church remained neutral. One of the members of his congregation was a Negro nursemaid, whom everyone assumed was a freed slave until a deputy U.S. marshal from Tennessee arrived with a warrant for her arrest. The woman had run away from her owner and the marshal was there to take her back.

When Chivington heard about it, he let the woman hide in the parsonage and waited on his porch for the lawman. It was a hot summer evening, and Chivington removed his outer shirt, leaving his thick, muscular arms bare. The deputy arrived, put his foot on the bottom step, and waved his warrant.

"Take your foot off that step," Chivington said, his deep, powerful voice a roar.

"I am an officer of the law," the deputy said, "armed and with authority to use force if necessary."

Chivington raised his fists and flexed his muscles.

"I, too, carry arms," he said. "Take your foot off that step."

The two men glared at each other in silence, then the marshal removed his foot and went back to Tennessee.

A few years later, in a parish in St. Joseph, Missouri, Chivington's antislavery activism was put to a stronger test. The Missouri–Kansas border area bristled with guerrilla warfare between proslavery and antislavery advocates long before the Civil War began. Threats and intimidation, beatings and murders were common, but that did not stop Chivington from speaking in his Sunday sermons against the institution of slavery.

He was put on notice that he would be tarred and feathered if he ever preached again in the county. He sent word back that he would preach the following Sunday and nobody was going to stop him. A group of militant proslavery men arrived at the church carrying a bucket of hot tar and a feather pillow. They took their seats with the rest of the congregation and waited to see whether the minister would dare to appear.

They did not have long to wait. Chivington entered the little wood-frame church and planted himself behind the pulpit. He gazed out at the assembly, then placed his Bible in the center of the lectern. Reaching inside his long black robe, he pulled out two revolvers and put them on either side of the Bible.

"By the grace of God and these two revolvers," he announced, "I am going to preach here today." He delivered his sermon and was not threatened again. It was then that people began to call him the "fighting parson."

Chivington fought everything he considered to be evil—slavery, gambling, prostitution, and liquor. After St. Joseph, his next parish was the wild, lawless town of Nebraska City, where he was sent to reorganize a church that had long been moribund. As Chivington drove his wagon down the main street, he recognized that the devil was in control. Lining the street were saloons, gambling halls, and brothels. It was time for righteousness to take a stand.

At each street corner, he halted the wagon, rose, and made a brief announcement.

"I am your new Methodist pastor. Services will be held in the Methodist church at eight tonight."

He visited the church that afternoon and found that it had been turned into a bar. He was furious.

"Who dares to profane the house of God?" he demanded.

Customers bolted for the door, but the bartender pulled out the deed to the building, which had been signed over to him by the last pastor, who had left to join the gold rush. Chivington grabbed the paper from the man's hand and tore it to shreds. He charged around the counter and wrestled the barrels of whiskey out into the street, where he split them open, spilling their contents in the dirt. A crowd gathered to watch this man of God go about his work. Someone asked him what right he had to destroy another man's property.

"The authority of Almighty God," Chivington bellowed.

No one else raised any objection, and at eight o'clock that night he preached a sermon in his new church.

Chivington arrived in Denver on Saturday, May 4, 1860. His first act was to buy enough lumber to build a house for his family. The following morning, he held services in a grove of cottonwood trees; the First Methodist Church of Denver was in operation.

After that, church services were held on the second floor of the Criterion Saloon, in a room Chivington shared with the Episcopal priest until each denomination built its own church. A parishioner recalled that "on that first Sunday the gambling was carried on on the first floor while preaching was proceeding on the second. The flooring was of rough boards with wide cracks between them, and every word uttered by the occupants of the saloon, including those at the gaming tables, was as plainly heard by the congregation as the sermon. On the next Sunday, the gambling was suspended for an hour while the preaching proceeded, which was considered quite a concession for that time."

There were other problems unique to frontier churches. Of the first twelve funerals conducted by the Episcopal minister, five of the deceased had been shot, two had been executed for murder, one had shot himself, and another had drunk himself to death. Preaching, like most other things, was different in the west, but even there a sin was a sin and had to be rooted out and destroyed. The Reverend Chivington was good at that.

As he had done in every other town, Chivington soon became a respected and valued member of the Denver community, a soldier in God's war. When the Civil War began a year later, he had the opportunity to become a soldier in the nation's war. It changed his life, just as it altered the lives of millions of Americans in both North and South. Chivington would never again be the same.

With the outbreak of the war, Colorado Territory and the other western lands found themselves virtually defenseless. Troops were ordered back east to fight the Confederates. Only thirty-nine soldiers of the Second Infantry remained on duty at Fort Larned on the Arkansas River. Fort

Wise had 33 men, Fort Kearny 125, and 90 were quartered at Fort Laramie. In all the vast plains covering some 200,000 square miles, fewer than three hundred troops patrolled.

If the Cheyenne and Arapaho had wanted war with the whites, this was their best chance. Never again would they hold such a commanding advantage in numbers over those small garrisons. The Indians took no action, however. Black Kettle and the other peace chiefs kept even the most warlike of their young braves under control, confining themselves to attacks on their old enemies the Ute. They roamed with the buffalo instead of staying fenced up on the reservation; and they still begged and traded and drank on the streets of Denver, appearing menacing and frightening to many settlers. But they did not make war.

The threat of war remained vivid in the minds of the whites, however. Other Indian tribes, especially those in New Mexico and California, were raiding. In addition, Denver, because of its goldfields, faced the danger of a Confederate invasion from Texas. If the government in Washington could not leave an army to protect the western settlers for the duration of the Civil War, they would have to protect themselves. Thus, under pressure from the territories, the U.S. Congress that summer authorized the formation of volunteer regiments to replace the regular army in the territories. So successful was this program that within one year, nearly fifteen thousand volunteer troops had signed on, about five thousand more than had been stationed there before the war.

The new troops of the western territories differed from the prewar army regulars. Most of the volunteers were physically and mentally superior to the men of the peacetime army. They were highly motivated and aggressive because they were charged with the defense of their own towns and homes and families. Although they did not take kindly to discipline—they would not parade as smartly or obey orders as unquestioningly as the regulars did—they were more knowledgeable about frontier life and the ways of the Indians.

The most important difference between these volunteers and the regulars—and what ultimately led to Sand Creek—was the attitude of the volunteers toward the Indians. It was simplistic and unforgiving: They believed in fighting rather than in negotiating. "Less frequently now did the [volunteer] army take the Indian side of a dispute, or discriminate between shades of guilt, or seek solutions other than armed might, or restrain tendencies toward barbaric excesses. The new military may well have provoked more hostilities than it quelled, but with the attitudes that shaped it came bolder and more effective fighters than the Indians had heretofore known."

Colorado was the first of the western territories to organize its militia. The newly appointed territorial governor, William Gilpin, a West Point graduate, lawyer, and politician—and altogether a peculiar man— formed the First Colorado Regiment without any authorization from Washington or so much as one dollar in funds. The outfit quickly became known as "Gilpin's pet lambs." To pay for his army, the governor took it upon himself to issue drafts on the U.S. Treasury, much to Washington's surprise. Influential Denver citizens were given military commissions. John Slough, a lawyer, was made a colonel of Gilpin's regiment; Samuel F. Tappan became lieutenant colonel, and Chivington was appointed major. Governor Gilpin had asked Chivington to serve as regimental chaplain, but Chivington said he would prefer a fighting to a praying commission. He got his wish.

Chivington's first fight was with the merchants and traders who had contracts to equip and supply the regiment. They objected to being paid with the governor's homemade Treasury Department drafts, but Chivington forced the merchants to accept them. "If they were not willing," he said, "we made them willing. I remember several instances where men said, 'I don't want those drafts. They are worth nothing and never will be.' We said, 'Now, this is only a question of whether you will take them as evidence of indebtedness or whether we take the property without any evidence of it.'"

In the end, the suppliers were stuck with about $375,000 in drafts before the U.S. Treasury decided to honor them later in the war. Until that time, the worthless paper nearly ruined the city's economy. Gilpin was forced to resign within a year because of his unorthodox financial practices.

The Gilpin drafts served their purpose, however, and the First Colorado Regiment was mustered into active duty on August 29, 1861. The men were well equipped and after a short period of training at Camp Weld outside of Denver, they were eager to go to war. But there was no war to go to—both the Indians and the Confederates in Texas remained quiet—and the men—ex-miners, farmers, ranch hands, and clerks— grew bored. "They did not like lying in camp," Chivington wrote. Restless now, the troops began to cause problems for the locals, stealing food, drinking, and raising hell. People referred to them as "chicken thieves, jayhawkers, turbulent and seditious, a disgrace to themselves and their country."

The bartender at the Criterion Saloon once made the mistake of denying entry to the men of the First. The soldiers responded by wrecking the place. They withdrew, and later returned to the bar, marching up to the door in their best military fashion with a loaded cannon in tow. "They deserted at will [and] cussed out their officers with impunity. Taps was merely a signal to head for the fleshpots in town." Chivington said, "They only came to camp to get their meals."

City officials organized a special unit of the police force to deal with drunken troopers, but that had little effect. Soldiers who were arrested knew they would not be in jail for long because their friends would batter down the door and free them. The behavior of the volunteers was not much better in camp. One company was notoriously slow and careless about morning formation. Their commanding officer decided to teach them a lesson and ordered that guard duty be assigned to those at the left end of the formation, where stragglers were forced to fall in. The men resolved to beat the C.O. at his own game. Soon there was no longer a left end to any formation. They huddled together in three circles!

Several companies had to be disarmed as a disciplinary measure, with officers and men placed under arrest for mutiny. Chivington, fearing that the men might decamp, wrote to the commanding general at Fort Leavenworth to explain the situation and ask that his outfit be sent into combat. The men wanted to fight—against Indians or Confederates or each other, if need be. They were brave, but they had not enlisted to play at parade-ground soldiering. Typical of the western pioneers, they were independent, wary of discipline, and reluctant to follow orders blindly, characteristics that were to be of major consequence at Sand Creek.

In the fall of 1861, a force of three thousand Texans under the command of Brigadier General Henry H. Sibley, known as the "walking whiskey keg," started out for Colorado Territory. By winter, they had captured Albuquerque and Santa Fe, and an urgent request was dispatched by the commander of Union forces in New Mexico to ask Governor Gilpin to send all available troops to help out. The situation was critical. The Confederates had to be stopped before they reached Denver's goldfields. Finally, the First Colorado Regiment was on the move.

They left Denver in deep snow and biting cold on February 22, 1862, and headed south toward Fort Union, New Mexico, the principal depot for military supplies for all the forts in the area. Fort Union was also the destination of the Confederates.

The morale of the Colorado volunteers improved rapidly, but their discipline did not. The men in one company, mostly German immigrants, believed they were being discriminated against because they had fewer wagons than other units. The company commander, Lieutenant Kerber, announced that his men would go no farther until they were given the same number of wagons as the others. Colonel Slough, the regimental commander, drew his pistol and ordered two other companies to train their weapons on the mutineers, disarm them, and force them to take up the march. The Germans raised their rifles, threatening the colonel. One of them shouted, "You shoot Kerber and we'll fill you full of holes." Colonel Slough wheeled his horse around and turned the problem over to Major Chivington. He placated the men by promising to give them more wagons as soon as they could be found—or stolen. The rebellious company resumed the march.

Chivington himself had occasion to be disobedient during the trek to New Mexico, according to his version of events. Colonel Slough decided to stop for a few days and make camp south of the Arkansas River to allow the horses and mules to rest. Chivington suggested that he use the time to train the men in military tactics. Slough disagreed. He did not plan to fight any large-scale battles. The two men argued so loudly that everyone in the camp could hear them. Chivington appealed directly to the men to support him, and about half the regiment did so, which angered Colonel Slough.

"You can take 'em and go to hell with 'em," Slough shouted. He strode off to his tent, muttering about a court-martial. Chivington had not heard the last of this incident.

Prodded by another frantic message from the Union army commander in New Mexico, Colonel Edward R. S. Canby (who was Confederate General Sibley's brother-in-law), the First Colorado Regiment made a forced march to Fort Union, covering sixty-four miles in twenty-four hours. It was a grueling and magnificent feat. Horses and mules died in harness from the terrible pace, but the spirits of the soldiers were undampened. As soon as they reached the fort, they raided the sutler's store and feasted on stolen champagne, cheese, and crackers.

Quite a few of them got drunk and no one would have minded except that it led to casualties. Sometime during the night, there was a confrontation between Lieutenant Issa Gray, the Officer of the Day, and one of the outfit's best noncoms, Sergeant Philbrook, who shot the lieutenant in the head. There could be but one outcome for the offense; Philbrook was sentenced to death by firing squad, which, Chivington said, was "a very hard fate."

Chivington's troubles with Colonel Slough were not over. The morning after the shooting, Slough and his exec, Lieutenant Colonel Tappan, called on Colonel Canby, only to find Chivington already there enjoying a cozy breakfast. Slough demanded that Chivington be placed under arrest, according to Chivington's account, and court-martialed for insubordination, mutiny, and dereliction of duty. Canby declined to act on Slough's request at that time.

"Our first business is to fight," he said. "Forget all of that until we have Sibley attended to, one way or another."

The conversation turned to how best to deal with the Confederate invasion. Slough made his position clear right away. He believed it was futile to attack Sibley's larger force. Instead, they should carry out delaying tactics to slow the Southern advance. Slough proposed diverting streams, making roads impassable, and burning the grass to starve the Confederates' horses. Chivington disagreed with Slough and did not hesitate to say so.

"My men didn't come here to burn grass," he said. "They came down here to fight. The best place to fight is at the highest possible point, right at the top of the pass. My men are used to high altitudes, Sibley's come from a low altitude. Give them 10 minutes at a mile high, and one of my men will be worth 10 of his."

Canby agreed. The troops would attack.

On the night of March 25, 1862, Colonel Slough led a column of 1,342 men, including 916 of his First Colorado Regiment, out of Fort Union. It was not an orderly procession. Some of the Coloradans lagged behind the column. Others rode ahead to stash a portion of their loot from the sutler's store. A soldier never could tell when champagne, cheese, and crackers might come in handy.

The troops spent the night in the town of Loma, where many of them amused themselves carousing with the Mexican women and fighting with their men. "Some of them fared badly," Chivington said, "if we may judge from their appearance the next day." He let them have their fun, for now. He did not expect them to behave like parade-ground puppets, but when the time came, they would fight like soldiers or answer to him. Few of the men, drunk or sober, wanted to answer to Chivington.

The next morning, Slough ordered Chivington to take two companies of the First Colorado, plus the cavalry, to scout ahead and make a hit-and-run raid on the rebels at Santa Fe. Slough would give Chivington his chance to fight, and if the major survived, then Slough could court-martial him. Slough put these thoughts in a letter, commenting that half his regiment had "gone off to hell with a crazy preacher who thinks he is Napoleon Bonaparte."

Chivington's men first encountered a group of Confederate scouts, who were passing the time playing cards, and captured them without firing a shot. Farther on, he spotted a force of some seven hundred Confederate soldiers proceeding through Apache Canyon. He deployed his infantry on both sides of the canyon, placed the cavalry in reserve, and waited as three gray-clad columns approached. His men held their fire until the rebel force reached a point midway down the canyon. Then they opened up.

The Southerners were caught in the open. They fought valiantly, but scores were killed and wounded. One of them later recalled the sight of Chivington in battle. "Their commander, the biggest man I ever saw, sat on his horse in the road, bellowing his orders like a great bull. Bullets must have been flying all around him, but he paid no attention to them."

By sundown, the rebels had fled. Chivington was left with sixty prisoners and many Confederate wounded. He sent them back under guard to Slough's camp, along with a message requesting reinforcements to deal with a larger Confederate force that he expected to appear at any moment. Slough himself arrived the next night, and the following day, the Confederates advanced on Apache Canyon with approximately one thousand troops.

Slough went forward to meet them, determined that the victory and the glory would be his this time, not Chivington's. He sent the crazy preacher with 430 men on a dangerous march through the mountains, to try to reach the rear of the Confederate force.

Chivington's Coloradans made their way up the mountains through tangles of low-limbed cedar and piñon trees to take up a position above Glorietta Pass, where the Confederate supply train of eighty wagons was located. At about noon, Chivington heard gunfire from the canyon floor where Slough's troops were engaging the enemy, and he began the difficult descent. The terrain was so steep that his troops had to use 125-foot ropes made of leather lines to keep from falling.

Chivington took the Confederate guards by surprise before they could organize any kind of defense. Within minutes, he had captured the fully loaded wagons, all the supplies for Sibley's entire army. All the Southerners had left was what they carried in their knapsacks, and the blow forced Sibley to return to Texas. Chivington's daring action almost certainly saved Colorado and New Mexico from Confederate occupation. The impact was so decisive that the action came to be called the Gettysburg of the West.

Chivington had all the Confederate wagons and supplies heaped together and burned, but a decision about the fate of the 1,100 mules and horses was more troublesome. He could not take the animals on the difficult trek back over the mountain, and he certainly would not leave them for the enemy. Finally, he ordered his men to fix bayonets and kill them. He later described it as the "hardest task I had during the war."

Colonel Slough and his troops at the canyon had taken heavy casualties and been forced to retreat several miles. When General Sibley learned of the loss of his supplies, however, he realized he was in no position to pursue, and he broke off the engagement. Colonel Canby ordered the men back to Fort Union. On April 9, angry at being recalled, Slough resigned his commission. All the officers and men of the First Colorado Regiment signed a petition requesting that Chivington be promoted to full colonel and given command of the regiment, passing over Lieutenant Colonel Tappan. Canby agreed, and he issued the order on April 14. Chivington had his victory, his glory, and now his command.

The regiment remained based at Fort Union for several months. During that summer, supplies were dwindling, especially the stock of tobacco. When the men learned that an army wagon train was approaching, some of them decided to raid it before it reached the fort so they would be assured of getting their tobacco.

Chivington found out about the plan, assembled the men, and told them that if they promised not to raid the train, he would guarantee that they got half the tobacco at no risk to themselves. That seemed like a fair deal, and they agreed. Chivington led the regiment out to meet the wagon train and made a formal request to the officer in charge for half the tobacco he carried. The officer said that the tobacco was for issue to regular army troops only, not volunteers.

"It is only a question, sir," said Chivington calmly, "as to whether we will have half or all of it. If we have to use force, we will take every ounce of tobacco your sutler has, and you will never get one chew. We have come down here, done the fighting and marching, endured the privations, relieved you from the grasp that the enemy had upon you, and we don't intend now that we will be cut off with anything less than fair, even-handed dealing."

Chivington got his tobacco. That matter attended to, he embarked on a trip to Washington to arrange to have his infantry re-equipped as cavalry. During his stay in the capital city, he claimed to have visited "my old-time friend, Mr. Lincoln," and to have turned down an offer from Secretary of War Edwin M. Stanton of a brigadier general's commission in the Union army in the east. "I would rather command the First Cavalry of Colorado than to command the best brigade you have got in the Army of the Potomac," he claimed he told Stanton.

On January 13, 1863, Chivington led the triumphant First Colorado, now a cavalry regiment, on its return to Denver. Crowds lined the streets to cheer the man who had saved them from the rebels, the newly appointed commander of the Military District of Colorado. People mobbed him to shake his hand. He was lauded, toasted, wined and dined, presented with scrolls, swords, and expensive gifts. He was the most popular man in all the territory, both with its civilians and its troops.

A newspaper reporter wrote, "It is only necessary for him to lead for them to follow, and where they both go, you bet your life something is going to be did."

5

The Foul Conspiracy

It happened six hundred miles from Denver on Sunday, August 17, 1862. To the people of Denver and the towns and cities throughout the west, it was their worst nightmare come true. If it could happen there, back east in Minnesota, then no one was safe, certainly not the folks of Denver living with savages in plain sight on every street. It was the most blood-chilling atrocity any Indians had ever committed, and it began with an argument over some eggs.

Four young Santee Sioux warriors were returning to their reservation from hunting when they came across a clutch of eggs laid by a hen that had strayed from a farmer's coop. One of the braves wanted to take the eggs but another warned him that the farmer might cause trouble if he did so. The first accused the second of cowardice. To prove he was not a coward, the second brave said he would kill the farmer. The dare escalated, the farmer and his wife and two neighbors were murdered, and the warriors returned to the reservation to boast of their deeds.

Chief Little Crow called a tribal council to discuss the situation. He argued for peace, saying that there were too many white settlers in the vicinity for them to fight. "The white men are like locusts," he said. "They fly so thick that the whole sky is like a snowstorm. We are only little herds of buffalo left scattered."

The Santee Sioux were considered to be "good" Indians. They lived quietly on their reservation, trying their hand at farming and sending their children to the white man's schools and mission churches. Many had become Christians. Chief Little Crow attended Sunday services at the local Episcopal church, and had spoken with the pastor just that morning.

The tribe remained passive even though their annual annuity had not been paid, the white traders had cheated them, and their crops had been poor. They had endured hunger and humiliation and had given up their lands—and now this. The tribal council voted to go to war, arguing that the Indians would be punished anyway for the crimes committed by the braves. Many years of resentment and bitterness were voted that night, and Little Crow agreed, reluctantly, to lead them.

In the morning, the Santee Sioux struck, and by sunset four hundred white settlers were dead, "dispatched with a savagery rarely equaled in the history of Indian uprisings—families burned alive in their cabins, children nailed to doors, girls raped by a dozen braves and then hacked to pieces, babies dismembered and their limbs flung in the mother's face."

Terror lay on the land and hundreds of whites fled to Fort Ridgely, the nearest army post, which was manned by only two officers and seventy-six men. The commanding officer led a force of forty-six troopers to the reservation, but they were ambushed on the way and only half that number returned to the fort. The following day, the fort itself was besieged. For forty-eight hours, some eight hundred warriors attacked, but the soldiers held them off, thanks to their effective use of three howitzers. The Indians regrouped and set out for the nearby town of New Ulm, where the fighting lasted another day, progressing from street to street, house to house. Much of the town was destroyed, but the locals held on and by dusk Little Crow ordered his warriors to withdraw.

The Sioux uprising was over. When all the bodies were found and counted, the toll of whites killed reached close to eight hundred. Several hundred more had been captured. Now the retribution began. The governor raised a militia force of 1,600 men to chase down the savages. They crossed paths on September 22 in the country's largest battle ever between white and Indian. Defeated in the field, some of the Indians fled to Canada, others surrendered, and the rest were hunted down.

A military commission was established to conduct a trial of nearly four hundred braves accused of rape, murder, and other crimes. Each proceeding lasted less than ten minutes. When they were finished, 303 Indians were sentenced to death. President Lincoln, responding to an appeal from an Episcopal bishop, examined the trial records himself and concluded that the evidence justified the execution of only thirty-eight of the accused. These were hanged together at Mankato, the thirty-eight traps sprung at the same instant. Chief Little Crow escaped to Canada but returned a year later to lead one last raid within sight of St. Paul. Some thirty whites were killed. The next day, he was ambushed and killed while picking blackberries.

The residents of Denver followed every detail of the Minnesota massacre with a morbid fascination. The Sioux had been docile for years, longer than the Cheyenne and Arapaho, and had turned like some tamed animal suddenly gone rabid. More frightening to the people of Denver was the fact that they were unprotected. Most of the regular army troops were committed to the fighting in the east, and the First Colorado Regiment was still in New Mexico. A second volunteer regiment had been organized earlier that summer, but it had already been sent to Kansas to fight the rebel bands from Missouri. Denver missed the jayhawkers and chicken thieves of the First Colorado about whom they had complained so much. They had caused a lot of trouble, but it would be comforting to see some blue uniforms around town again.

Not that the Cheyenne and Arapaho were troublesome. More men had died that year in saloon brawls than had been killed by Indians. Even Chivington agreed that the Indians were peaceable. "We passed the winter of 1862 and 1863 without any very great amount of open hostility," he wrote, "just stealthy work." There had been one disturbing incident, however. Some Cheyenne went to a ranch to beg for food. The rancher and his friends, Denton and Peter Shook, gave them some provisions, but the Indians wanted more. In the ensuing struggle over a side of bacon, Denton Shook was struck in the head, but he fought back and the Indians left.

Some time later, the braves returned with sixty more and began shooting arrows at the ranch house. A few entered the house, grabbed Peter Shook, and tried to drag him outside. Also in the house were several women, and they engulfed Shook in their arms and held on to him. "The feminine phalanx turned the trick, and the Cheyenne moved on to scenes where begging was less complex and women didn't interfere in a man's work."

It was a petty incident, as were others that occurred during that period, but the people were jittery nonetheless. Rumors spread of a vast conspiracy that the Indian tribes were organizing, to rise up and slaughter every white person west of the Missouri. Even William Byers, whose editorials in the *Rocky Mountain News* had been conciliatory the year before, was caught up in an unreasoning panic.

Byers treated the incident with the Shooks as akin to mayhem and murder. "Such outrages have gone quite far enough," he wrote. "It is time the redskins learned to behave themselves; they are paving the way for extermination faster than nature requires." A month earlier he had written that "Indian affairs in our territory are in anything else but a desirable state, just at this time. A growing animosity to the white settlers is manifest in the disposition of our immediate neighbors, the Arapaho and Cheyenne."

These remarks were published before Denver received news of the Minnesota massacre. Fear, prejudice, and hatred hardened after the horrors in Minnesota. Throughout the country, the contagion spread. The Ute, Shoshone, Kiowa, Comanche, and the Southern Oglala and Brulé Sioux ran rampant, marauding and killing. Blue-garbed columns of cavalry rode hard after them. In Colorado Territory, however, the Cheyenne and Arapaho ran off a few horses and mules from the stagecoach stations, begged or stole food, got drunk and made nuisances of themselves. Though how could a settler be sure that the band of five, or maybe twenty-five, warriors riding up to his isolated ranch house only wanted a little food?

The new governor for the Colorado Territory arrived during the summer of 1862, and he exploited and aggravated the undercurrents of suspicion and distrust. His name was John Evans, and as much as any other single individual, he was responsible for sending Chivington and his men marching off to Sand Creek. An impressive figure, five feet ten inches tall and weighing two hundred pounds, Evans had a full beard, aquiline nose, brown hair, and penetrating blue eyes.

A philanthropist and expert whittler, Evans was a physician who had made his fortune in real estate in Illinois. The city of Evanston was named for him, and he was a founder of Northwestern University and later of the University of Denver. He was active in Republican politics and had supported Lincoln's 1860 campaign for the presidency.

A capable organizer and administrator, Evans was also cold-blooded, mercenary, and not reluctant to use his office for political ends. He had two overwhelming ambitions when he arrived in the territory: to develop Colorado's natural resources as quickly as possible and to become its first United States senator. As a result, every action he took was guided by these goals, particularly the latter. He would permit nothing to stand in the way of his political future.

Evans, Chivington, and newspaperman Byers became close friends and allies. All three shared the dream of statehood for Colorado and of high political office and power for themselves. If Evans was to be the first senator, then Chivington would be the first congressman. Byers was content to be the power behind both thrones; a congressional investigating committee later referred to Byers's newspaper as the "official organ" of the Evans administration.

Evans's position as governor also made him ex officio Superintendent of Indian Affairs, a regrettable arrangement because he was not well informed about Indian matters. Nevertheless, he exerted considerable influence on relations between whites and Indians. In his first report to the legislature, he urged the passage of a law authorizing him to raise a militia whenever the need might arise. To justify the measure, he argued that Colorado was surrounded by Indians who could be incited to violence at any time. Evans's 1862 report to the Bureau of Indian Affairs in Washington said that the Cheyenne and Arapaho were restless, but he hoped that the impending return of the First Colorado would keep them docile.

He expected to do more than merely keep the Indians quiet; he wanted them out of the way, confined to the Upper Arkansas Reservation established by the Fort Wise Treaty. The rest of the territory belonged to whites, to the miners and farmers and ranchers. As governor, Evans believed it was his duty to clear the Indians off the land so that it could be developed, farmed, and mined as God had intended.

However, the Indians had no desire to settle in the barren terrain set aside for them. Some of them thought at the time of the signing of the treaty that its provisions were unfair. By now, all of them felt cheated. The land provided for farming had not been irrigated, nor had any of the other promised improvements been made. Only the surveying of the reservation was complete. It was a bad treaty, the Indians believed, and the whites had not lived up to its terms. If the Great Father in Washington refused to honor his commitments, then why should the Cheyenne and Arapaho? Obviously, the white man was not to be trusted.

Governor Evans needed some way to force the Indians off the territorial lands and onto their reservation. If they had been preying on the settlements, then he would have been justified in calling up his newly authorized militia, but the Indians continued to live, almost obstinately, in peace. Evans spread the word, however, that he had begun to receive reports that the Cheyenne and Arapaho were planning to wage war.

The first such evidence, received in April 1863, stated that Southern groups were meeting with the Indians in the northern territories to try to induce them to go on the warpath and attack Fort Larned and Fort Lyon. The Confederates sent some Indians north from Texas to meet with various tribes to enlist their aid. The Osage agreed, but the Kiowa and Comanche refused to take part in the scheme. The Cheyenne and Arapaho also refused, thanks in part to the influence of the trader William Bent, and the efforts of Black Kettle and the other peace chiefs. With so little support forthcoming, the Confederates abandoned their plan for an Indian uprising.

That same month, Denver was visited by a natural disaster. During the night of April 19, a fire broke out in the Cherokee House and by dawn the heart of the city lay in smoke-covered ruins. More than seventy buildings were destroyed, many of them deliberately blown up or razed by teams of mules to create a firebreak. Businesses were wiped out, and the economic losses staggering. Food grew scarce and prices climbed, until the next wagon freight trains reached the city. The indomitable spirit that had built a city in the wilderness only four years before reasserted itself, however, and reconstruction began almost overnight. This time, the builders used brick instead of wood.

Dealing with the aftermath of the fire was easier than dealing with the Indians. In May, Governor Evans claimed he had been told—by whom is unclear—that the Cheyenne and Arapaho had been invited to join the Sioux to drive the whites out of the area. Charles Bent recalled that the Cheyenne and Arapaho chiefs refused to smoke the war pipe, however, "showing that they intended to remain at peace." Evans was unwilling to take the risk, or perhaps he was impatient that the Indians refused to show any hostile intentions, so he sent a warning to the Arapaho camp that they would all be exterminated if they sought war with the whites. He told the Indians to spread the word to all other tribes in the territory.

Events were not moving fast enough for Evans. Despite his threat, the Indians showed no inclination to retreat to their unfinished reservation. He decided to call a meeting with the chiefs to force the issue, and he dispatched the government's Indian agents and other whites friendly with the tribes to tell them that a council would be held in September. The messengers reported back that the chiefs agreed to meet with him

but only with reluctance. When Evans traveled to the council site, however, he found no Indians there.

Furious, he sent Elbridge Gerry, a rancher who was married to a
Sioux woman, to ferret out the Indians. Gerry found a Cheyenne camp a
few miles away, but, in his view, the chiefs were even less receptive to
the idea of a council than they had been before. They complained to him
about the Fort Wise Treaty, saying that they had not understood what
they were signing. Gerry did his best to persuade the chiefs to change
their minds, but they remained adamant. Even descriptions of the many
gifts the governor was offering failed to move them.

Chief Bull Bear was especially truculent.

"Does the Great Father want us to live like white men?" he asked.

"The Great Father," Gerry said, "will help you to live comfortably.
He will build schools and educate your papooses."

"Does the Great Father want us to live like white men?" Bull Bear
asked again.

"Yes, that is what he wants."

"You tell white chief," Bull Bear said, "Indian maybe not so low
yet."

When Gerry reported the Indians' response, Evans was indignant and
insulted. Stronger measures would have to be taken. According to one
military historian, Evans "moved systematically to prove that the Plains
Indians were hostile. His motivation was simply to force a situation
which would enable him to clear Indians from all settled regions of Colorado territory. If the Indians' hostility could be proved, military actions
against them could be justified." It would also help his bid for statehood
and open the way for his election as senator.

In October, Evans reported some news that fit his plan perfectly. It
came from Robert North. An illiterate white man married to an Arapaho
woman, he had lived with the tribe for many years. North told the governor that recently he had rescued an Arapaho woman enslaved by the
Ute. For his bravery, North had been honored by a number of tribes at a
medicine dance held at an encampment fifty-five miles south of Fort
Lyon.

While there, North said, he learned that the Comanche, Apache,
Kiowa, Northern Arapaho, Sioux, and Cheyenne had pledged to make
war on the whites in the spring, as soon as they could gather enough

weapons. Any Indian who opposed this plan was threatened with death if he revealed it.

"I saw the principal chiefs pledge to each other that they would shake hands with and be friendly with the whites until they procured ammunition and guns," North said.

A few weeks later, Evans received apparent confirmation of North's report from John Smith, a trader and interpreter of long standing. Smith believed that the threat of a combined Indian uprising in the spring was real. He had seen large numbers of Sioux, who had never gone so far south before, along the Arkansas and Smoky Hill rivers. Smith also told the governor that Little Raven, the Arapaho peace chief, was reluctant to meet with the Cheyenne and the Sioux. He feared that if he was seen with them, he would be considered an accomplice in the attack that was sure to come in the spring.

On November 9, Evans met with Roman Nose, a Cheyenne chief. Smith was present as interpreter. Roman Nose said he wanted to be friends with the whites, which Smith doubted, but that the other Cheyenne, and the Sioux and Kiowa, desired war.

Evans no longer had any doubt about the inevitability of an Indian uprising. He sent a written copy of Robert North's statement to H. P. Dole, the Commissioner of Indian Affairs in Washington. In a covering letter, Evans said that he was fully satisfied with the truth of North's observations and that he would uncover "each step of progress in this foul conspiracy among those poor degraded wretches."

Other whites with close ties to the Indians, such as Charles Bent, continued to maintain that the Cheyenne and Arapaho refused to smoke the war pipe, but Governor Evans preferred to believe North, Smith, and Roman Nose. War was coming in the spring. On December 14, Evans wrote to Secretary of War Stanton requesting military aid, the authority to call up the militia, and a stationing of troops along the wagon train and stagecoach routes.

He also told Stanton that he had been working with the local Indian agent, Samuel G. Colley, in an attempt to maintain the peace, but that such efforts were futile because the tribes had disappeared. The Indians apparently were far from their usual winter camp. Evans's attempt to locate them was probably not very thorough. There were several Cheyenne villages in sight of Fort Lyon and Fort Larned all during the winter of 1863–1864, and Indians visited the trading posts daily.

The weather that winter was unusually severe, and the Cheyenne and Arapaho were too concerned with their own survival to create problems for the whites, even if they had desired to. H. T. Ketchum, the special agent for Indian affairs, had no trouble finding the Indians. He reported that they were destitute, sick, and starving. Smallpox was rampant; he vaccinated as many people as he could. He wrote that the Indians were friendly and pleased to see him but they were so short of food that they were eating cattle known to be diseased.

The Indians expressed bitterness that white hunters had killed so many buffalo just for the hides and had left the carcasses—vital to the Indians for food—to rot on the prairie. Still, Ketchum noted, they remained at peace. The only disturbance had involved a party of young Arapaho who ran off some horses from a ranch east of Denver. When the chief learned of it, he had the horses returned to their owner.

Traders routinely cheated the Indians, exchanging cheap trinkets for their valuable buffalo robes. The Indians received junk worth less than a dollar or food worth no more than two dollars for a robe with a value of at least eight dollars. At Fort Lyon, agent Ketchum saw Indians trade the robes off their backs for whiskey, despite winter temperatures below freezing. He also saw civilians and soldiers at the fort urging Indians to steal cattle in return for money and whiskey. He watched a white man club an Indian in the face with a whiskey bottle because the Indian had looked "wistfully and longingly" as the man drank the bottle dry.

Ketchum described these things in a letter to Governor Evans. "While citizens and soldiers are permitted to enter their villages with whiskey in daytime and at night; to make the men drunk and cohabit with the squaws, disseminating venereal diseases among them; while the commanding officer at [Fort Larned] continues to get drunk every day and insult and abuse the leading men of the tribes, and make prostitutes of their women; you cannot expect to have any permanent peace with these Indians."

Fort Lyon's commanding officer, Major Scott J. Anthony, who would eagerly ride to Sand Creek with Colonel Chivington, held a different view of the Indians. He summed up the situation by noting that the Indians were indeed destitute. The government should either provide food for them or let them starve to death. The latter, Anthony concluded, would be the easiest way of disposing of them all.

More responsible citizens worked to prevent war. In January 1864, H. P. Bennett, a delegate to the U.S. Congress from Colorado Territory, wrote to the Commissioner of Indian Affairs in Washington. He recounted how the Fort Wise Treaty was supposed to have provided land for the Indians, on which they could be protected from further trespasses by white men and live in peace.

"Three years have elapsed and they are still wanderers from their lands; the buffalo on which their forefathers depended for subsistence are passing rapidly away, by the encroachment of the whites upon their hunting grounds, and already the red man finds hunger and starvation staring him and his in the face."

Bennett added the suggestion, offered by some of the Indians themselves, that the troops at Fort Lyon be posted on the border of the Indians' land to form a barrier between them and the white settlers. That, Bennett concluded, would prevent whites from entering Indian lands and Indians from going into the settlements, and also keep whiskey away from the young warriors.

The Commissioner of Indian Affairs forwarded the letter to the Secretary of the Interior with the recommendation that the matter be decided by the War Department. Somewhere in that shuffle of paper, Bennett's proposal was lost or misplaced, or simply not acted upon. Nothing more was heard of the idea.

As spring and the war Evans predicted got closer, the people of Colorado faced a new problem, the threat of another Confederate invasion from the south. On March 26, 1864, Major General Samuel R. Curtis, in command of the Department of Kansas, which included Colorado Territory, informed Evans that he would have to send every available soldier south of the Arkansas River to meet the threat.

Evans was concerned about leaving the territory defenseless and at the mercy of the Indian tribes. Strangely enough, Evans had never informed Curtis—a man of modest ability and no experience in Indian matters—of his belief that Denver would face an Indian uprising in the spring. Curtis was responsible for the military security of the Colorado Territory and was Chivington's commanding officer, but neither Chivington nor Evans raised the issue of an Indian attack with him. So far as Curtis knew, the Cheyenne and Arapaho were friendly and were expected to remain so.

Ten days before Curtis ordered the removal of the troops from Colorado to prepare for the Confederate threat, Evans told Chivington that Indian agent Sam Colley believed that the Indians were quiet and had no hostile intentions. Colley did say that the Sioux to the north were planning to bring war to the plains in the spring, but that information was not passed on to Curtis, either. Evans asked Colley to find proof of the Indian plans for war.

"I hope you will use all diligence," Evans wrote to Colley, "to ascertain the true character of the threatened Indian hostilities. It is of the utmost importance to the preservation of proper relations with the Indians themselves, as well as the preservation of our citizens from outbreaks and butchery, and all the horrors of Indian war, that the utmost vigilance be observed. If possible, get spies who can get into their confidence and report promptly all you can learn."

As it turned out, there was no time for spies, nor was there any need. Evans, and Chivington, soon got what they wanted.

6

The Indians Are Coming!

In early April, when the first tentative signs of spring began to appear, war—as predicted—came to the plains. But it did not begin the way people expected. No sweeping hordes of warriors thundered across the prairie, raiding and pillaging and murdering. It started when some Indians stole some cows—or so it was said. Maybe the cattle wandered away on their own and the Indians were blamed. In the end, it made no difference; the outcome was the same.

On April 9, a messenger from Irwin and Jackman & Co., government contractors to supply beef to the army, reported to Chivington that 175 head of cattle had been stolen in the vicinity of Sand Creek by Indians who, when last seen, were heading north. When the government investigated the incident a year later, no testimony was taken to support the allegation of theft. The herders who claimed to have seen the Indians chasing off the cattle were never called to testify. Indeed, their names were never mentioned.

The Indians maintained that the cattle had stampeded, spooked for some reason, and that the herders blamed the Indians for their own carelessness. That was a common practice. The scout Kit Carson often said that herders lost stock through their own negligence and blamed Indians for it. The Cheyenne denied stealing the stock, but they did report that they had seen a large herd drifting across the plains and had brought some of the cows into their own camp. The Indians also said that they were not anywhere near Sand Creek when the cattle were reported lost.

No matter how it happened, the damage was done. The fears and expectations of the white population appeared to be confirmed, and Chivington was called upon to do his duty as commander of the Military District of Colorado. The fighting parson ordered out a detachment of fifty-four men, two twelve-pound howitzers, and ten wagons—under the command of Lieutenant George S. Eayre—to pursue the hostiles.

After several days on the trail, made more difficult by unexpected snowstorms, Eayre sighted an Indian village. By the time he reached it, it was deserted. The Indians, a small band of Cheyenne, said they were frightened by the rapid approach of so many soldiers. One Indian had stayed behind, and when Eayre sent two men to get him, he killed one and ran away. According to Eayre's report, the Indian camp consisted of five lodges and contained large quantities of beef and buffalo meat plus a cache of supplies, all of which he put to the torch.

The next day, Eayre's detachment came upon another deserted village fifteen miles away. They found nineteen head of cattle, which Eayre's civilian guide identified as part of the missing stock. Eayre burned the village and returned to Denver for additional supplies and lighter wagons so he could continue his pursuit of the Indians. He obtained the wagons simply by commandeering them on the city streets. He reported to Chivington that the cattle had been stolen by the Cheyenne and that they had obviously planned the hostilities since they had opened fire first.

After Lieutenant Eayre resumed his patrol to find the rest of the herd and the thieving Indians, Chivington received a report from a rancher named Ripley complaining that Indians had run off his mules, destroyed telegraph lines, and harassed ranchers in the northern part of the territory. Chivington ordered Lieutenant Clark Dunn and forty men to recover the mules and to disarm the Indians and take them prisoner.

Stopping to water their horses at the Platte River, Dunn and his troopers spotted what they said was a village of about twenty Indians with some mules camped about a mile upstream. (According to Charles Bent's account, the party consisted of fourteen Cheyenne Dog Soldiers on their way north to visit another tribe; they said they had found the mules wandering on the prairie and were taking them along.) Lieutenant Dunn sent the rancher Ripley and a soldier ahead to examine the mules. The rancher claimed they were his. The soldier reported that the Indians confronted them with drawn rifles and were ready to fight.

Dunn had divided his command to cover more territory and had with him only fifteen men. He formed them in a line and advanced on the Indian camp. Halting about five hundred yards away, he dismounted and indicated with hand gestures that he wanted to talk. One Cheyenne brave approached Dunn and the two men shook hands. Believing that the tension had been broken, the rest of the Indians rode up to the line of soldiers and dismounted. It was then that Dunn ordered his men to disarm the braves.

Dunn later claimed that the Indians fired first—the Indians said the soldiers did—and when the fight ended, four soldiers and three Cheyenne lay wounded. Dunn reported that the battle lasted at least a half hour and that he had killed "quite a number" of the Indians. The soldiers chased the Cheyenne for several miles but gave up at nightfall when it started to snow.

When Dunn returned to Denver on April 15, a report was received that the same band of Indians he had confronted had attacked a ranch, killing two persons and wounding a third, and had run off all the cattle. Although stealing cows and mules was serious, murdering ranchers was quite another matter. Dunn and his men rode to the site of the reported killings and found nothing—no bodies, no wounded men, no signs of a fight. However, the rumors persisted and the fear spread. The Indians were on the warpath.

Colonel Chivington took a hard line against the Indians immediately. He sent a warning to all posts in the territory to be alert for cattle rustlers, and set forth a prescription for dealing with the Indians. "There is but one course for us to pursue, to make them behave or kill them, which latter it now seems we shall have to do."

To an officer in command of a post along the Indians' expected line of march, Chivington wrote, "Be sure you have the right ones, and then kill them." In a message to the C.O. at Fort Laramie, warning that Cheyenne were heading in their direction with stolen stock, he said, "Look out for them and kill them." A dispatch to his superior, General Curtis, was less vindictive, however. Chivington merely said that he would "chastise the Cheyenne severely" unless Curtis instructed him otherwise.

Chivington, too, was on the warpath. The push for Colorado's statehood was under way and he was deeply committed to it, along with his cronies Evans and Byers. Chivington's political future, if he was to have one, depended on statehood so that he could run for Congress. He was not alone in these ambitions. Other influential and well-connected men sought the office. The cheers and acclaim he had received for his actions at Glorietta Pass two years before had long faded and he had done nothing since to keep his name in the public mind, except, perhaps, to alienate some supporters with his arrogant behavior as commander of the military district.

Chivington's high-handed manner when the First Colorado Regiment was organized, forcing merchants to take the worthless Gilpin treasury drafts in lieu of cash, had created resentment. These feelings lingered among the businessmen and were inflamed with every peremptory action, such as Lieutenant Eayre commandeering wagons off the streets. Chivington was, after all, responsible for the behavior of his men.

No, the glory had faded and for many former admirers the praise had turned to grumbles, the admiration to indignation. Chivington needed to demonstrate his courage again, to restore his heroic image. Since the Confederates were apparently content to leave Colorado in peace, Chivington would have to do battle with the savages. If he could save the populace of Denver from the marauding hordes of Indians, he would soon be on his way to the U.S. Congress.

Stealing a few cows did not count as marauding, however. The pace of the war would have to pick up if Chivington was to find glory. When, on April 16, he received a report that some drunken Indians had terrorized a rancher, he ordered Major Jacob Downing—a lawyer before he joined the First Colorado—to investigate. Downing was a hard-liner like Chivington. "I think and earnestly believe," he said, "the Indians to be an obstacle to civilization, and should be exterminated." With a force of sixty men, Downing rode out along the South Platte River. He spoke with many settlers and learned that they feared an Indian uprising, but he did not find any Cheyenne or any evidence of their crimes.

Two weeks later, his luck changed. He reported to Chivington that he had captured an Indian—half Cheyenne and half Sioux—but had not killed him because of his Sioux blood. (Apparently, Downing had an understanding with Chivington that only Cheyenne were to be killed.) If he obeyed his own impulses, Downing said, he would kill the Indian, but instead he questioned the man by "roasting his shins" over a small fire, and he disclosed the location of a Cheyenne camp.

Guided by his prisoner, Downing led his detachment toward Cedar Canyon, north of the South Platte River, arriving shortly after sunrise. The campsite was occupied by women, children, and old men—the warriors were off hunting—and the Cheyenne had no inkling of any trouble between Indians and whites, according to the report of the trader John Smith. These Indians were peaceful, friendly, and virtually defenseless.

That made no difference to Downing. So far as he was concerned, he was at war. "I made my attack on the Indians from the fact that constant statements were made to me by the settlers of the depredations committed by the Indians on the Platte, and the statements of murders committed; and I regarded hostilities as existing between the whites and Cheyenne before I attacked them." The murders Downing mentioned had been committed only in a rancher's imagination, but soon that would change.

Downing gave the order to charge. "I ordered the men to commence killing them," he said. "I burned up their lodges and everything I could get hold of. I took no prisoners." He recounted that the battle lasted three hours and that he and his men killed twenty-six Indians and wounded thirty, with a loss of one soldier killed and one wounded. He also reported that there were no women or children among the dead. How they managed to escape while only the men were killed was a feat he did not explain.

He told Chivington that he had punished the Indians severely but that the battle was only the beginning of a war that could have only one result—the extermination of the Cheyenne. Downing's actions that morning in Cedar Canyon were both a preview and a rehearsal for the later events at Sand Creek.

On May 10, Lieutenant Eayre and his men, hunting Cheyenne with authorization from Chivington to burn lodges and kill Indians wherever he found them, spotted a band of four hundred Indians led by Chief Lean Bear. The Indians had been camped for the winter near Fort Larned and were on their way north, trying to avoid the soldiers. Having heard about Downing's attack, they decided that it was no longer safe to stay there, so when Eayre caught up with them, they were about 160 miles southeast of Denver.

Eayre later reported that the Indians attacked first and that he defeated them in a seven-hour battle. He claimed to have killed twenty-eight, with a loss to his own forces of four dead and three wounded. The Indians had a different version, according to George Bent. They were alarmed by the sight of the soldiers with their cannon and prevailed upon their chiefs to meet with the whites to tell them they were friendly and meant no harm.

"A number of us mounted our horses and followed Lean Bear, the chief, out to meet the soldiers," recalled Wolf Chief many years later. "We rode up on a hill and saw the soldiers coming in four groups with cannon drawn by horses. Lean Bear, the chief, told us to stay behind him while he went forward to show his papers from Washington which would tell the soldiers that we were friendly. The officer was in front of the line."

Lean Bear wore a medal given to him by President Abraham Lincoln. It hung around his neck and he displayed it proudly and with the assurance that it would protect him from harm. The soldiers would not dare shoot at a man who wore a medal from the Great White Father himself. As Lean Bear came within twenty feet of Eayre, the lieutenant ordered his men to open fire. Lean Bear fell at once. The soldiers raced toward him and riddled his body with bullets.

Eayre ordered the howitzers to fire, and the battle was on. Wolf Chief did not say how long it lasted or how many were killed, but he insisted that the fighting ended when Black Kettle, the Cheyenne peace chief, rode out from the camp. "He told us we must not fight with the white people, so we stopped."

According to Wolf Chief, the younger braves were so angry over Lean Bear's murder that they chased Eayre and his men back to Fort Larned. They no longer saw any reason to live at peace with the whites, and nothing Black Kettle said could subdue their rage. They raided a ranch at Walnut Creek, owned by a white man with a Cheyenne wife. She bargained for his life. The Indians took her and told the rancher to clear out because they intended to kill every white person they could find. For several days, bands of Cheyenne warriors ranged up and down the stagecoach line, ransacking stations and ranches. They found them abandoned. The whites had fled.

Next it was the turn of the Arapaho. Shortly after Lieutenant Eayre brought his men to Fort Larned, a band of Kiowa came to the post. The fort's commander, Captain Parmeter, had been warned by the Arapaho peace chief, Left Hand, that the Kiowa intended to steal the horses. Parmeter ignored the warning and was drunk when the Kiowa arrived. Kiowa women distracted the soldiers by dancing for them, and during the dance, the braves ran off the herd, including 240 of Eayre's horses and mules.

Bearing a white flag, Left Hand visited the post to offer his help in recovering the horses. Captain Parmeter, who later was relieved for drunkenness, ordered his men to fire on Left Hand and his band of Arapaho. An Indian was an Indian, after all. The Arapaho escaped unhurt, but, incensed by the soldiers' actions, they ran off all the horses from their own agency and so terrified the settlers in the area that they abandoned their homes. It wasn't long before the settlers demanded revenge.

Yet there were some who still thought, or hoped, that a full-scale war could be averted. It is significant that those who held this view were mostly regular army officers. For example, Major H. D. Wallen of the Seventh Infantry wrote to the army's adjutant general that "an extensive Indian war is about to take place between the whites and the Cheyenne, Kiowa, and a band of Arapaho. It can be prevented by prompt management."

Major T. I. McKenny, a staff officer sent to Colorado by General Curtis to investigate the situation, reported that "if great caution is not exercised on our part, there will be a bloody war. It should be our policy to try and conciliate them, guard our mails and trains well to prevent theft, and stop these scouting parties [of Chivington's men] that are roaming over the country, who do not know one tribe from another and who will kill anything in the shape of an Indian. It will require only a few more murders on the part of our troops to unite all these warlike tribes."

It was too late for conciliation, however. As Major McKenny was drafting his report, war parties of Cheyenne and Arapaho were roaming the plains to clear out the whites along the Platte and Arkansas trails.

Thus the war began—over some missing cattle. It was to be a total, merciless war: a war that ultimately would cost the U.S. government $30 million and result in the deaths of uncounted numbers of settlers and Indians; a war that would terrorize the Colorado Territory and reach its bloody climax at Sand Creek. By May of 1864, Black Kettle and the other peace chiefs had lost all influence over their warriors.

The spring and summer of 1864 would not soon be forgotten by the residents of Denver and its outlying ranches and settlements. Each day brought grisly rumors of atrocities and raids all along the Platte. No one in Denver had actually seen the victims, or the Indians, but everyone knew someone who had heard from someone else . . . and people remembered the horrors in Minnesota. Every shadow on the horizon and night coyote wail became an Indian. Even nature conspired to add to the terror.

A light rain fell on May 19, just enough to dampen the dust in the streets. At dusk, a rainbow arched gracefully across the sky, but west of the city, thick black clouds hid the Great Divide and dull booms of thunder rumbled down from the unseen mountains. For weeks, it had been raining heavily in the mountains, just as the deep winter snows began to melt. Some of the mines had been flooded, but it was nothing to worry about. That often happened in the spring.

Around midnight, those who were not yet asleep heard a strange noise. It sounded like the roar of the wind and it seemed to be getting louder and closer. A huge wall of water, some twenty feet high, appeared out of the darkness and surged down the bed of Cherry Creek, carrying with it the ruins of houses and barns, horses, cattle, and sheep.

Enormous waves tore through the city in minutes, sweeping buildings loose from their foundations and inundating everything with tons of mud. A schoolteacher and reporter for the *Rocky Mountain News,* "Professor" O. J. Goldrick, described the scene.

> About the midnight hour of Thursday, the nineteenth instant, when almost all in town were knotted in the peace of sleep, dead to all noise and blind to all danger, snoring in calm security, a frightful phenomenon sounded in the distance, and a shocking calamity presently charged upon us. Hark! What and where is this? A torrent or tornado? And where can it be coming from, and wither going? Presently the great noise of the mighty waters, like a roaring Niagara, burst upon us.

No more than a dozen people lost their lives in the flood, but there was plenty of damage to property. Many buildings within the city simply disappeared, among them the Methodist church, offices, the jail, and city hall. The town's safe, which contained municipal court records, maps, and other important papers, was never found. And the *Rocky Mountain News* building, built on stilts in the middle of the creek bed, went down in grand style, according to the garrulous Professor Goldrick.

> Down it sank, with its Union flagstaff, into the maelstrom of the surging waters, soon to appear and disappear, between the waves, as, wild with starts, in mountains high, they rose and rolled, as if endeavoring to form a dread alliance with the clouds.

Four employees were trapped in the bobbing, twisting wreckage, but they escaped through the upper-story windows and clung to ropes thrown to them by people on the riverbank. Not a trace of the building remained in the creek bed, and rubble from the structure was uncovered along the banks over the next thirty years. The newspaper presses, weighing several thousand pounds each, were found miles away. Editor Byers and his family, stranded on the top floor of their farmhouse outside of town, were rescued by Chivington and a boatload of soldiers.

Hundreds of people lined the banks of the creek to witness the destruction of the town, many of them clad in nightclothes, having been rescued from their homes by the men of the First Colorado Regiment from Camp Weld. One, a Mrs. Sanford, recorded her impressions in her diary.

> By the light of bonfires along the creek, we could see the inky waves, 15 to 20 feet high, carrying trees, houses, cattle, and sheep, and, for all we knew, human beings, to certain destruction. It was a wild, weird night, never to be forgotten. Early dawn revealed scenes of pitiful desolation.

In a few days the waters receded, leaving the residents of Denver with a massive cleanup and rebuilding effort while they continued to look over their shoulders and across the empty prairie for signs of the Indian attack they knew was coming.

On May 28, Governor Evans was told by Elbridge Gerry that all the Cheyenne were bitter and hated the whites because of the recent expeditions against them and the murder of Lean Bear. The governor sent a worried message to General Curtis noting that the Cheyenne were "in strong force" and that the punishment meted out to them by Major Downing at Cedar Canyon had only whetted their appetite for revenge. Evans predicted a prolonged war unless a new expedition was sent out to deal decisively with the Indians. Otherwise, the lines of communication between Denver and the states would be cut.

He received no reply from Curtis. A few days later, he dispatched a more emotional appeal. "It will be destruction and death to Colorado if our lines of communication are cut off, or if they are not kept so securely guarded as that freighters will not be afraid to cross the plains. We are now short of provisions and but few trains are on the way. I would respectfully ask that our troops may be allowed to defend us and whip these redskin rebels into submission at once."

Denver's geographical situation made it vulnerable. All provisions and supplies had to be brought from the east over the Platte River trail, and if passage was obstructed, the city would be isolated and under siege. Curtis responded to Evans's second plea the day he received it. He sent a telegram to Chivington in care of the governor.

"Send out force to crush the Indians that are in open hostility, as requested by Governor Evans."

Four days later, having received no acknowledgment from Chivington, General Curtis sent another message.

"What troops have moved, and where are they? What can you send forward? The sending of supplies, as well as Indian troubles, makes it important to know."

Chivington apparently made no reply and Curtis did not inquire again. The fighting parson ignored his orders and did not assign a force to crush the Indians, not at that time.

On June 8, a council was held between the local U.S. Indian agents and chiefs of the Oglala and Brulé Sioux tribes at Fort Cottonwood in Nebraska Territory. The purpose of the meeting was to assess the hostile intentions of the Cheyenne. The Sioux said they wanted to remain friends with the whites and were afraid of being mistaken for Cheyenne and attacked by soldiers. The chiefs reported that the Cheyenne boasted of killing every white person along the Platte River trail. The Cheyenne were said to be arming themselves heavily, but as far as the Sioux were concerned, they believed the Cheyenne were fools for going to war with the whites. They would surely all be killed.

The skirmishes with the Cheyenne had not yet reached Denver. Raids were reported farther east, between Fort Lyon and Kansas, but no guns had been fired near the city. To the residents, the Indian uprising remained mostly exaggeration and rumor. That all changed on June 11.

That morning, Ward Hungate, the manager of a ranch near Box Elder Creek, twenty-five miles east of Denver, was with his hired hand, Miller, looking for stray cattle. They reached the crest of a hill several miles from home, looked back, and saw pillars of smoke rising from the ranch house. That could mean only one thing. Hungate was frantic. His wife and two young daughters were back there.

Miller said he would ride to Denver to get help, and he urged Hungate to go with him. The Indians would kill him if he went back to the ranch. There was nothing he could do for his family now. But Hungate wheeled his horse around and raced home. Miller reached Denver and contacted the owner of the ranch. The man hitched up his team and wagon and headed out alone, unable to find anyone else willing to accompany him.

He found Hungate's body some distance from the house, riddled with more than eighty bullets. Every outbuilding had been burned to the ground and all the stock driven off. He searched the grounds for Mrs.

Hungate and the children and finally found them in a well. Their bodies had been mutilated, the girls' throats slashed so deeply that their heads had nearly been severed. They had all been tied together and tossed in the well.

News of the killings spread rapidly. Chivington ordered out a detachment to find the Indians and said not to encumber themselves with prisoners. Tales of huge war parties riding through the territory became commonplace. It was not until several months later that it was learned that the Hungates had been killed by four Arapaho braves on their way north.

The ranch owner took the battered bodies of the Hungate family into Denver and placed them on public exhibition in a box in a downtown store. If someone deliberately desired to inflame the already-aroused passions of the white population, he could have found no better way than by displaying those decaying human remains. Although no one seems to know who recommended it, Governor Evans could surely have prevented the spectacle had he so wished. However, if his goal was war with the Indians, then the public viewing of the Hungates was a master stroke. (Chivington might well have been capable of ordering the ghoulish display, but he was not in Denver at the time.)

Whether deliberate or not, the sight of the bodies, especially the two little blond-haired girls, ages three and six, hardened the hatred of everyone who saw them. The Hungates in death now became for the whites what Lean Bear was for the Cheyenne—martyrs, a focal point, a rallying cry and symbol. And, as symbols often do, they led to greater outrages on both sides.

Rumors ran like wildfire through dry grass that the Indians were poised to attack the settlements and ranches, and farmers streamed into Denver for protection. A newly formed militia was drilling on East Fourteenth Street when a man galloped into town shouting, "The Indians are coming! The Indians are coming!"

Other riders carried the alarm throughout the countryside. Those settlers who had remained on their ranches headed for town as fast as their teams and buckboards could take them. The sight of terrified families pouring into Denver with the few possessions they had taken the time to pack galvanized the locals into action. The women and children were shepherded into the two strongest buildings, the U.S. Mint and the Lindell Hotel on Larimer Street. Iron shutters were bolted in place across the windows and armed men patrolled outside.

A group of residents demanded weapons and ammunition from the military storeroom. Nervous guards held them back for a time, but when they threatened to destroy the building, the guards unlocked the doors and let them take whatever they wanted.

By midnight, scouts who had been sent out to reconnoiter reported no sign of Indians. An investigation revealed that the scare had been started by one panicky rancher who mistook a group of Mexican ranch hands— who were waving and yelling to round up some cattle—for an Indian war party.

Governor Evans imposed martial law in Denver on the day of the great Indian scare, ordering all businesses to close at 6:30 P.M. so that every able-bodied man could report for military drill at 7:00. He sent an impassioned, and distorted, statement of Denver's situation to Secretary of War Stanton in Washington, bypassing General Curtis.

"Indian hostilities on our settlements commenced, as per information given you last fall. One settlement devastated 25 miles east of here; murdered and scalped bodies brought in today. Our troops near all gone. Can furnish 100-days men, if authorized to do so, to fight Indians."

Two days later, Evans made a direct request of General Curtis. The Indian alliance was so powerful, he said, that it was impossible to protect the settlements and supply lines without additional military forces. The people of the Colorado Territory were depending on General Curtis to subdue that alliance of "infernal barbarians." He included two statements to support his position that the Indians were at war. One was from Robert North, who earlier had told Evans of a planned uprising among the Cheyenne.

North now said that he had learned that an Indian war was imminent. It would be led by the Cheyenne to take back their lands and drive the whites from the territory. The Indians believed they had been cheated by the traders and they would no longer listen to their peace chiefs.

The second statement was from Jack Jones, sometimes known as William McGaa, who claimed to be the son of a lord mayor of London. Generally drunk, McGaa was a trader who had lived with Indians for twenty years and purported to know all the Cheyenne chiefs. He told Evans that the Cheyenne had been raiding small wagon trains for eight years, and that he knew personally of eight such incidents in which men, women, and children had been murdered, but that the Indians had taken care to leave no traces of their attacks.

The Cheyenne, McGaa continued, were the ringleaders of a conspiracy. They and other tribes had been secretly gathering guns and ammunition. They knew they had been robbed of their country by the whites and they would no longer abide by past treaties or make new ones. Only the recapture of their land would satisfy them. McGaa added that the Cheyenne intended to so impoverish the whites that they would clear out. His statement was a damning indictment of the Cheyenne, not only of their plans but also for past depredations. More reputable traders, such as William Bent, never confirmed McGaa's claims, but Governor Evans did not take the trouble to seek verification.

General Curtis did not relish being pushed into a war by a nervous and ambitious politician, and he made it clear to Evans that he did not agree about the threat of an Indian uprising. He was not convinced that a war had begun or that it was even likely.

Evans was greatly distressed by Curtis's attitude of disbelief. He renewed his pleas on June 22, noting that it was only because of advance information he had received from North and McGaa that he had been able to avert another Minnesota massacre. The governor was a bit short on detail as to how he had accomplished that, but he apparently believed it. He asked General Curtis to approve a three-pronged attack on the hostile Indian alliance—Chivington from the south, Curtis from the east, and General Mitchell, from Nebraska Territory, from the north.

Then, trying to control his anger at Curtis's skepticism and his failure to see the situation to be as dangerous as Evans claimed, the governor wrote, "I had supposed that the information I have given you was sufficient to satisfy you that this Indian war is no myth but a terrible reality. If you have evidence that my information of Indian hostilities and alliances for war are not well founded, I shall be most happy to be informed of it; yes, to satisfy me that I am mistaken will be the greatest favor you can confer upon me and the people of Colorado generally. But how any evidence can disprove the facts which are furnished I am at a loss to perceive, and how the multiplied and numerous assurances from friendly Indians, Indian traders, and people who suffer, and our troops who have had several engagements with them, can fail to prove our dangers, I am at a loss to understand."

At the same time, Evans set in motion a plan to separate friendly Indian tribes from the hostiles. He directed the Indian agent Sam Colley to arrange food and other supplies for friendly Indians at Fort Lyon and Fort Larned. The idea, he explained to Colley, was to provide refuges for those braves who did not choose to fight, places where they would be free from attack by soldiers. Perhaps, Evans added, other Indians who grew tired of fighting would also come, thereby reducing the size of the Indian forces with which the troops and settlers would have to contend.

Accordingly, on June 27, Evans issued a proclamation to be distributed to as many Indians as could be reached.

> To the friendly Indians of the plains:
>
> Agents, interpreters, and traders will inform the friendly Indians of the plains that some members of their tribes have gone to war with white people.
>
> They steal stock and run it off, hoping to escape detection and punishment. In some instances, they have attacked and killed soldiers and murdered peaceable citizens. At this the Great Father is angry, and will certainly hunt them out, and punish them. But he does not want to injure those who remain friendly to the whites. He desires to protect and take care of them. For this purpose I direct that all friendly Indians keep away from those who are at war, and go to places of safety.
>
> The object of this is to prevent friendly Indians from being killed through mistake; none but those who intend to be friendly with the whites must come to these places. The families of those who have gone to war with the whites must be kept away from among the friendly Indians.
>
> The war on hostile Indians will be continued until they are all effectually subdued.

The intent was clear. Friendly Indians would be provided with havens where they could be protected from attacks by soldiers. Evans listed the sanctuaries to which the friendly Indians should go: Kiowa and Comanche to Fort Larned; Sioux to Fort Laramie. "Friendly Arapaho and Cheyenne belonging on the Arkansas River will go to Major Colley, U.S. Indian agent at Fort Lyon, who will give them provisions and show them a place of safety."

That place of safety was on the banks of what some called the Big Sandy, but which was known to others as Sand Creek.

7

Kill and Scalp All

"Dead cattle, full of arrows, are lying in all directions. A general Indian war is anticipated." So wrote William Byers in the *Rocky Mountain News* on July 18. The threat of an Indian war was much more than just anticipated by then, however, especially by the emigrants and settlers along the Platte River trail. The day before Byers's article appeared, war parties had made scattered raids along the trail, hitting stagecoach stations and freight trains. Buildings were torched, stock run off, and an undetermined number of people killed. The next day, Indians attacked a wagon train at Walnut Creek, only fifteen miles from Fort Larned, killing ten men and scalping two others, who survived the ordeal.

No doubt existed about the identity of the braves responsible. They were Arapaho, Cheyenne, and Sioux. Indian agent Sam Colley, who had not been sympathetic even when the Indians were docile, wrote to Governor Evans a week later to say that the Indians could no longer be trusted. His solution was a simple and popular one: "a little powder and lead is the best food for them."

The army issued orders to bar all small wagon trains from proceeding through the territory until enough wagons could be assembled to form trains sufficiently large that the Indians would refrain from attacking them. Orders were also sent to the military posts requiring them to keep their stock penned up at night and permitting grazing during the day only under guard. In addition, no Indians were to be allowed inside any of the forts unless they were blindfolded first, a precaution taken so that the Indians would not learn the extent of the forts' defenses or the number of available troops. "Neglect of this military concealment," the notice read, "will be followed by the most severe and summary punishment."

Throughout this tense period, Chivington was shuttling between Denver and the outlying forts, sending detachments against marauding bands, arranging troop escorts for the U.S. mail, and providing protection for the smaller posts and camps. On the rosters of the Military District of Colorado, he had slightly in excess of two thousand men under his command—the First Colorado Regiment plus some small units of regulars—but the number fit for duty at any one time was usually fewer than fifteen hundred, and these were spread thinly over a vast territory. The Indians hit at random, like tornadoes skipping across the prairie, touching down where wind and whimsy took them, only to disappear quickly, leaving destruction and dreadful memories in their wake.

There were many dreadful memories to live with that August and September. The strikes increased in frequency and boldness, and the death toll among whites edged higher. Ranches were burned and sacked in greater numbers, men were killed, and women and children carried into captivity. Savvy white settlers under attack saved a last bullet for themselves. Each day brought reports of fresh depredations.

August 8: Wagon train burned; eleven men killed; one woman and one child kidnapped.

August 10: Ranch on the Platte River attacked; two women and three children captured.

August 19: Wagon train raided; ten men tortured to death; wagons burned.

Between August 8, the first day of the outbreak, and August 28—a period of only three weeks—more than fifty whites along the Platte River trail were murdered. On August 18, Chivington sent a dispatch to General Curtis's chief of staff: "Have honor to report that Indians all around us. Can easily raise a company for 100 days, most likely two or three [companies]; can I do it? Needed immediately for defense against Indians."

The residents of Denver felt themselves under siege and isolated from the rest of the country. Martial law remained in effect throughout the summer. Men carried guns with them at all times. The people would not have been surprised to see the Indians riding up Larimer Street at any moment. Women and children sheltered in solid brick buildings at night. Shops closed early. Farmers abandoned their fields, ready for harvest, and left the crops to wither. Locusts swarmed over the plains, blotting out the sun, devouring what remained. A biblical sense of doom hung over the land.

Along the Platte River trail, hundreds of stagecoach passengers were left stranded at military posts, together with scores of freight wagons and their crews. The trail was effectively closed for nearly six weeks, host only to Indians and the swirls of dust and sand. No mail from the east could reach Denver. Finally, the mail was shipped to Panama, then San Francisco, and taken overland from the west to Denver.

As food grew scarce, prices soared. The cost of flour jumped at once from nine dollars to sixteen dollars per hundred pounds, eventually reaching forty-five dollars. The inflation was not all the fault of the Indians, however. One Colorado historian explained it simply: "A group of leading businessmen and officials seized opportunity by the forelock. They bought up all the flour and boosted the price."

The city ran out of coal oil, leaving people to depend on candles. William Byers, established in new quarters after the flood, faced a severe shortage of newsprint. Before supplies were restored, he published the *Rocky Mountain News* on brown wrapping paper, pink and white tissue paper, and yellow butcher paper. Some days, the paper was small, but Byers never missed an issue. During the September election, he even managed to combine reporting and advertising.

> INDIAN MURDERS. The most revolting, shocking cases of assassination, arson, murder, and manslaughter that have crimsoned the page of time have been done by Indians, in former days and recently, but nevertheless we hold ourselves hourly prepared to strike you off from 1 to 20,000 election [leaflets] at lowest panic prices, and in the type of the art, that's sure to make you win.

While the citizens of Denver were learning to live with shortages of necessities, the Indians were prospering. George Bent, still trusted by them, wrote that as he rode through the Indian villages, he saw "scalp dances constantly going on; warriors were filled with plunder taken from the captured wagon trains; warriors were strutting about with ladies' silk cloaks and bonnets on, and the Indian women were making shorts for the young men out of the finest silk."

Governor Evans bombarded the War Department in Washington with frantic appeals for help, including a plea for authority to organize a regiment of one-hundred-day volunteers. On August 10, he wrote to the

Commissioner of Indian Affairs that Colorado was facing the most massive Indian war the continent had ever seen. If Evans was not allowed to raise the one-hundred-day regiment, the white population of the territory would be slaughtered. On the following day, the governor issued a proclamation "authorizing all citizens of Colorado, either individually or in such parties as they may organize, to go in pursuit of all hostile Indians on the plains, to kill and destroy, as enemies of the country, wherever they may be found, all such hostile Indians."

"The conflict is upon us," Evans wrote, "and all good citizens are called upon to do their duty for the defense of their homes and families."

The declaration was published in the *Rocky Mountain News,* along with an editorial comment from Byers. "A few months of active extermination against the red devils will bring quiet and nothing else will."

On August 18, after Evans had been informed that a man and a boy had been killed south of Denver, he sent his most strongly worded appeal to Secretary of War Stanton.

"Extensive Indian depredations, with murder of families, occurred yesterday 30 miles south of Denver. Our lines of communication are cut, and our crops, our sole dependence, are all in exposed localities, and cannot be gathered by our scattered population. Large bodies of Indians are undoubtedly near to Denver, and we are in danger of destruction both from attack of Indians and starvation. I earnestly request that Colonel Ford's regiment of Second Colorado volunteers be immediately sent to our relief. It is impossible to exaggerate our danger."

Evans also wrote to General Curtis, asking again for enough troops to keep the Platte River trail open. Otherwise, the position of the territory would be "hopeless."

Two days later, the governor received another alarming report. Elbridge Gerry rode the sixty-five miles between his ranch and Denver nonstop to pound on Evans's door at midnight. Two Cheyenne friends had warned him that over the next two nights, every settlement between the Platte and Arkansas rivers would be attacked simultaneously by war parties.

This development was particularly frightening because previous Indian raids had involved small, uncoordinated bands. If Gerry's information was correct, up to one thousand Apache, Comanche, Cheyenne, and Arapaho braves were uniting for this campaign, and no local militia or regiment of volunteers would be capable of stopping them. Chivington rushed the few men he could spare to the outlying settlements, but he fully expected that they would be overwhelmed.

The attacks came two nights later, but the raiding parties were small and quickly driven off. Ironically, the ranch that suffered the greatest loss of stock—150 head—belonged to Elbridge Gerry.

Evans renewed his request to Secretary of War Stanton: "Pray give positive orders for our Second Colorado cavalry to come out. Have notice published that they will come in detachments to escort trains up the Platte on certain days. Unless escorts are sent thus we will inevitably have a famine in addition to this gigantic Indian war. Flour is $45 a barrel, and the supply growing scarce, with none on the way. Through spies we got knowledge of the plan of about 1,000 warriors in camp to strike our frontier settlements, in small bands, simultaneously in the night, for an extent of 300 miles. It was frustrated at the time, but we have to fear another attempt soon. Pray give the order for our troops to come, as requested, at once, as it will be too late for trains to come this season."

General Curtis did not send the Second Colorado Regiment back to Denver. He needed to commit all his forces to the Confederate threat in Arkansas and Missouri and the larger Indian wars in Nebraska and Kansas. Compared with those problems, the troubles in Colorado were minor. To placate Evans, however, he did authorize the formation of a new regiment of Colorado volunteers.

The Third Colorado Volunteer Cavalry Regiment, called the hundred dazers or the Bloodless Third, had no trouble finding recruits. At the same time enlistment began, someone started a rumor that all able-bodied men in Colorado, except those already in some sort of home-guard service, would be drafted and sent east to fight the Confederates. The tale was untrue, but, conveniently, it had the desired effect; in a matter of weeks, 650 men joined the Third.

Command was given to twenty-eight-year-old Colonel George L. Shoup of the First Colorado, who had served under Chivington at Glorietta Pass. In the military chain of command, it was nominally Chivington's regiment because, as commander of the Military District of Colorado, he outranked Shoup. The Third Colorado wore the same uniforms as all U.S. Army cavalry units, but when it came to a choice of weapons, they were given whatever was left over, unwanted by the huge armies in the east. "The guns given us were old," one of the troopers recalled, "out-of-date Austrian muzzle-loading muskets of large bore, and our ammunition consisted of paper cartridges from which one had to bite off the end when loading. These guns sent a bullet rather viciously, but one could never tell where it would hit."

The men of the Third included the best and worst types to be found in the territory, depending on who was describing them. "I wish to emphasize the fact that a large majority of that regiment were high-class representative men," wrote a member of the Third. Nearly all of the officers were "men of high standing in their respective communities."

Other more objective observations were less charitable. "Recruited from the dregs of the territory's population," wrote one historian, "the 'hundred dazers' left much to be desired." And another said, "they looked upon their military service as a lark, a welcome change from life's humdrums. Miners down on their luck saw a chance to earn a little money; cowpokes tired of ranch work jumped eagerly at the invitation to 'go for a soldier.'"

Whatever their origins and qualifications, the men of the Third lived up to the riotous reputation of the First: "chicken and melon stealing, casual AWOLs, late sleeping, trout fishing, bitching, drunken officers, saloon fights, and tumbles in the hay with country maidens much impressed by new blue cavalry uniforms. No one wanted to drill, guard duty was ignored, and none of the volunteers, apparently, obeyed any order unless the mood was on him and the tone of the command suitably civil."

These were the men Colonel John Milton Chivington would lead to Sand Creek.

Chivington remained in Denver toward the end of the summer. He had an election to win and he waged his war against the Indians primarily in church sermons and speeches on the campaign trail. Wherever he spoke in his campaign for Colorado statehood and a congressional seat for himself, he echoed and incited popular sentiment by urging a war without mercy. The only way to deal with the savages, he thundered, was to "kill and scalp all, little and big." Even papooses should be killed because they would grow up to become warriors. "Nits make lice," he liked to say.

When a rumor circulated that four hundred Ute braves were on the warpath against Cheyenne and Arapaho, Chivington said he would place no obstacles in their path through his jurisdiction. "Now," he added, "if these red rebels can be killed off by one another, it will be a great savings to the government, for I am fully satisfied that to kill them is the only way to have peace and quiet."

Expressing such thoughts seemed a sure way of getting elected, but in August, Chivington got caught in a controversy that caused some people to revise their opinion of him. Perhaps, after all, he was not the man he made himself out to be.

For some months, a band of twenty-two Confederates led by a petty criminal named Jim Reynolds, who had escaped from Denver's jail in 1862, had roamed the territory, adding to the mayhem while ostensibly on a mission to recruit Coloradans for the Southern cause. More likely, they were outlaws executing a string of robberies, which included taking $3,000 from a stagecoach and $63,000 from a wagon train. In mid-August, Reynolds and four of his cronies were captured and brought to Denver.

Chivington wanted to put them on trial immediately, charging them in a military court as enemy guerrillas rather than in a civil court as thieves. He set up a commission, took testimony, and asked General Curtis for permission to have the men executed if they were found guilty. Curtis replied that he was the only one who could pronounce a sentence of death. Chivington had no choice but to pack them off to Fort Lyon, the nearest military post. He ordered one of his officers, Captain T. G. Cree, to escort the prisoners with a one-hundred-man detail. He did not think that Indians would attack a detachment of that size, or that the prisoners, in chains, would have any chance to escape.

The detachment expected to cover the 240 miles between Denver and Fort Lyon in nine days, but, strangely, after the troops departed, it was found that no rations had been drawn for the prisoners. On the second day of the journey, they were shot—while trying to escape, it was said. Captain Cree reported that the prisoners had been extremely abusive and insolent to the guards, despite repeated warnings. They made an attempt to get away, despite their chains, and all were shot. "They died for want of breath," Cree said.

An attempt was made to keep the incident secret. "The statements given to the press were shadowy in the extreme," concluded a local historian. "Whether the culprits were regarded as prisoners-of-war, or as transgressors of the civil law, the method of their taking off was unworthy a civilized people."

In one version of the killings, the prisoners had faced a firing squad, one of whose members was a stagecoach driver who had been robbed by Reynolds and his band. Most of the troops refused to fire; in the end, two sergeants drew their pistols and did the deed. Uncle Dick Wootton, who passed the site of the executions some time later, reported seeing the skeletons "bound with ropes to as many trees. The flesh had been picked clean from the bones, but a bullet hole in each skull showed how the men had met their death. Each skeleton stood in a pair of boots, which was all that was left about them in the way of clothing."

The U.S. attorney, S. E. Browne, sent a strongly worded protest to General Curtis. "The whole five were butchered, and their bodies, with shackles on their legs, were left unburied on the plains. Our people had no sympathy with these thieves, but they feel that our common manhood has been outraged, and demand that this foul murder not be sloughed over in quiet. When the news was first brought to Chivington of the death of these persons, and of the manner of their death, he sneeringly remarked to the bystander: 'I told the guard when they left that if they did not kill those fellows, I would play thunder with them.' There is no doubt in the minds of our people that a most foul murder has been committed, and that, too, by the express order of old Chivington. With such men in power our people feel that they have but little security in person or property."

There is no evidence that General Curtis ordered an investigation into the matter, or that U.S. Attorney Browne pursued it, but the "Reynolds business" became a frequent topic of conversation among the Denverites, and many of them pointed accusing and damning fingers at old Chivington. With the election approaching, the timing of this criticism was, for him, unfortunate.

The vote, scheduled for September 11, was the culmination of a bitter political fight over the issue of Colorado's territorial status. It also turned on the character of the two men most closely identified with the push for statehood, Chivington and Governor Evans. The campaign had been always acrimonious, often unscrupulous, with neither side claiming virtue for its tactics.

Proponents of statehood, calling themselves the Union Administration Party, were so confident of victory that they had pushed for the elections for U.S. Congress and Senate on the same ballot, with Evans and Henry Teller standing for Senate and Chivington for Congress. Thus, a vote for statehood was automatically a vote for them. Statehood appealed to some people because it promised home rule and better representation in Washington for Colorado's interests. Others supported it because of their personal political ambitions. Every newspaper in the territory except one endorsed the statehood movement, and Byers in his *Rocky Mountain News* was among the most ardent supporters.

Most of the residents, on the other hand, were opposed to the idea of statehood. The population of the territory numbered about 25,000, and the majority of them believed that the drive for statehood was premature.

They did not want the burden of taxation that statehood would impose on them. Their campaign focused on those issues but devoted most of its energy to capitalizing on the personal unpopularity of Chivington and Evans. The antistatehood forces charged that the two had fomented the current Indian troubles in a clumsy attempt to demonstrate the importance of direct representation in Washington and to form the Third Colorado Regiment, thus exaggerating the Indian threat.

The campaign rhetoric grew so vitriolic that Evans, in a move to save statehood, announced that he would withdraw his name as a candidate for the Senate. His action came too late to defuse the opposition. The criticisms continued because it was well known that he supported Chivington's bid for Congress. Chivington himself was the object of enough hostility to kill the statehood measure.

Even General Curtis at Fort Leavenworth in Kansas was critical of Chivington. As election day neared, he pointedly suggested that Chivington was more interested in his political career than in his duties as commander of Colorado's military district. Curtis was annoyed that Chivington was spending virtually all of his time in Denver, electioneering, instead of attending to the Indian troubles throughout the territory.

Chivington could not let the accusation go unchallenged. "I assure you, general," he wrote, "that I have not spent an hour nor gone a mile to attend to other matters than my command. My return from [Fort] Lyons to Denver was caused by terror and alarm created by the Indian massacre in that neighborhood and at the earnest request of all concerned in the peace and quiet of the whole territory. If representations have been made to the contrary, and you cannot come out yourself, a member of your staff could see by visiting this district who are true and who are false in their statements."

Chivington may have convinced Curtis of his earnestness, but he failed to persuade the voters. He, and statehood, lost by a three-to-one vote, and his dreams of political glory were now as moribund as the military glory that had faded so fast after Glorietta Pass. What he needed was a victory over the Indians that would restore his luster as a hero, but the Indians were making peace overtures, threatening to bring the war, such as it was, to a close—much too soon.

The move toward peace began at Fort Lyon, a desolate outpost on the flats of the Arkansas River. It was a cheerless place to be stationed, according to Mrs. Byron Sanford, the wife of one of the officers. "It looks lonely here," she wrote in her diary on her arrival in 1862, "with hardly a tree in sight and back as far as the eye can reach, a level plain. There is a sutler's store, where canned goods and general supplies are kept, but no vegetables, not even potatoes, just ordinary soldier rations."

The only vegetation was a fringe of slender willow trees along the banks of the river and a puny grove of cottonwoods to the south. Beyond the trees, barren prairie stretched unbroken to the horizon. There was nothing special to do at Fort Lyon and nothing to see, nothing to break the numbing monotony. Three-foot walls of red sandstone and adobe mud enclosed several nondescript structures with flat dirt roofs and windows made of cowhide stretched over a wooden frame. The enlisted men's barracks had a dirt floor. Rain poured through leaky roofs, turning the floor to mud.

Fort Lyon's commanding officer was twenty-five-year-old Major Edward Wynkoop, a tall, handsome man with wavy black hair and a long, drooping mustache. Born to an affluent family in Pennsylvania, Wynkoop had come west in 1856 looking for adventure. He became involved in the founding of Denver, discovered gold, sold his claim, and was elected sheriff. When the First Colorado Regiment was formed, he received a commission as a captain and served with Chivington at Glorietta Pass. He won a promotion for his part in the battle.

When Wynkoop assumed command of Fort Lyon on May 9, 1864, he asked Chivington what course of action should be taken with regard to the Indians. Chivington told him that the Cheyenne would have to be soundly whipped. If Wynkoop's men caught any Indians, the only thing to do with them was to kill them.

At the time, Wynkoop shared Chivington's sentiments, and he aggressively pursued bands of Indians throughout his sector of the territory. He wrote to Chivington in mid-August that until he received orders to the contrary, he would kill every Indian he came across.

On September 4, three soldiers rode out from Fort Lyon for Denver, where they were due to be discharged from the service. The fact that the three were willing to travel the 240 miles to Denver unescorted indicates that the threat of Indian raids had died down. Not far from the fort, they spotted three Cheyenne—two old men and an old woman—on horseback. The troopers raised their rifles to fire: with Indians in 1864, a man shot first and asked questions later—besides, those were Major Wynkoop's orders. They hesitated, however, when one of the old warriors waved a piece of paper at them. It may have been because the Indians were elderly, or because one of them was a woman, or because the soldiers were glad to be getting out of the military. Whatever the reason, they lowered their rifles and, honoring the Indians' request, took them back to the fort.

Wynkoop was enraged. The soldiers had deliberately disobeyed the standing orders to kill Indians. Indian agent Sam Colley was present when the group rode up to the headquarters building. "The major, as well as the balance of us, felt like using them a little rough," Colley remembered, "for we were all feeling a little hard toward the Indians. I went out and saw they were two Indians with whom I was well acquainted, and who I knew had been trying to keep peace between the Indians and the whites. Just as I went up to them the major came up and spoke very harsh to them, and told them to get down off their horses. I told the major that I knew them, and that they were both friendly."

The Indians known to Colley were Cheyenne subchiefs called One-Eye and Min-im-mie; the woman was One-Eye's squaw. The paper they had waved at the soldiers, and which may have saved their lives, was a letter from Black Kettle and other Cheyenne peace chiefs, written for them in English by Edmond Guerrier, a trader whose father was French and whose mother was Cheyenne. Guerrier had prepared two identical letters, one addressed to Indian agent Colley and the other to William Bent.

Cheyenne Village
August 29, 1864
    We received a letter from Bent, wishing us to make peace. We held a council in regard to it. All came to the conclusion to make peace with you, providing you make peace with the Kiowa, Comanche, Arapaho, Apache, and Sioux. We are going to send a messenger to the Kiowa and to the other nations about our going to make peace with you. We heard that you have some Indian prisoners at Denver. We have seven prisoners of yours which we are willing to give up, providing you give up yours. There are three Cheyenne war parties out yet, and two of Arapaho. They have been out some time and expected in soon. When we held this council there were a few Arapaho and Sioux present. We want true news from you in return. That is, a letter.
                                        Black Kettle [and other chiefs]

The letter from Bent to which Black Kettle referred had described Governor Evans's proclamation in June urging friendly Indians to go to designated places of refuge where they would be safe from soldiers and settlers. Arapaho and Cheyenne had been told to report to Colley at Fort Lyon. Black Kettle hesitated to lead his people into the fort, however. There had been too much killing on both sides for that kind of trust to endure, if it ever existed in the first place. But Black Kettle still hoped to make peace, and the letter was the safest way to try to do so.

Wynkoop read the letter carefully and questioned the Indians about the size of the war parties. One-Eye told him that there were two thousand Cheyenne and Arapaho camped at the headwaters of the Smoky Hill River, along with forty lodges of Sioux. The war parties were being called in while the Indians awaited the government's reaction to Black Kettle's letter. One-Eye urged Wynkoop to go in person to Smoky Hill as soon as possible.

Wynkoop faced a difficult decision. The letter could be a ruse designed to lead him and his men into an ambush. His forces were much smaller than those of the Indians and could easily be massacred. True, Black Kettle was known as a peace chief, but it was not unthinkable that the war chiefs were falsely using his name. On the other hand, the letter could be a sincere call for peace. If Wynkoop went to the Indians at Smoky Hill, he might be able to put a stop to the months of raiding and killing, and thus end the war.

Another consideration crossed Wynkoop's mind. The Indians were holding seven white prisoners. He could not pass up a chance to save them, even if it meant risking an ambush. He would have to trust the Indians, a startling departure for him under the circumstances. So in the end, it was the fate of the captives that decided the affair. Wynkoop would go to Smoky Hill.

8

What Shall I Do with the *Third*?

Major Wynkoop decided that he had no choice but to trust the Indians. He was not about to be foolhardy, however, and would take all necessary precautions to protect himself and his men. Therefore, he told One-Eye and Min-im-mie that they would accompany him, as hostages. If the Indians attacked Wynkoop and his men, the chiefs would be killed on the spot. Even though they were only subchiefs, they were still men of importance to the tribe. The Cheyenne would not be willing to forfeit their lives so easily, or so Wynkoop hoped. He also counted on the two howitzers he would take with him to give the Indians second thoughts about attacking.

One-Eye remained impassive when told he would be taken along as a hostage. Wynkoop recalled that the Indian "appeared to be perfectly satisfied and said he was willing to sacrifice his life if his tribe did not act in good faith toward me." The Cheyenne always kept their word, One-Eye told him, and if they failed to do so this time, he would not choose to live. Without honor, life held no meaning. Min-im-mie agreed.

Although Wynkoop had dutifully echoed Chivington's feelings about Indians, his personal dealings with them had thus far been minimal. He was greatly surprised and perplexed by the quiet dignity and apparent integrity of the old chiefs. "I was bewildered," he wrote, "with an exhibition of such patriotism on the part of the two savages and felt myself in the presence of superior beings; and these were the representatives of a race that I heretofore looked upon without exception as being cruel, treacherous, and bloodthirsty without feeling or affection for friend or kindred." The conversion of Major Edward Wynkoop had begun.

On the morning of September 6, Wynkoop led a column of 127 cavalry and the two howitzers through the gates of Fort Lyon for the four-day ride to the Indian camp on the Smoky Hill River. He placed the three Indians who had brought the proposal to him at the head of the column, surrounded by troopers. Although he was impressed by them, he meant to stick to his pledge. If the column was attacked, they would be killed outright. He made that quite clear to his troops.

Almost as an afterthought, Wynkoop took along a fourth hostage, an old Cheyenne known as "the Fool," who lived near the post. The man was of little importance to the tribe, but Wynkoop felt it could not hurt to have another hostage. Wynkoop did not minimize the danger he was facing. He knew that his name might go down in the history books as the man who had led 127 soldiers to their death in an Indian ambush.

On the first day of the march, he sent One-Eye's squaw ahead to deliver a letter to Black Kettle. She was to tell the chief that Major Wynkoop was coming to talk about peace and to receive the white prisoners.

Edmond Guerrier, who had handwritten Black Kettle's letter, was with the chief when One-Eye's squaw arrived at the Indian camp. He translated Wynkoop's letter for the Cheyenne. "The substance of Wynkoop's letter, as I now recollect," said Guerrier a year later, was this: that there were no Indian prisoners, to Wynkoop's recollection or knowledge, at Denver; that he would come out to talk to the Indians and would meet them at the Smoky Hill River; that he did not come to fight but to talk; and that he expected the Indians to bring the white prisoners along. "I read the letter to the Indians," Guerrier said. "They saddled up their horses and started [for the council site] immediately."

Shortly after dawn on September 10, Wynkoop and his men spied a line of eight hundred battle-ready warriors drawn up across the plain. "They lined up facing the troops," said George Bent, "with bows strung, and for a time, it looked very much like war."

Wynkoop formed his wagon train in a circle for defense. He had received no reply from Black Kettle and did not know if One-Eye's squaw had delivered the message. The idea of an ambush weighed on his mind. The cavalry was outnumbered nearly eight to one, but now there was no place to hide. His command could not outrun the Indian braves.

"Putting on as bold a front as I could, under the circumstances," Wynkoop recalled, "I formed my command in as good order as possible for the purpose of acting in the offensive or defensive, as might be necessary, and advanced toward them."

The sight of the soldiers in line and riding toward them agitated the warriors. As Wynkoop approached, he saw arrows at the ready, and he also noticed that many of the braves were armed with rifles and pistols.

The tense silence was broken only by the jangling of canteens against the hard leather cavalry saddles. Two hundred yards from the line of Indians, Wynkoop raised his right hand and gave the order for his small command to halt. He called for One-Eye and John Smith, the interpreter, to be brought up. He told One-Eye to ride ahead and let Black Kettle and the other chiefs know why the cavalry had come. One-Eye rode toward the warriors, his horse kicking up a trail of dust that linked the two lines. Nothing else moved, and the minutes dragged by.

One-Eye emerged from the Cheyenne line and announced to Wynkoop that Black Kettle agreed to talk. The Indians fell back—sullenly, resentfully, it seemed to Wynkoop—and the troopers edged forward to take up a position on the riverbank. Warriors on horseback encircled them, riding fast and howling wildly. The sight made the soldiers increasingly uneasy.

Wynkoop formed up the men, howitzers in the middle, the wagons corralled behind. Guards were deployed around the perimeter with orders to keep the Indians out unless Wynkoop gave permission for them to enter. Both camps watched each other warily, the braves galloping and shouting, the soldiers grim, carbines at the ready.

A few hours later, at about 9:00 A.M., a small procession of Cheyenne and Arapaho chiefs, led by Black Kettle, made its stately way to Wynkoop's camp. The council began. Wynkoop said that he had come in response to Black Kettle's letter, whereupon Black Kettle asked why, if he had come in peace, he had brought so many soldiers with him. Wynkoop replied that he had none but peaceful intentions but he still had to be able to protect himself if need be.

Black Kettle seemed to accept this and Wynkoop continued to talk, choosing his words with care, knowing how many lives depended on his skill in expressing himself. He paused periodically to allow Smith to interpret his remarks to the chiefs. Smith, too, was worried, lest he give even the slightest inappropriate shading to any of Wynkoop's remarks or utter Cheyenne language that might inadvertently offend the chiefs.

A year later, in testimony before the congressional committee investigating the Sand Creek affair, Smith recalled: "Major Wynkoop stated through me to the chiefs apart that he had received their message; that acting on that, he had come up to talk with them; asked them whether they had all agreed to and endorsed the contents of the letter which he had in his possession, and which had been received from One-Eye."

The chiefs said they agreed with the letter and Wynkoop put forward his proposal, all he was empowered to offer the chiefs that day.

Addressing Black Kettle, Wynkoop said, "I told him that I had not the power to offer them terms of peace; that I was not big enough chief; that I had come out there for negotiating with them, if possible, for the return of the white prisoners, and that I had a proposition to make to them, which was [that] I would use my utmost endeavors to procure peace for them. I stated that I would take any delegation of chiefs that they might select from both tribes with me to the governor of Colorado Territory, who was also Indian superintendent, and that the fact of their having delivered up the white prisoners into my hands would in all probability assist them, it being an evidence that they were sincere."

Wynkoop also suggested that the Indians take their families to Fort Lyon, where they could wait in safety for the chiefs' return from Denver. He was careful not to offer them more than he could provide. He emphasized that he was acting on his own responsibility and could pledge nothing beyond safe passage for the chiefs to Denver and back. Wynkoop turned to his aides and to John Smith and asked each in turn whether he endorsed this pledge to the chiefs. To a man, they agreed—Smith, Captain Silas Soule, Lieutenant Charles Phillips, and Lieutenant Joseph Cramer. It was a pledge that was to bring much anguish to Cramer and Soule.

Without warning, the meeting turned nasty. Bull Bear, chief of the Cheyenne Dog Soldiers, rose to speak. John Smith, the interpreter, recognized the harshness and hostility in Bull Bear's words. Smith turned to Wynkoop and said quietly, "I have now got to talk for my life."

Bull Bear said that he had tried to live in peace with the whites but they would not let him do so. His brother, Lean Bear, had been killed by soldiers while he was trying to talk peace. The Cheyenne and Arapaho were not to blame for the present troubles. Whites had started the war. It was not possible for the Indians to have peace with them. The only course for the Indians to follow was to fight.

Angry murmurings from some of the chiefs supported Bull Bear's remarks, but old One-Eye stood up and hushed them. In a voice hoarse with passion, he told how he had taken the chiefs' letter to Fort Lyon at the risk of his own life, a risk well worth taking if it led to peace. He counted on the chiefs to act in good faith, but if they would not now do as they had agreed, he did not wish to live, not if Cheyenne broke their word.

John Smith remembered that One-Eye said "he was ashamed to hear such talk in the council as that uttered by Bull Bear. He then appealed to the other chiefs to know if they would act like men and fulfill or live up to their word. If the chiefs did not act in good faith he should go with the whites and fight with them, and that he had a great many friends who would follow him."

One-Eye's comments calmed tempers, but there were still grievances to air and injustices to parade in front of Wynkoop, the "tall chief," as the Indians were calling him. Next it was the turn of Left Hand, an Arapaho chief. He explained that he, too, had always been friendly with the whites and had never had trouble until the last few months. He spoke of his difficulties at Fort Larned when Captain Parmeter ordered his men to fire on the Indians even though they were carrying a white flag. After that, Left Hand said, he could no longer restrain his younger braves from going on the warpath. In spite of these incidents, he did not want war and would prefer to live in peace.

Little Raven, another Arapaho chief, was less conciliatory, adopting the same militant tone as Bull Bear. He had lived for years with the whites and had tried to be friendly and to shake hands, but he no longer believed that peace was possible.

Throughout the speeches, Black Kettle sat cross-legged on the ground, listening in silence with a slight smile on his face. Wynkoop recalled him as appearing serene and dignified. He was about sixty years old, well built, with solemn eyes and what others described as an intelligent and highly animated face. He wore leggings, breechclout, and a deerskin shirt, all heavily decorated. In his hair was a cluster of eagle feathers, and three silver coins hung from a leather thong around his neck.

When the other chiefs had finished, Black Kettle rose slowly to his feet and started to speak. "He was glad to hear his white brother talk," John Smith reported. Black Kettle said that "he believed [Wynkoop] was honest in what he said, and that he welcomed [the soldiers] as friends; that he believed that their troubles were over if they would follow the advice of the tall chief, meaning Major Wynkoop; that there were bad white men and bad Indians, and that the bad men on both sides had brought about this trouble; that some of his young men had joined in with them; that he was opposed to fighting and had done everything in his power to prevent it; that he believed the blame rested with the whites, that they commenced the war and forced the Indians to fight."

Black Kettle recounted the events of the previous spring, the attacks by the soldiers Eayre, Dunn, and Downing, the killing of Lean Bear, and the shooting at Left Hand. After these incidents, many of the Cheyenne concluded that war was inevitable. Even so, the chiefs did not want war and several times had attempted to go to the forts for protection, as Governor Evans's proclamation of June had asked them to do. Each time, Black Kettle added sadly, they had been driven off by the soldiers.

Despite what he called this unjust treatment from his white brethren, Black Kettle desired peace. Smith recalled that the chief then "shook hands with Major Wynkoop and his officers, stating that he was still what he had always been, a friend to the whites, and, as far as he was concerned, he was willing to deliver up the white prisoners, or do anything that was required of him, to procure peace, knowing it to be for the good of his people; but that there were other chiefs who still thought they were badly treated by their white brethren, who were willing to make peace, but who felt unwilling to deliver up the prisoners simply on the promise of Major Wynkoop that he would endeavor to procure them peace. They desired that the delivering up of the white prisoners should be assurance of peace.

"He also went on to state that, even if Major Wynkoop's propositions were not accepted then by the chiefs assembled, and although they had sufficient force to entirely overpower Major Wynkoop's small command, yet, from the fact that he had come in good faith to hold this consultation, he should return unmolested to Fort Lyon."

The two sides had reached an impasse. No white prisoners would be released without a guarantee of peace, which Wynkoop had no authority to give. He explained to them again that he could not make peace, that it was up to the Great Father in Denver, and he repeated his offer to conduct the chiefs there. By two o'clock that afternoon, with no resolution in sight, the council adjourned, agreeing to meet the following day.

Wynkoop withdrew his troops twelve miles to a better defensive position and waited, whether for a peace overture or an attack, he did not know. Although Black Kettle had said they would not be molested, he and the other chiefs freely admitted that they could not always restrain their young braves. The troopers were edgy and apprehensive. During the council that morning, there had been a potentially explosive situation in the camp. Despite Wynkoop's orders, the soldiers had been unable to keep the Indians away. Cheyenne and Arapaho roamed freely among the soldiers, poking at equipment, hefting knapsacks, even shoving grapes down the barrels of the howitzers.

A soldier shoved an Indian back from one of the guns. A guard drew his pistol. The brave and his companions pulled arrows from their quivers, and Lieutenant G. H. Hardin quickly put his men into formation. Bloodshed at close quarters awaited nothing more than a brusque gesture or a surly look. Lieutenant Phillips rushed out to the council site to fetch Lieutenant Cramer. Phillips told Cramer that he "would have to stop it or we would be massacred, and that our only show now was to show them a reckless indifference." Cramer told the men that they "must take the thing cool, and keep but a few in place, only a sufficient number to defend themselves, for if we did anything that looked like fighting, I thought it would bring on a fight with the Indians, and also to keep near the wagons so as to use them to fight behind in case we were attacked."

The soldiers grew more agitated. Not keen on the expedition in the first place, they were now talking of mutiny, of heading back to the fort on their own. A few confronted Wynkoop, demanding that he lead them out before they were slaughtered. He tried to calm them by explaining about the meeting with the chiefs, the opportunity to free the white prisoners, and Black Kettle's pledge that the troops would not be harmed regardless of the outcome of tomorrow's sessions. The talk seemed to placate the men but no one got much sleep that night.

At noon, Left Hand and a small party of Indians called at Wynkoop's camp with sixteen-year-old Laura Roper in tow. She had been captured by the Cheyenne in Kansas a month before. A woman and three children had been taken at the same time, but the woman had been traded to the

Sioux. Left Hand said that Black Kettle would bring more white captives the next day.

Black Kettle appeared the following morning with word that the chiefs had agreed to go with Wynkoop to Denver to see Governor Evans. He delivered the three children into Wynkoop's hands and said that three other prisoners had been traded to the Sioux and that steps would be taken to recover them. (These captives were not released for nine months, during which time one hanged herself.) In contrast to the usual Indian practice with prisoners, Laura Roper and the three younger children now in the care of the soldiers had been treated well. One of them even said he would like to stay with the Indians.

Wynkoop's dangerous gamble had paid off. He had retrieved four white prisoners and was about to escort all the Cheyenne and Arapaho chiefs to Denver for a council of peace. For the first time since the early spring, there was reason to believe that the Indian war would soon be over.

Wynkoop and his men returned in triumph to Fort Lyon. Agent Sam Colley distributed the government annuities to the chiefs and Wynkoop handed over a large supply of army rations. The chiefs sent the supplies back to their camp on the Smoky Hill River, along with the reassuring message that "everything was all right and that they were going to Denver to make peace."

Wynkoop agreed that everything *was* going to be all right. The Indians wanted an end to the hostilities and had turned over prisoners as a sign of good faith. They were trying to secure the release of other captives and they had been able to keep their warriors from attacking Wynkoop and his soldiers, whom they easily outnumbered. Wynkoop was proud of what he had accomplished.

He sent a report on the Smoky Hill council to Governor Evans and told him he would take the chiefs to Denver as soon as possible. He rode on ahead of the Indians and their forty-man escort, directly to the governor's home. Evans, he was told, was too sick to see him. The next morning, however, Evans arrived unannounced at Wynkoop's hotel room, showing no sign of illness.

Evans declared that he was sorry the chiefs had been brought to Denver: He did not want to have anything to do with them. Wynkoop was stunned. Evans was refusing to talk with the chiefs even though they had come to secure peace! The Indians had declared war on the United States, the governor said, and their fate was now in the hands of the military. Evans added that he did not consider it proper policy to guarantee peace

with them until they had been sufficiently punished for their recent depredations.

Wynkoop listened in disbelief as the governor explained that if he
made any agreement with the savages, he would be acknowledging that
they had beaten the United States. "I said it would be strange," Wynkoop reported later, "if the United States would consider themselves
whipped by a few Indians, and drew his attention to the fact that, as a
United States officer, I had pledged myself to these Indians to convey
them to Denver, to procure an interview with himself. I had brought
these Indians a distance of 400 miles from their village with that object
in view, and desired that he would furnish them an audience. He replied
querulously that he was to start the next day to visit the Ute agency on
business; besides, he did not want to see them anyway."

Then Evans mentioned the real reason for not wanting to make
peace. With his voice rising, the governor recounted how through his
own persistent efforts he had been granted authority to raise the Third
Colorado Regiment. He had sent repeated warnings to Washington
pleading that the citizens of Colorado faced certain extermination unless
the hundred dazers were enlisted. "They had been raised to kill Indians,"
the governor told Wynkoop, "and they must kill Indians." Evans had
created a monster and now he had to feed it.

If Evans offered the Cheyenne and Arapaho peace, Washington
would think he had misrepresented the danger. There would have been
no need to bear the expense of raising, equipping, and training the new
regiment. Evans begged Wynkoop to understand his position. "What
shall I do with the Third Regiment if I make peace?" Wynkoop persisted, however, and, reluctantly, Evans consented to meet with the
chiefs. It was clear, however, that he had no interest in making that
meeting a success.

Evans did commend Wynkoop for retrieving the prisoners but he
added that he would not have done it in the same way. Instead, Evans
said, he would have "gone out and fought them and killed them, and
made them deliver up the white captives." Wynkoop reminded him that
he had been outnumbered eight to one, and Evans did not pursue the
point.

Throughout their lengthy discussion, Evans kept returning to his
basic dilemma: What would he do with the Third if he made peace with
the Indians? He and Chivington had kept the telegraph lines and mail
service busy with their dire predictions of the expected disaster. Byers
had inflamed the Denver residents with fiery editorials against the Indi-

ans. The public exhibition of the murdered Hungate family had led to a lust for revenge. And Evans kept asking what to do with the Third. It had been formed to kill Indians and that was what it must do.

News of the arrival of Black Kettle and his fellow chiefs met a divided reaction from the people of Denver. Some were relieved that months of fear and uncertainty might be coming to an end. Others, perhaps most, agreed with Evans and Chivington that there should be no treaty until the Indians had been punished. On the day before Evans was supposed to meet with the chiefs, Byers reflected the majority view in the pages of the *Rocky Mountain News.* "We are opposed to anything which looks like a treaty of peace with the Indians who have been actively engaged in the recent hostilities. The season is near at hand when they can be chastised and it should be done with no gentle hand."

Some people talked about sabotaging the talks by capturing the chiefs or gunning them down in the street, and as Wynkoop's wagon train approached the city, the tension and feelings of peril were palpable. Because of the possibility of violence, a group of Denver's leaders met the Indians at the edge of town and escorted them through the streets. Muttered threats and shaken fists greeted them from the wooden sidewalks, but there were no incidents.

Chivington worked hard to undermine the talks. As soon as he learned of them, he informed General Curtis. The Third Regiment was up to strength and ready, he wrote, and the Indians wanted peace only because they knew they would be disciplined by the hundred dazers for their outrages. He added that he hoped Curtis would order the Indians to make full restitution.

Chivington received Curtis's reply on the morning of the conference. "I shall require the bad Indians delivered up; restoration of equal numbers of stock; also hostages to secure. I want no peace till the Indians suffer more. I fear the agent of the interior department will be ready to make presents too soon. It is better to chastise before giving anything but a little tobacco to talk over. No peace must be made without my directions."

Curtis, Evans, Byers, and Chivington had already written the lines for the parts they would play in the Sand Creek drama.

"No peace till the Indians suffer more."

"Third Regiment is full."

"It should be done with no gentle hand."

"They must kill Indians."

"What shall I do with the Third?"

"Kill and scalp all!"

The peace conference, conceived in trust and hope at Smoky Hill, was doomed before it even began.

9

Assurances of Safety

B lack Kettle and his fellow chiefs shook hands solemnly with the white men present—Governor Evans, Colonel Chivington, Colonel Shoup, Major Wynkoop, and several other officers including Captain Soule and Lieutenant Cramer, who had accompanied Wynkoop to Smoky Hill. John Smith was there to interpret, and the Ute Indian agent, Simeon Whitely, stood ready to make a verbatim record of the proceedings. The peace pipe was lit and passed in silence from one man to the next. It was September 28, 1864, and the council was being held at Camp Weld, Denver, Colorado Territory. The time for peace, or more war, was at hand.

Governor Evans asked the Indians what they had come to say. Black Kettle spoke for them. He said he had come to talk about the governor's proclamation of June 27, the one that offered places of refuge for all friendly Indians. He explained that he accepted the terms of the proclamation, but it had taken some weeks to gather his people to hold a council on it. The Indians had lived up to the terms of the proclamation by delivering their white prisoners. Black Kettle continued with great eloquence.

I followed Major Wynkoop to Fort Lyon, and Major Wynkoop proposed that we come to see you. We have come with our eyes shut, following his handful of men, like coming through the fire. All we ask is that we may have peace with the whites. We want to hold you by the hand. You are our father. We have been traveling through a cloud. The sky has been dark ever since the war began. These braves who are with me are all willing to do what I say. We want to take good tidings home to our people, that they may sleep in peace.

I want you to give all these chiefs of the soldiers here to understand that we are for peace, and that we have made peace, that we may not be mistaken by them for enemies. I have not come here with a little wolf bark, but have come to talk plain with you. We must live near the buffalo or starve. When we came here we came free, without any apprehension, to see you, and when I go home and tell my people that I have taken your hand, and the hands of all the chiefs here in Denver, they will feel well, and so will all the different tribes of Indians on the Plains, after we have eaten and drunk with them.

There was silence in the room when the old chief sat down on the floor among the other Indians. His eyes searched the governor's face impassively. Evans looked down at him and immediately accused him of making an alliance with the Sioux, who were pursuing their war against the whites. The governor's words were harsh, his tone strident.

You have done a great deal of damage—have stolen stock, and now have possession of it. However much a few individuals may have tried to keep the peace, as a nation you have gone to war. While we have been spending thousands of dollars in opening farms for you, and making preparations to feed, protect, and make you comfortable, you have joined our enemies and gone to war.

Hearing, last fall, that you were dissatisfied, the Great Father at Washington sent me out on the plains to talk with you and make it all right. I sent messengers out to tell you that I had presents, and would make you a feast, but you sent word that you did not want to have anything to do with me, and to the Great Father at Washington that you could get along without him.

Black Kettle agreed that they had on that occasion refused to meet with the governor, but he and several other chiefs protested that they had not joined forces with the Sioux. They admitted, however, that their actions may have justified Evans's belief in such an alliance.

Evans announced bluntly that he was in no mood to make a treaty with them.

"Your young men are on the warpath," he said. "My soldiers are preparing for the fight. You, so far, have had the advantage, but the time is near at hand when the plains will swarm with United States soldiers."

Since the chiefs had been unable to control their braves and prevent the raids of last spring, so far as Evans was concerned they would not be able to conclude a peace that would last beyond the coming winter. After that, the braves would surely go on the warpath again. Evans continued:

> The time when you can make war best is in the summertime. The time when I can make war best is in the winter. So far you have had the advantage; my time is fast coming. I have learned that you understand that as the whites are at war among themselves, you think you can now drive the whites from this country, but this reliance is false. The Great Father at Washington has men enough to drive all the Indians off the plains and whip the [Confederates] at the same time. Now, the war with the whites is nearly through, and the Great Father will not know what to do with all his soldiers except to send them after the Indians on the plains. My proposition to the friendly Indians has gone out. I shall be glad to have them all come in under it. I have no new propositions to make. Another reason that I am not in a condition to make a treaty is that war is begun, and the power to make a treaty of peace has passed from me to the great war chief. My advice to you is to turn on the side of the government, and show by your acts that friendly disposition you profess to me.

One chief asked what he meant by turning on the side of the government. Evans replied that it meant making some arrangement to help the soldiers. Black Kettle said they would return to Fort Lyon with Major Wynkoop and talk to their braves about helping the soldiers. He did not believe there would be much difficulty in getting them to agree.

Evans repeated his warning that if the Indians did not keep the peace, they would be treated as enemies. At that, Chief White Antelope rose, fingering the medal that hung around his neck. It had been given to him by President Lincoln. When speaking, he held it out in front of him as if it were a tiny shield that would protect him from harm.

"I understand every word you have said, and will hold on to it. The Cheyenne, all of them, have their ears open this way, and they will hear what you say. I am proud to have seen the chief of all the whites in this country. I will tell my people. Ever since I went to Washington and received this medal, I have called all white men as my brothers, but other Indians have since been to Washington and got medals, and now the soldiers do not shake hands but seek to kill me. I fear these new soldiers who have gone out [the Third Colorado Regiment] may kill some of my people while I am here."

"There is great danger of it," Evans said.

"When we sent our letter to Major Wynkoop," White Antelope said, "it was like going through a strong fire or blast for Major Wynkoop's men to come to our camp. It was the same for us to come to see you. When Major Wynkoop came, we proposed to make peace. He said he had no power to make peace, except to bring us here and return us safe."

"Whatever peace you make," Evans said, "must be with the soldiers and not with me."

Evans switched tactics and began to fire questions at the Indians about raids that had occurred in the territory that year.

"Who committed the depredations on the trains near the junction about the first of August?"

"Who committed the murder of the Hungate family?"

"Who stole soldiers' horses and mules from Jimmy's camp 27 days ago?"

"What were their names?"

"Where is Roman Nose?"

"Who stole Charley Antobe's horses?"

White Antelope answered each question, supplying names when the perpetrators were known to be Cheyenne or Arapaho, and blaming the other incidents on Kiowa, Comanche, or Sioux. He also pointed out that soldiers had started the war by firing on Indians who had found stray stock on the plains.

Neva, an Arapaho subchief, leaped to his feet to protest.

"I want to say something. It makes me feel bad to be talking about these things and opening old sores. Mr. [John] Smith has known me ever since I was a child. Has he ever known me to commit depredations on the whites? I went to Washington last year; receiving good counsel, I hold on to it. I am determined always to keep peace with the whites. Now, when I shake hands with them they seem to pull away. I came here to seek peace, nothing else."

"We feel that you have, by your stealing and murdering, done us great damage," Evans said. "You come here and say you will tell us all, and that is what I am trying to get."

"The Comanche, Kiowa, and Sioux have done much more injury than we have," Neva replied. "We will tell you what we know, but cannot answer for others."

In the tense moments that followed, the chiefs acknowledged certain raids made by their people, then Evans shifted the questioning to the activities of the Sioux. He asked what the Sioux were planning to do next.

"Their intention is to clear out all this country," Bull Bear said. "They are angry and will do all the damage to the whites they can. I am with you and the troops to fight all those who have no ears to listen to what you say. My brother, Lean Bear, died in trying to keep peace with the whites. I am willing to die in the same way, and expect to do so."

Neva reiterated the Indians' peaceful intentions. "I know the value of the presents which we receive from Washington; we cannot live without them. That is why I try so hard to keep peace with the whites."

Colonel Chivington, who had been sitting quietly throughout the council, rose to his feet and planted himself squarely in the middle of the floor. His towering size and booming voice commanded everyone's attention.

"I am not a big war chief," he said, "but all the soldiers in this country are at my command. My rule of fighting white men or Indians is to fight them until they lay down their arms and submit to military authority. You are nearer to Major Wynkoop [at Fort Lyon] than anyone else, and you can go to him when you get ready to do that."

The meeting was over. The chiefs were pleased with the outcome and told interpreter John Smith that they believed everything was all right. Black Kettle embraced Governor Evans and Major Wynkoop, and everyone shook hands. Photographs were taken. The war was over. The Indians thought they had made peace with the whites.

As Evans and Chivington understood it, however, they had not made peace with the Indians. On the day after the council, Evans wrote to Sam Colley, the Indian agent for the Cheyenne and Arapaho, stating his position.

> The chiefs brought in by Major Wynkoop have been heard. I have declined to make any peace with them, lest it might embarrass the military operations against the hostile Indians of the Plains. The Arapaho and Cheyenne Indians being now at war with the United States government, must make peace with the military authorities. You will be particular to impress upon these chiefs the fact that my talk with them was for the purpose of ascertaining their views and not to offer them anything whatever. They must deal with the military authorities until peace.

A short time later, in his annual report to the Commissioner of Indian Affairs in Washington, Evans noted that only a few of the Indians wanted peace. Most remained hostile and would have to be conquered by force. He added his conviction that there should be no peace treaty until they were beaten.

Evans also wrote to the commissioner noting that the chiefs he had met with at Camp Weld were "earnest in their desire for peace, and offered to secure the assent of their bands to lay down their arms, or to join the whites in the war against the other tribes of the Plains. I advised them to make immediate application to the military authorities and to accept the terms of peace they might be able to obtain, and left them in the hands of Major Wynkoop, who took them back to Fort Lyon." This letter contradicts the sentiments Evans expressed in his annual report.

The Commissioner of Indian Affairs was displeased with Evans's performance at Camp Weld. On October 15, he wrote that it was the governor's duty "to hold yourself in readiness to encourage and receive the first intimations of a desire on the part of the Indians for a permanent peace." Washington believed that Evans had done nothing to encourage Black Kettle's offer of peace. Nor had Chivington. The commissioner continued: "I cannot help believing that very much of the difficulty on the Plains might have been avoided if a spirit of conciliation had been exercised by the military and others."

To the Cheyenne and Arapaho, Evans and Chivington were seen as having agreed to make peace. The governor's proclamation of June 27 remained in effect. Cheyenne and Arapaho who went to Fort Lyon would receive protection. The governor had not publicly rescinded the proclamation, and when Black Kettle mentioned it at the beginning of the council, Evans had not indicated it might no longer be applicable. He had said, "I shall be glad to have them all come in under it."

The chiefs present at the council with Evans had no reason to suspect that by taking their families to the fort, they would be in any jeopardy. Even Colonel Chivington supported that conclusion, telling them that they could go to Major Wynkoop at Fort Lyon when they were ready. Before Wynkoop left Denver, he confirmed to Evans and Chivington that he would ask the Indians to bring their families to stay at Fort Lyon until something definite had been decided about a treaty. The Indians there would be under Wynkoop's protection, the protection of the American flag. The Indians knew it, Wynkoop knew it, Evans and Chivington knew it.

*   *   *

Wynkoop and his men escorted the chiefs on the long journey back to Fort Lyon during the first week of October. Settlers and farmers along the Arkansas River returned to their homes and began to gather their crops. Before the Camp Weld conference, they were afraid to stay in these remote dwellings, but now they happily went home with the assurances of Major Wynkoop that all was well. "I told them," Wynkoop recalled, "that they could consider themselves in perfect safety until such time as I could give them warning to the contrary, and told them to return to their ranches and take in their crops."

At Fort Lyon, Wynkoop held a meeting with Black Kettle and the other chiefs, asking them to bring their families to the vicinity of the fort so that he could keep watch over them and prevent them from being attacked by other soldiers. He also arranged to distribute rations to them. John Smith remembered that Wynkoop said "he preferred to have [the Indians] under his eye and away from other quarters, where they were likely to get into difficulties with the whites. The chiefs replied that they were willing to do anything Major Wynkoop might choose to dictate, as they had perfect confidence in him. Accordingly, the chiefs went after their families and villages and brought them in; they appeared satisfied that they were in perfect security and safety."

Formally, Fort Lyon belonged to the District of the Upper Arkansas, headquartered at Fort Riley, Kansas, commanded by General Curtis. Therefore, Wynkoop prepared a full report for Curtis about the Smoky Hill mission, the Denver council, and the current status of the Indians camped near Fort Lyon. Wynkoop suggested to Curtis that if peace terms were offered to the Indians, he could guarantee their fidelity by having all the Indian villages located near the fort, where they would be subject to his control. He also noted that the Cheyenne and Arapaho chiefs had expressed a willingness to help the soldiers fight the Kiowa and Comanche.

Curtis was away from Fort Riley when Wynkoop's report arrived. It was read by the general's aide, Major B. S. Henning, who did not approve of Wynkoop's actions. Acting on what he knew to be Curtis's attitude toward the Indians—"I want no peace till the Indians suffer more," Curtis had wired Chivington on the day of the Camp Weld conference—Henning decided that Wynkoop had acted against policy. Wynkoop was unaware of Curtis's views; Chivington had never told him of the message.

In addition, Henning felt that Wynkoop had violated Curtis's order forbidding Indians from entering the forts unless blindfolded, and he had left his district without orders by taking the chiefs to Denver. Henning had also received what he called "disturbing rumors" that Wynkoop had been issuing food and other supplies to hostile Indians, another violation of regulations. He never revealed the source of these rumors, however. Some people have suggested that it was to Chivington's advantage to have Wynkoop removed from his post, but there is no evidence that Chivington instigated the rumors.

On October 17, Major Henning drafted an order relieving Wynkoop of command of Fort Lyon and directing him to report to district headquarters at Fort Riley to explain his actions. The man Henning chose to replace Wynkoop was Major Scott J. Anthony of the First Colorado Regiment.

Anthony had been a merchant in Leavenworth, Kansas, before going to the Colorado goldfields in 1860. He failed to find gold, but he opened a general merchandise store in Leadville. A cousin of the suffragist Susan B. Anthony, he had served in the First Colorado since 1861 and had fought at Glorietta Pass.

His orders from Henning were clear. He was to take command of Fort Lyon and investigate the suggestion that "certain officers" had issued supplies and goods to hostile Indians in direct violation of orders. Henning said he wanted an officer at the fort who showed good judgment and would not commit the kind of foolish actions rumored to have taken place. He also said that Anthony was to make no agreement with the Indians without General Curtis's approval. He was not to allow Indians in the vicinity of the fort for any reason. Further, no officer was to leave the district without authorization. Henning expected to put a stop to the overstepping of authority seen at Fort Lyon.

Major Anthony arrived at Fort Lyon on November 5 to formally take command. Wynkoop was surprised—he had not been informed in advance that he was about to be relieved. Anthony's first order on taking over stated that any Indian who entered the post would be arrested.

He visited the nearby camp of 652 Arapaho to inform them that he was now in charge. His orders were that the soldiers would have nothing to do with the Indians. He demanded to know "by what authority and for what purpose they were encamped there. They replied that they had always been on peaceable terms with the whites, had never desired any other than peace, and could not be induced to fight. That other tribes were at war, and, therefore, they had come into the vicinity of a post, in order to show that they desired peace, and to be where the traveling public would not be frightened by them, or the Indians be harmed by travelers or soldiers on the road."

Anthony was startled by their attitude. He had been assured by Henning that the Indians near the post would be hostile. He told the chiefs that he would write to headquarters to say that they had been peaceful and intended to remain so. To be safe, however—they were, after all, Indians—he told them they could stay camped there only if they surrendered their weapons and stolen stock. If they did so, they would be considered prisoners of war.

The chiefs agreed to these terms and turned over their few weapons. Anthony's troopers combed the Indian herds and selected ten mules and four horses that looked as if they might at one time have belonged to whites. Anthony noted that the Indians' horses were in poor condition. The people themselves were hungry and Anthony issued ten days' worth of army rations, in defiance of his orders. Wynkoop commented that "after learning all the circumstances in regard to them, [Anthony] assured me that, notwithstanding his stringent orders, he was obliged to follow the same course almost that I had adopted. He made issues to these same Indians, and of a greater quantity than ever I had issued."

Ten days later, Anthony changed his mind. He told the Arapaho that he could no longer provide them with food. He released them as prisoners of war, returned their weapons, and recommended that they kill game to live on. He did this, he explained, because he had decided they were not dangerous. In a report to General Curtis written a day after his arrival at Fort Lyon, Anthony had said that the Indians there "could make but a feeble fight if they desired war."

Shortly thereafter, Black Kettle and a band of almost seventy Cheyenne approached the fort. Because Anthony would not allow them inside the stockade, they met with him at a commissary building a half mile away. Black Kettle wanted to know what their status was now that their protector, Major Wynkoop, was no longer in command. The Arapaho had told Black Kettle that things looked dark since the arrival of Major Anthony, the "redeye" chief (whose eyes were red from a bout with scurvy). Are we at war, Black Kettle wanted to know, or is there still a chance for peace?

Major Anthony said he did not have the authority or the instructions to make peace with them but would inform them immediately if and when he received such instructions. In the meantime, Anthony said, Black Kettle should establish a camp for his people forty miles away, along the banks of Sand Creek. Major Wynkoop, who had delayed his departure from Fort Lyon to reassure the Indians about the change of command, also spoke to Black Kettle and the other chiefs at that meeting.

"I told them how I was situated," Wynkoop recalled, "having been relieved from the command by Major Anthony, and that I was no longer in authority, but that Major Anthony, who was now in command, would treat them the same as I had done, until something definite could be heard from proper quarters in regard to them, and advised them to rely upon what he told them; that he was a good chief."

Anthony had told the Indians that he was waiting to hear from General Curtis about whether they could make peace; Wynkoop had said the same thing when he was in command. Anthony told them to camp at Sand Creek, that he would let them know when he received instructions to make peace. Thus, the Indians had every reason to feel secure.

That night, Black Kettle and a few other Cheyenne chiefs stayed at the home of John Wesley Prowers, a twenty-six-year-old trader and interpreter who had worked at Bent's Fort and who was married to the daughter of One-Eye. The Indians trusted Prowers and discussed their situation with him.

"They said they were perfectly satisfied with the way things were going," Prowers recalled, "and hoped the matter would soon be settled. They said that they were very sorry that Major Wynkoop had been removed, but thought that Major Anthony would do all he could for them, and that they felt perfectly easy. Black Kettle asked me what I thought of the council. I told him that I thought it was all right; that from all I could learn I thought everything favorable. They all appeared much pleased with what I had told them, and hoped that it would all be so.

"Next morning before leaving my place, I made them a few presents, sugar, coffee, flour, rice, and bacon. I also gave them some tobacco which had been purchased by the officers at this post, and sent me to give them. They were well pleased, and thanked the officers for giving them the tobacco and shook hands all around [some of the officers being present]. Major Anthony had agreed to come up and see them at my place, and for some reason did not come. He sent John Smith up to talk for him. John Smith told them that he was sorry [Anthony] could not come up to see them, but would be glad at any time to see them at the post, and for them to remain on Sand Creek with their lodges; that they should be

In November 1858, William Larimer staked out the towns of Auraria on the west bank of Cherry Creek and Denver City on the east bank. (*Courtesy Colorado Historical Society, F484.*)

A wood engraving shows Larimer Street, named for Denver's founder, in 1859. (*Courtesy Colorado Historical Society, F1288.*)

As gold fever seized the country, Denver grew, and Larimer Street soon boasted such thriving businesses as the Pikes Peak Jewelry Store. (*Courtesy Colorado Historical Society, F42932.*)

Reports of easy pickings for gold at Pikes Peak, at left, brought thousands of miners, schemers, and gamblers to town. (*Courtesy Colorado Historical Society, F7036.*)

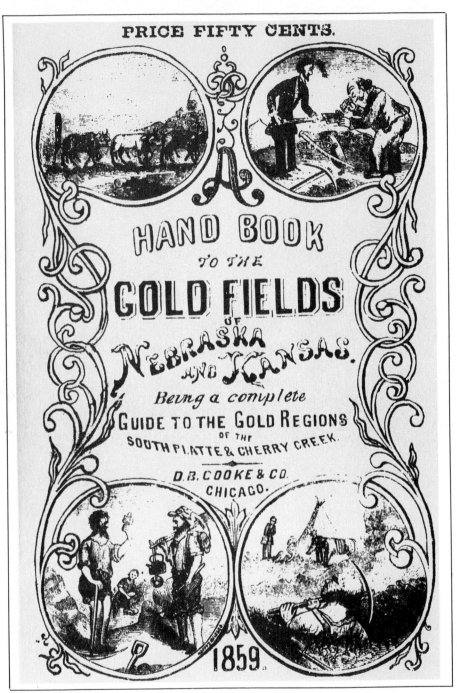

The *Hand Book to the Gold Fields* sold for fifty cents and promised that gold could readily be found in the Cherry Creek region—on the plains, in the mountains, and by the streams. (*Courtesy Colorado Historical Society, F33597.*)

Bent's Fort had adobe brick walls three feet thick. Round towers at two corners were thirty feet high and ten feet in diameter, offering a broad field of fire for musket and cannon. (*Courtesy Colorado Historical Society, 378WPA.*)

The Reverend, later Colonel, John Milton Chivington, born in rural Ohio in 1821, arrived in Denver in 1860 to bring "right and decency" to the citizenry. (*Courtesy Colorado Historical Society, F24623.*)

John Evans, who became Governor of Colorado Territory in 1862, had made a fortune in Illinois real estate and was a founder of Northwestern University. A physician and expert whittler, he also served as ex officio Superintendent of Indian Affairs for the territory. (*Courtesy Colorado Historical Society, F28.*)

William Byers brought a printing press by covered wagon from Omaha to Denver and founded the *Rocky Mountain News*. Byers, Evans, and Chivington became allies, sharing the dream of statehood for Colorado and political power for themselves. (*Courtesy Colorado Historical Society, F2086.*)

Described as dignified and intelligent, the Cheyenne Chief Black Kettle desired peace with the whites but believed that the U.S. government deceived him and treated the Indians unjustly. (*Courtesy Colorado Historical Society, drawing by John Metcalf, F4911.*)

Cheyenne Chief White Antelope wore around his neck a medal given him by Abraham Lincoln. White Antelope died at Sand Creek chanting, "Nothing lives long except the earth and the mountains." (*Courtesy Colorado Historical Society, F12876.*)

ATTENTION!
INDIAN
FIGHTERS

Having been authorized by the Governor to raise a
Company of 100 day

U. S. VOL CAVALRY!

For immediate service against hostile Indians. I call upon all who wish to engage in such
service to call at my office and enroll their names immediately.

Pay and Rations the same as other U. S.
Volunteer Cavalry.

Parties furnishing their own horses will receive 40c per day, and rations for the same,
while in the service.
The Company will also be entitled to all horses and other plunder taken from the Indians.

Office first door East of Recorder's Office.

HAL SAYR.

Central City, Aug. 13, '64.

The Third Colorado Volunteer Cavalry Regiment had no trouble finding recruits in the
summer of 1864. The hundred dazers included men of high standing in the community as
well as the "dregs of the territory's population." These were the troops Chivington led to
Sand Creek. (*Courtesy Colorado Historical Society, F42630, F4232.*)

Cheyennes and Arapahoes arrived in Denver in September 1864 for the Camp Weld council with Governor Evans. The large building in the center is the Methodist Church. (*Courtesy Colorado Historical Society, F1897.*)

The Camp Weld council, September 1864. Kneeling (front row, left to right): Edward Wynkoop, Silas Soule. Seated (middle row, left to right): Neva, Bull Bear, Black Kettle, One-Eye, Left Hand. Standing (back row, third from left): the interpreter John Smith. (*Courtesy Colorado Historical Society, 834WPA.*)

Major Scott J. Anthony assumed command of Fort Lyon in October 1864. He told the Cheyennes that he could not yet admit them to the fort or formally make peace. He suggested that they camp along the banks of Sand Creek, about forty miles away. (*Courtesy Colorado Historical Society, F2276.*)

Jim Beckwourth, a black trapper, hunter, and guide, was an honorary Indian chief. He rode with Chivington as the colonel's scout. (*Courtesy Colorado Historical Society, F17954.*)

A painting of the Sand Creek battle by Robert Lindneux, 1936. Historians have questioned the placement of the American flag. (*Courtesy Colorado Historical Society, F40341.*)

The dashing and impulsive George Armstrong Custer, Seventh Cavalry, in a uniform of his own design. (*Courtesy Colorado Historical Society, F33596.*)

perfectly safe there. Then they shook hands all around, and the talk broke up, and the Indians left for the camp on Sand Creek."

John Prowers's young daughter, Mary, watched the meeting with intense interest, and she waved goodbye as they rode off. "That was the last any of us saw of my grandfather, Chief One-Eye."

Major Anthony was apparently a master of duplicity. While persuading Wynkoop and the Indian chiefs that all was well and that he was the Indians' protector, he was telling General Curtis something quite different. In a report written on November 6, the day after he reached Fort Lyon, he told Curtis that the Indians "pretend that they want peace, and I think they do now, as they cannot fight during the winter, except when a small band of them can find an unprotected train or frontier settlement. I do not think it is policy to make peace with them now, until all perpetrators of depredations are surrendered up to be dealt with as we may propose."

Two weeks later, he reported to Curtis that he had told the Indians he had no desire for trouble but that he could not authorize peace until so advised by headquarters. This would keep matters quiet for the moment, but only until he had enough troops to enforce any demands the government might want to make. Anthony believed he could easily conquer the Arapaho in the vicinity of the post, but that if he attacked them, other tribes would retaliate by raiding settlements and wagon trains. Fort Lyon did not have enough soldiers to fight large war parties. His intention was to wait until reinforcements were sent to Fort Lyon so he could take to the field against all the Indians. He mentioned, specifically, a small band within forty miles of the fort, Black Kettle's village at Sand Creek.

Anthony clearly planned to fight, and so did Chivington. His Third Colorado Regiment chafed with boredom and frustration. The men had enlisted to kill Indians and so far they had hardly even seen any. Their one-hundred-day enlistment period was nearing its end.

Only one company of the Third had been in action, a month before. On October 10, they came across two lodges of Cheyenne south of the Platte River. This was a peaceful camp of families, not a war party, but the troopers attacked anyway, reportedly killing six braves, three women, and a boy. The company commander said that the Indians raised a white flag, but too late, and so no prisoners were taken. He also reported that they found bills of lading from a freight train, along with a white woman's scalp and blood-covered shoes.

There had been no more fighting for the Third and they were becoming ever more unruly and intractable. Chivington himself was still smarting from his loss in the statehood election. He moved companies of the Third out of Denver to a point sixty miles southeast and requested carbines for the men, noting that he would be going after the Indians as soon as his troops were equipped.

On October 22, Chivington received a telegraphed message indicating that he might have competition in his drive to fight the Indians. Acting on orders from the Secretary of War to protect the Overland Stage Line, Brigadier General Patrick Edward Connor of the Department of Utah wired Chivington that he was coming to Denver with two companies of cavalry.

"Can we get a fight out of Indians?" General Connor asked. "How many troops can you spare for a campaign?"

If there was to be any glory from a battle with the Indians, Chivington wanted it to be his. If Connor engaged the enemy, Chivington and the Colorado troops would be his subordinates. To be successful, Chivington would have to act before Connor arrived and before the enlistments of the Bloodless Third ran out.

Connor may well have been both an inspiration and a threat to Chivington. An instantaneous hero for leading his troops 140 miles in freezing weather to make a surprise attack on a village of Shoshone and Bannock Indians in Idaho the year before, Connor had killed 224 and been rewarded with a promotion to the rank of brigadier general. However, a Denver historian wrote, Connor was also a "definite threat to Chivington's dignity, his authority in his military district, the integrity of his jurisdiction. Connor's influence, added to all of the other possible pressures on Chivington, may well have contributed the stimulus necessary to drive him to extreme and desperate measures."

On November 13, Chivington ordered the units of the Third to assemble at Boone's ranch on the Arkansas River, a spot on the way to Fort Lyon. A tempting target awaited them not far from there, a band of Cheyenne under Black Kettle.

While the Third Colorado was gathering, General Connor arrived in Denver. Chivington was suspicious of his motives. He was taken with the idea that Secretary of War Stanton had sent Connor to check on whether Chivington was being sufficiently zealous in carrying out the war against the Indians. Why Stanton, concerned about the life-and-death fighting in the Shenandoah, should be interested in the activities of a colonel of Colorado volunteers in a skirmish that was winding down somewhere in the distant western territories is perhaps a testament to Chivington's exaggerated sense of self-importance.

Chivington made it plain to General Connor that he stood ready to lead the Third Colorado Regiment against the Indians, but he was not about to tell Connor which Indians or where. He planned the battle to be his victory, no one else's. As he mounted his horse to join his men, Connor approached.

"I think," Connor said, "from the temper of the men that you have and all I can learn, that you will give these Indians a most terrible thrashing—if you can catch them." He added that if Chivington managed to get the Indians in a canyon with a river at one end and his men blocking the other, then in the event of such an obvious trap, the Coloradans might get them. "But I am afraid on these plains you won't do it."

"Possibly I may not," Chivington said, ignoring the taunt, "but I think I shall."

Connor expressed his doubts again and asked where the Indians were that Chivington was going after.

A smile spread over Chivington's face. "General," he said, "that is the trick that wins in this game, if the game is won. There are but two persons who know their exact location, and they are myself and Colonel George L. Shoup."

Connor looked expectantly at Chivington, waiting for information, but Chivington said nothing.

"I won't tell anybody," Connor said.

"I will bet you don't," Chivington replied.

"Well," Connor said, finally conceding defeat, "I begin to think that you will catch the Indians."

While Chivington was riding to Boone's ranch to join his troops, two other players in the drama were also traveling. On November 16, Governor Evans left for Washington to argue for more troops with which to mount a large-scale winter campaign against the Indians. Chivington had probably told Evans of his plan to attack the Indian encampment at Sand Creek, and no doubt Evans was supportive of it. The Indian war had grown quiet. If it could be stirred up again, a renewed drive for statehood might be successful.

Evans also must have realized that an attack on the Indians camped at

Sand Creek, believing they were under the protection of the American flag, would enrage the rest of the Cheyenne and the other tribes, as well. If the Indians took to the warpath in retaliation for Sand Creek, the news would reach Washington while Evans was there and would lend considerable weight to his argument. Instead of being granted additional troops, however, Evans found himself, months later, still in Washington defending Chivington's actions.

Another person heading east in late November was Major Wynkoop, who departed Fort Lyon on November 26, three weeks after he had been relieved of command. Having been ordered to report to Fort Riley to justify to General Curtis his actions at Smoky Hill and Camp Weld, Wynkoop carried with him two letters.

One was signed by all the officers stationed at Fort Lyon, expressing regret that he had been relieved of command. It testified "to the fact that the course adopted and carried out by you was the only proper one to pursue, and has been the means of saving the lives of hundreds of men, women, and children, as well as thousands of dollars' worth of property."

Wynkoop was praised by his officers for rescuing the white captives and for arranging the Camp Weld council, which was "productive of more good to the Indians, and did more to allay the fears of the inhabitants in the Arkansas valley, than all that has been done by all other persons in this portion of the department."

"Since that time," the letter went on, "no depredations have been committed by these tribes, and the people have returned to their houses and farms, and are now living as quietly and peaceably as if the bloody scenes of the past summer had never been enacted."

The letter ended with the hope that Major Wynkoop would soon be restored to his command. This ringing endorsement from Wynkoop's officers was supported by Major Anthony. He would later reverse his position, but on November 26, he wrote that "had it not been for the course pursued by Major Wynkoop toward the Cheyenne and Arapaho Indians, the travel upon the public road must have been entirely stopped and the settlers upon the ranches all through the country must have abandoned them or been murdered. I think Major Wynkoop acted for the best in this matter."

The second letter Wynkoop took with him was signed by twenty-seven ranchers and settlers in the Arkansas River valley. They praised his actions and congratulated him for pursuing what they considered to be the only right course.

Black Kettle also expressed gratitude and support for Wynkoop. Two days after the major and his small cavalry escort left Fort Lyon, three Indians overtook them with a message from Black Kettle: A large band of Sioux was massing in their path. Black Kettle's information was correct, and his warning probably saved Wynkoop's life.

On the same day that Wynkoop departed Fort Lyon, three white men—the interpreter John Smith, Private David Lauderback, and Watson Clark, a teamster who worked for Indian agent Sam Colley—left for Sand Creek. They had Major Anthony's permission to trade with the Indians. Anthony also had asked Smith to find out how many Indians were camped there.

They arrived at Black Kettle's village on November 27, intending to stay several days.

Chivington and the men of the Third Colorado Regiment were less than forty-eight hours behind them.

10

Take No Prisoners

Chivington reached the troops of the Colorado regiments at their camp at Boone's ranch on Wednesday evening, November 23. "Chivington takes command," Major Hal Sayr wrote in his diary that night, "which gives pretty general dissatisfaction." Not even his own command thought well of him anymore. The triumph of Glorietta Pass had indeed faded.

The next morning, they broke camp at nine and headed east along the Arkansas River toward Fort Lyon. The force numbered 575: 450 troops of the Third Colorado and 125 of the First. It was bitterly cold and the men drove their horses through snowdrifts two feet high. They burrowed deep in their heavy army overcoats and "cursed the maggoty hardtack given them for breakfast. They were saddle-sore, cold, and already sick of soldiering." The men covered fifteen miles before setting up camp on the riverbank.

The weather improved the following day. "Warm," Major Sayr recorded in his diary. Most of the snow melted and the men were in better spirits when they made camp that night at Spring Bottom, a stagecoach depot. They found plenty of water and wood for their needs. Chivington and his officers commandeered the cabin, ate a decent meal, and spent the evening relaxing in comfort. A trader named James Combs, who was traveling from Fort Lyon to Pueblo, called at the station, and Chivington questioned him about conditions at the fort.

"They don't expect me down there, do they?" Chivington asked.

"I told him no," Combs recalled. "I did not think that anybody from there to the post, or at the post, knew of his coming."

"No, sir," Chivington said, "nor they won't know it till they see me there."

Chivington asked the trader who was in command at Fort Lyon. Major Anthony, Combs told him. And who was in command before that? Major Wynkoop, was the answer.

"Oh! You must be mistaken," Chivington said with a laugh. "I think that Left Hand was in command."

Chivington then wanted to know how the Indians felt about Major Anthony. Did he feed them well? Exactly where were they located? Were they armed? Had they caused any trouble? Combs answered as best he could. Chivington turned the conversation to the purpose of his expedition.

"Scalps are what we are after," he said bluntly.

"I told him," Combs recalled, "that I thought he could get, any way, some 400 or 500 of them within one day's march of Fort Lyon; that I thought there was about that number—warriors, squaws, and papooses—in all, and told him that I thought he ought to do it with that party; that there had been no time, for some time past, when they could not have been taken with 50 men."

As Combs was leaving, he saw Chivington draw himself up straight in his chair and say to his officers, "Well, I long to be wading in gore."

On Saturday, November 26, Chivington and his command set off at dawn and rode all day, making twenty-eight miles. At the front of the long column of soldiers rode Jim Beckwourth, a black sixty-nine-year-old mountain man and guide. Although Beckwourth had spent most of his life as a trapper and hunter, he possessed the manners of a gentleman and a store of information envied by many with a more formal education. The Crow Indians had made him a chief, and he had lived among the Cheyenne for many years. They called him Medicine Calf. He rode in silence, his rifle cradled across his arms and one leg hooked up over his saddle. His eyes missed nothing.

Chivington sent off patrols periodically to the ranches along the route to make sure that nobody warned the Indians that such a large force of soldiers was on the way. Mary Prowers remembered the soldiers coming to her father's ranch, disarming him and his seven ranch hands and imprisoning them all in the house for two days and nights. No explanation was provided. At every ranch the occupants were kept under house arrest by the soldiers. The ranchers were not permitted to tend their stock, and many cattle wandered off. Chivington's troopers stopped stagecoaches and the U.S. mail. For three days along that stretch of the Arkansas, no one moved who was not wearing a blue uniform.

Chivington knew that most large-scale expeditions against Indians failed because the Indians learned about the troop movements and faded away. He was not about to let that happen. The Indians at Sand Creek were going to be taken by surprise.

The men rode for thirty-eight miles the next day, making camp only fourteen miles from Fort Lyon. That evening, two officers from the post, Captain Silas Soule and Lieutenant W. P. Minton, who were out riding west of the fort, spotted some horsemen in the distance. They assumed the riders were Indians and reported the sighting to Major Anthony. Anthony ordered Soule to lead a patrol out before dawn to investigate. At sunrise on the twenty-eighth, Soule and his twenty-man unit came across a mule train edging down the north bank of the river toward the fort. He asked the driver whether he had seen any Indians.

No, was the reply, but he had observed Colonel Chivington with ten or twelve companies of hundred dazers about two miles back. For all Chivington's precautions, he and his troops had been spotted by a mule skinner ambling along ahead of the column. The man had come close enough to recognize Chivington but had not been seen himself.

Soule was greatly surprised to hear this news. No one at Fort Lyon expected Chivington, and it was highly irregular for a detachment to arrive at a military outpost without advance notice. Soule and his men galloped off in the direction indicated by the mule driver, and within two miles spied the unmistakable figure of John Milton Chivington at the head of the column of blue-coated cavalrymen.

Chivington was furious. He demanded to know whether he was expected at Fort Lyon. Soule said that no one there knew he was coming. Chivington seemed relieved and proceeded to ask Soule whether there were any Indians near the post. The captain said that some were camped nearby but they were not dangerous and were considered to be prisoners while the C.O. awaited instructions from General Curtis. Soule overheard one of Chivington's officers remark that the Indians would not be prisoners after *they* got there.

Chivington made rapid plans to reach Fort Lyon before the mule train. Taking an aide with him, he rode as fast as he could for the post, catching everyone by surprise, just as he had hoped. He issued orders to seal off the fort and placed a ring of troops around the perimeter. No one, not even Fort Lyon's own cadre, would be allowed to enter or leave without Chivington's permission. The penalty for disobedience was death.

The fort's soldiers and Chivington's own command established a camp a half mile away, isolated in accordance with Chivington's general field order number two, issued that afternoon.

1. Hereafter, no officer will be allowed to leave his command without the consent of the colonel commanding, and no soldier without a written pass from his company commander, approved by the commander of his battalion.
2. No fires will be allowed to burn after dark, unless especially directed from these headquarters.
3. Any person giving the Indians information of the movements of troops will be deemed a spy and shot to death.

Major Anthony welcomed Chivington and said that he had been waiting for reinforcements so as to be able to deal with a band of hostile Indians living forty miles away at Sand Creek. After a few minutes of conversation about them, Chivington announced that he would march to Sand Creek that night. Anthony volunteered to accompany him with a battalion of 125 of his men, but he suggested that Chivington also attack the larger settlement of several thousand Cheyenne at Smoky Hill. Chivington agreed that it would be desirable to clear out that encampment but that his decision to do so would depend on the outcome of the attack at Sand Creek.

Anthony raised the matter of the friendly Indians and the three white men at Sand Creek who should be rescued. "My recommendation," he told Chivington, "is to surround the Sand Creek camp so that none may escape to warn the main body; and then, as soon as the first action is concluded, to push on to the Smoky Hill without delay. Further, by first surrounding the village, we will give our friends and agents in the camp an opportunity to escape before any fighting begins."

Anthony mentioned specifically Chief One-Eye (whom he said he was paying $125 a month to serve as a spy), Left Hand, and Black Kettle, as well as John Smith, Private David Lauderback, and the teamster Watson Clark. The latter three were at Sand Creek to trade and to spy. "All of these should be saved," Anthony said. "To get them out safely, notice should be given in advance of an attack."

Chivington did not appear interested in saving Black Kettle, describing him as chief of a tribe that "has been engaged in bloody war with the whites since April. His claim of friendship seems to have arisen with the ending of the summer season and the approach of cold weather when Indians fight at a disadvantage. However, it is not my intention to attack without warning. Actual operations must, of course, depend on conditions which we find on arrival, but I propose to first immobilize the Indians, if possible, and then to offer them a parley on terms of surrender."

Anthony seemed satisfied, and he wrote to General Curtis that day to report on the arrival of Chivington's forces "on expedition against Indians. This number of men has been required for some time, and is appreciated by me now, as I believe the Indians will be properly punished— what they have for some time deserved. I go out with 125 men and two howitzers to join his command."

Chivington issued marching orders for eight o'clock that evening. The men would have to ride hard and travel light to reach Sand Creek by sunrise. He ordered the wagon train with all the reserve supplies and baggage to be left behind at the fort. The troopers would take only what they could jam into their saddlebags, enough ammunition, bacon, and hardtack for twenty-three days.

While the men were drawing their rations and supplies, the Indians camped at Sand Creek waited for General Curtis's decision about a peace treaty. On November 28, the day Chivington and his men arrived at Fort Lyon, Curtis wrote to his superior, Major General James Carleton, that the Cheyenne and Arapaho "insist on peace or absolute sacrifice, as I choose. Of course, they will have to be received, but there still remain some of these tribes and all of the Kiowa to attend to, and I have proposed a winter campaign for their benefit. This, if successful, must be secret and well arranged beforehand." Curtis did not know that Chivington and his Colorado regiments were about to undertake just such a campaign. Indeed, Chivington had not even told Curtis that he was moving his troops to Fort Lyon.

Before General Curtis learned of Chivington's march on Sand Creek, he wrote to his aide, Major Henning, that he hoped Wynkoop had been "disposed of" and that a change for the better (with Major Anthony commanding) had been instituted at Fort Lyon. Even if the Cheyenne and Arapaho came to the fort to surrender, Curtis said, the military was under no obligation to receive them, feed them, or allow them inside the post. "At the proper time," he added, "a campaign would be undertaken against the hostiles, and to assure its success, the march of his troops would be masked from the view of the public." To Governor Evans, Curtis confessed that he was still "undecided and uncertain" over what to do about the Cheyenne and Arapaho—the "nominal prisoners," as he called them—encamped near Fort Lyon.

But Curtis would not have to make a decision about the Indians at Sand Creek. Chivington was about to do that for him.

There was no hope of a reprieve for the Cheyenne and Arapaho. As preparations were being made for the attack, however, several officers who had accompanied Major Wynkoop on his trip to Smoky Hill were attempting to intercede. Major Anthony had designated them as part of Chivington's force to attack Black Kettle's village.

The officers objected, pointing out to Anthony that Black Kettle could easily have massacred Wynkoop's command at any moment during the Smoky Hill expedition. But there was more to their objections than a sense of gratitude. There was also the question of honor. Wynkoop and his officers had guaranteed the safety of Black Kettle, and all the Indians at Sand Creek, until such time as General Curtis reached a decision about a peace treaty. Lieutenant James Cannon protested an attack on these Indians, "as I was aware that they were resting there in fancied security under promises held out to them of safety from Major E. W. Wynkoop, former commander of the post at Fort Lyon, as well as by Major S. J. Anthony, then in command." Lieutenant Minton, and C. M. Cossitt, the quartermaster, also argued against the operation on the grounds that the "Indians were recognized as friendly by all parties of this post."

Captain Silas Soule spoke to Anthony that afternoon, expecting him also to oppose the attack. Soule was surprised to hear Anthony say that "he was in for killing all Indians, and that he was only acting or had been only acting friendly with them until he could get a force large enough to go out and kill all of them."

Soule reminded Anthony of the pledge made to the Indians. Anthony said that Chivington had told him that the Indians to whom the pledge was made—plus John Smith and the two other white men in the camp—would not be killed. The ultimate objective of the expedition was to go after the larger encampment at Smoky Hill. Anthony tried to persuade Soule that some of the Cheyenne and Arapaho at Sand Creek deserved to die, but that the friendly chiefs—Black Kettle, One-Eye, White Antelope, and Left Hand—would be spared.

Failing to convince Soule, Anthony then told him that his honor would not be compromised if he joined the expedition since he had formally expressed his opposition to it. Later that day, however, Soule was warned by several fellow officers to stay away from Chivington; they had heard the colonel make threats against Soule because of his outspoken opposition. Soule sent a note to Chivington stating his reasons for opposing the campaign, but the note was returned unopened.

Lieutenant Joseph Cramer also took exception to Chivington's plan. He told Major Anthony that "I was perfectly willing to obey orders, but that I did it under protest, for I believed that he directly, and all officers who accompanied Major Wynkoop to the Smoky Hill indirectly, would perjure themselves both as officers and men; that I believed it to be murder to go out and kill those Indians, as I felt that Major Wynkoop's command owed their lives to this same band of Indians."

Anthony replied tersely that he had made no pledges that would compromise his honor. The promise of safety he had given the Indians was not binding because he had received no word from General Curtis. The only promise he had made was to let them know when he heard from the general—nothing more.

Cramer persisted, pointing out that Black Kettle and his people had acted in good faith, had spared the lives of 127 men at Smoky Hill, and had indicated their willingness to help the soldiers fight other Indian tribes. Anthony assured Cramer that "Black Kettle would not be killed; that it was a promise given by Colonel Chivington that Black Kettle and his friends should be spared; that the object of the expedition was to surround the camp and take the stolen stock and kill the Indians that had been committing depredations during the last spring and summer."

Still not satisfied, Cramer took the courageous decision to confront Chivington. He repeated the arguments he had made to Anthony and expressed his belief that an attack on Black Kettle and his band would be nothing less than murder. "I feel," he said, "that you are placing us in a very embarrassing circumstance by requiring us to fight the same Indians that saved our lives."

Chivington maintained an icy silence until Cramer had finished. Then he exploded with anger, looming over the lieutenant and shouting as he waved his clenched fist in Cramer's face. "The Cheyenne nation," he roared, "has been waging bloody war against the whites all spring, summer, and fall, and Black Kettle is their principal chief. They have been guilty of robbery, arson, murder, rape, and fiendish torture, not even sparing women and little children. I believe it right and honorable to use any means under God's heaven to kill Indians who kill and torture women and children. Damn any man who is in sympathy with them!"

He turned on his heel and strode out of the room, remarking loudly that men like Cramer and Soule should get out of the service of the United States.

That night, not long before the command was due to leave, there was one more protest, this one made by a group including lieutenants Cossitt, Minton, and Maynard, the Indian agent Sam Colley, and several civilians living at the post. They argued that it would be a crime to attack Indians who had been given assurances of safety and had gone to Denver to see Governor Evans in good faith and with good intentions. Colley told Chivington that the Indians had been misunderstood, misrepresented, and maltreated, especially by Captain Parmeter and others like him. Chivington paced around the room while the men were speaking. When they finished, he glared from one to another.

"Damn any man who is in sympathy with an Indian!"

There were no more objections.

Chivington ordered the troops into formation at eight o'clock that night and gave the command to move out, believing he was leading them to glory and everlasting fame. They traveled in a column of fours across the grassy, gently rolling plains. Throughout the long cold night, the troops varied their pace in standard U.S. cavalry manner—walk, trot, gallop, dismount and lead the horses. The men who had made the five-day march to reach Fort Lyon were already exhausted, and heads dropped against chests as they fought to stay awake in the saddle.

Despite the fatigue, the morale of the Colorado Third was high. The hundred dazers were finally going after Indians, which was why many of them had joined up in the first place. They did not know which Indians they were about to attack, or where—only their officers knew that—but most of them did not care so long as they killed some. They wanted revenge for the months of raids and terror, and one Indian was just as good as another for that.

Approximately seven hundred men marched toward Sand Creek that night. Major Anthony led 125 troops of the Colorado First from Fort Lyon; Lieutenant Luther Wilson commanded 125 soldiers of the Colorado First who had made the grueling march with Chivington to the fort; and Colonel Shoup had 450 men of the Colorado Third. They were a mixed force in both experience and appearance. The two units of the First had combat experience, proper uniforms, and considerable military bearing and discipline. They looked and acted like soldiers, and had been in service for more than two years. The men of the Third—the hundred dazers—appeared seedy, carried an assortment of weapons and hats, and marched like the raw recruits they were.

The temperature dropped steadily and the wind grew bitter as the night wore on. Old Jim Beckwourth became so stiff from the cold he could no longer make out the right course. Accompanying Chivington from Fort Lyon was Robert Bent, William Bent's half-breed son, and Chivington ordered him up to the head of the column to take over from Beckwourth as guide. Many of the men distrusted Robert Bent, not only because he was a half-breed but also because they believed him to be more Indian than white in his sympathies. Some said he had ridden with the Cheyenne in their war parties and had even killed white settlers.

Chivington and his officers kept a watchful eye on Bent. Toward midnight, he led them through a shallow lake. Many thought he did so deliberately in order to get their ammunition wet. He may, indeed, have been trying to lead the troops astray, to guide them to a different part of Sand Creek, where there were no Indians, so that he could announce that the Indians must have fled. Bent had three sisters and a brother in the village at Sand Creek. Near daybreak, he told Chivington, "Wolf, he howl. Injun dog he hear wolf, he howl, too. Injun hear dog and listen, hear something, and run off."

Chivington looked at Bent and tapped his revolver. "I haven't had an Indian to eat in a long time," he said. "If you fool with me, and don't lead us to that camp, I'll have you for breakfast."

As the first morning light spread over the plains, Chivington and Shoup urged their horses up a rise less than a mile from the Indian camp. They studied the scene through their binoculars. All was peaceful. Chivington had achieved complete surprise. Victory was his.

The column was south of the dry riverbed at the spot where the creek changed course from a southerly to an easterly direction. About one hundred tepees of Black Kettle's camp gleamed white in the pale dawn light. These lodges stood on the far bank of the creek, arrayed in a vast circle over a half mile in diameter, the distance of three arrow flights from a strong bow. Just west of the Cheyenne village were ten Arapaho lodges. The creek bed was about two hundred yards wide at that point and the bank on the Indians' side ranged from two to ten feet high. On Chivington's side of the creek was a small herd of ponies and about six hundred horses.

Chivington first made certain that the Indians could not reach their horses in a bid to escape. He ordered Lieutenant Wilson to take three companies of the Colorado First and scatter the horses. Captain McCannon was to employ a company of the Third to run off the ponies. Major Anthony and his men followed Wilson to approach the east end of the village to prevent the Indians from fleeing in that direction.

Chivington turned in his saddle to address his troops.

"Off with your coats, men," he shouted. "You can fight better without them. Take no prisoners. Remember the slaughtered white women and children. Remember the Hungates. I don't tell you to kill all ages and sex, but look back on the plains of the Platte, where your mothers, fathers, brothers, sisters have been slain, and their blood saturating the sands on the Platte."

With the fighting parson in the lead, the troops galloped forward. The massacre of Sand Creek had begun.

A mile away in the Indian village, the women were preparing to walk down to the creek bed, as they did early every morning, to draw water from its few puddles. The Cheyenne and Arapaho never drank water that had sat in containers overnight, calling that dead water. They drank only living water, drawn fresh from the earth. In one of the lodges, the three white men from Fort Lyon—Smith, Lauderback, and Clark—were already awake. John Smith's grown half-breed son, Jack, was with them. The entrance flap was flung open and a woman burst in, shouting that many buffalo were coming. Moments later, a chief entered the lodge and announced that soldiers were riding toward the camp. He asked John Smith to find out what they wanted.

The thunder of seven hundred galloping horses had awakened the entire village. Men, women, and children poured out of the lodges and milled about in confusion, yelling and gesturing at the troops. Black Kettle hoisted a large American flag and a smaller white flag over his lodge. The American flag had been given to him four years earlier by Commissioner of Indian Affairs A. B. Greenwood, who had instructed him to display it whenever he was approached by soldiers. The flag would protect the Cheyenne, Greenwood had said. Black Kettle called out to his people not to be afraid. They were in no danger. The camp was under the protection of the American flag. And that was when the troops opened fire.

The first shots came from Lieutenant Wilson's men. They had cut the horses off from the settlement and had started shooting from the north-

east. Chivington led his Colorado Third toward the eastern end of the
camp where Major Anthony's men were waiting. The hundred dazers
dismounted and opened fire, right through Anthony's position. His
troops fled to the creek, to avoid the hail of bullets from Chivington's
line of fire. With that, all semblance of organization and military control
was lost, and Chivington made no attempt to regain it. The tactical ge-
nius he had displayed at Glorietta Pass was nowhere in evidence at Sand
Creek.

The situation deteriorated as soldiers fired wildly and at random—at
Indians and at one another. Most of the troops, but especially the Third,
were no longer an army; they were a mob. "After that," said Captain
Soule, "I could see no order to the battle. The command was scattered
and every man firing on his own hook on both sides of the creek."

As the men advanced haphazardly, the Cheyenne chief White Antelope, wearing the medal from President Lincoln around his neck, decided that he no longer wished to live. For months he had been assuring
his people that the white man was good and that peace would soon be at
hand. He had been wrong. The white man had betrayed them. He ran
toward the soldiers waving his hands in the air, shouting in English for
them to stop killing his people. Bullets kicked up dust at his feet.

Black Kettle called out to him to run away from the soldiers, but
White Antelope halted in the center of the creek, folded his arms across
his chest, and waited to die. He stood there impassively, chanting his
death song, as bullets tore into his chest.

> Nothing lives long
> Except the earth and the mountains.

When the troops reached his fallen body, they scalped it, and cut off his
ears and nose.

Chief Left Hand of the Arapaho stood silently outside his lodge, telling
all those around him that he would not fight the white men. They were
his friends. Moments later, he was dead. Many other Indians, out of
confusion, a lingering and misplaced trust, and resignation, also made no
effort to fight or to flee. Lieutenant Cramer remembered that "a great
many started toward our lines with hands raised, as if begging for us to
spare them." The troops cut them all down.

John Smith walked slowly toward Lieutenant Wilson's men, waving a white handkerchief on the end of a stick.

"Shoot the old son of a bitch," one of the soldiers shouted. "He's no better than an Indian."

Smith froze, terrified, as bullets flew past him. Sergeant George Pierce spurred his horse forward in an effort to save Smith, but before he could reach him, Pierce's horse stumbled. When the sergeant got to his feet, he was shot dead, probably by one of his own men. Smith turned and raced back to the lodge, convinced that he would never see another sunrise.

Private Lauderback, dressed in his blue cavalry uniform, was fired on when he tried to approach the soldiers, and he, too, retreated to the lodge. Watson Clark, the teamster, attached a tanned buffalo skin to a pole and raised it over his head. He climbed up on a wagon but was quickly forced back inside to escape the gunfire.

Lauderback peered around the tepee's entrance flap, spotted Chivington about fifty yards away, and called out to him. Chivington told him to come out. Lauderback started toward the colonel but after a few steps, a soldier opened fire. Chivington told the men around him to hold their fire and he directed Lauderback to fall in at the rear of his command.

John Smith crept out and hailed Chivington.

"Run here, Uncle John," Chivington yelled. "You are all right." Smith and Watson Clark ran toward him and fell in behind the troops.

Three groups of soldiers were moving in the same direction: Men on horseback rode along both sides of the creek, and Chivington with his hundred dazers of the Third Colorado came along on foot at the edge of the village in the creek bed itself. Only one detachment of troops was not engaged in the fighting—the command of Captain Soule. Opposed to killing the Indians to whom he had pledged safety, Soule had ordered his men not to fire. They rode along the south bank of the creek watching the battle.

About one hundred Indians fled along the creek bed west of the village to a spot a mile away where the banks were gouged by gulleys and ravines. Foot soldiers were behind them and mounted troopers ahead, some two hundred in all, cutting off their retreat. Using their knives and bare hands, the Indians quickly dug holes and crude trenches in which the warriors could make a stand and the women and children—the bulk of the group—could hide. Soldiers lined up on both sides of the creek and fired at them at will.

George Bent took refuge in one of the trenches. "We fought back as well as we could with guns and knives," he said, "but we had only a few guns. The troops did not rush in and fight hand to hand, but once or twice after they had killed many of the men in a certain pit, they rushed in and finished up the work, killing the wounded and the women and children that had not been hurt."

The Indians held off the soldiers for almost four hours before the troops broke off the fight and returned to the village. Major Anthony later wrote to a friend that he "never saw more bravery displayed by any set of people on the face of the earth than by these Indians. They would charge on the whole company singly, determined to kill someone before being killed themselves. We, of course, took no prisoners."

About seventy of the Indians in the trenches were killed. The rest, including George Bent, who had taken a bullet in the hip, escaped after the troops withdrew.

Scattered bands of soldiers chased stray Indians among the sand hills. By mid-afternoon, most of the troopers were tired of fighting and riding, and they drifted back to the encampment. The combat had ended but the killing and atrocities had not. Throughout the day they continued, forming a haze of fragmented memories that some men carried with them like scars for as long as they lived. Others put the events out of their minds before the week was over.

Chivington's men were a mob—primitive, unrestrained, crude, barbaric—stripped for that time of even the thinnest veneer of civilization. They avenged the Hungates and the other dead whites tenfold. Chivington did nothing to stop them, if, indeed, the hatred and passion fired over the previous months by the fighting parson, the newspaper editor Byers, and Governor Evans were capable of being stopped. However, Chivington was the only one of the three present at Sand Creek and he did not try to restrain his men.

The descriptions of the actions of the Colorado volunteers became part of his record, his trial, his life, and his legacy. They brought him not the fame he was seeking but infamy, not the glory he was desperate to recapture but ignominy.

> I saw one man dismount from his horse; he was standing by the side of Colonel Chivington. There was a dead squaw there who had apparently been killed some little time before. The man got down off his

horse, took hold of the squaw, took out his knife and tried to cut off her scalp.

There was one little child, probably three years old, just big enough to walk through the sand. The Indians had gone ahead, and this little child was behind following after them. The little fellow was perfectly naked, traveling on the sand. I saw one man get off his horse, at a distance of about 75 yards, and draw up his rifle and fire—he missed the child. Another man came up and said, "Let me try the son of a bitch; I can hit him." He got down off his horse, kneeled down and fired at the little child, but he missed him. A third man came up and made a similar remark, and the little fellow dropped.

I saw five squaws under a bank for shelter. When the troops came up to them they ran out and showed their persons to let the soldiers know they were squaws and begged for mercy, but the soldiers shot them all. I saw one squaw lying on the bank whose leg had been broken by a shell; a soldier came up to her with a drawn saber; she raised her arm to protect herself, when he struck, breaking her arm; she rolled over and raised her other arm, when he struck, breaking it, and then left her without killing her. There were some 30 or 40 squaws collected in a hole for protection; they sent out a little girl about six years old with a white flag on a stick; she had not proceeded but a few steps when she was shot and killed. I saw a little girl about five years of age who had been hid in the sand; two soldiers discovered her, drew their pistols, and shot her, and then pulled her out of the sand by the arm. I saw quite a number of infants in arms killed with their mothers.

One old squaw wandered sightless through the carnage. Her entire scalp had been taken, and the skin of her forehead fell down over her eyes to blind her. Several troopers got into a quarrel over who should have the honor of scalping one body. The issue could not be decided; so all took scalps from the same carcass.

A group of soldiers paused amid the firing to take turns profaning the body of a comely young squaw, very dead. Indians' fingers were hacked away to get their rings as souvenirs. One soldier trotted about with a heart impaled on a stick. Others carried off the genitals of braves. Someone had the notion that it would be artistic work to slice away the breasts of the Indian women. One breast was worn as a cap, another was seen stretched over the bow of a saddle.

I saw a little boy covered up among the Indians in a trench, still alive. I saw a major in the Third regiment take out his pistol and blow off the top of his head. It was the Third Colorado men who did these things.

During the massacre [I] saw three squaws and five children, prisoners in charge of some soldiers; that, while they were being conducted along the road, they were approached by Lieutenant Harry Richmond, of the Third Colorado Cavalry; that Lieutenant Richmond thereupon immediately killed and scalped the three women and the five children while they were screaming for mercy; while the soldiers in whose charge the prisoners were shrank back, apparently aghast.

Colonel Chivington was in position where he must have seen the scalping and the mutilation going on.

To the best of my knowledge and belief these atrocities that were committed were with knowledge of J. M. Chivington, and I do not know of his taking any measures to prevent them. All these matters were a subject of general conversation, and could not help being known by Colonel J. M. Chivington.

When it was over, more than one hundred Indians were dead, although Chivington would later claim as many as five hundred. About five hundred Indians escaped. John Smith later reported that there were probably fewer than seventy armed warriors in the village, yet they held off seven hundred soldiers while the majority of the Indians got away. Chivington's command lost nine men killed and thirty-eight wounded, some of whom were shot by other soldiers. As a military exercise, it was a fiasco.

After their orgy of murder and mutilation, many of the troopers fell into a restless sleep. "I was so utterly exhausted," one of the Third Colorado volunteers wrote, "from want of sleep and food, as were many others, that I hunted up a buffalo robe, of which there were large numbers scattered around, threw myself down on it, and was asleep almost as soon as I touched the ground."

Chivington and his officers wandered over the desolate area as John Smith tried to identify the dead chiefs. The condition of the bodies made a number of them unrecognizable. "It was very hard for me to tell one from another," Smith said. As far as he could determine, all the chiefs had been killed, including Black Kettle, and One-Eye, the grandfather of Mary Prowers.

The soldiers were awakened at dusk for supper and told to sleep with their guns in their hands that night. Shortly before midnight, they were roused again and ordered to fall in line to repel an attack. Indians were out there somewhere in the darkness, the officers warned.

"We rushed out," a trooper in the Third recalled, "but were in such a sleepy condition that we had difficulty in forming a line, as hardly any of us knew what we were doing. We heard occasional shots in various directions, and out in the light of the fire could be seen what looked like hundreds of Indian ponies running hither and thither. Apparently there were no riders, but we knew that Indians, in an encounter, always try to conceal their bodies from the enemy by lying over on the far side of their mounts. From the number of what appeared to be horses that could be seen in every direction, it seemed that surely we were due to be overwhelmed."

Shots were heard throughout the next hour, and the pickets were driven back from the perimeter, by Indians, they said. Someone figured out that the "horses" were actually dogs, scores of the Indians' dogs running wild, searching for their masters. The men were allowed to stand down, but many kept their fingers on the trigger the rest of the black night.

At sunrise, the men ate a cold breakfast. In one of the few lodges still standing, Private Lauderback cooked breakfast for John Smith, his squaw and child, another white man's squaw, three children, a baby, and Smith's son Jack. Outside, speculation was rising among the men of the Third about Jack Smith. He was part Indian and he was still alive. Some of the troopers questioned why Lauderback and Watson Clark had not been killed. After all, they had been found in the camp with the Indians.

Major Anthony got wind of the talk and went immediately to Chivington to argue for Jack Smith's life. The half-breed could be useful as a guide and scout, Anthony said, "but unless you give your men to understand that you want the man saved, he is going to be killed."

"I have given my instructions," Chivington said. "[I] have told my men not to take any prisoners."

Anthony persisted, pointing out how helpful Jack Smith could be, but Chivington was adamant.

"I said at the start that I did not want any prisoners taken, and I have no further instructions to give."

Later that afternoon, about fifteen soldiers forced their way into the lodge. As Lauderback described it, they told Jack Smith that he was "a son of a bitch and ought to have been shot long ago. Jack told the man that was talking to him that he did not give a damn; that if he wanted to kill him, shoot him. When Jack said this I thought it was time for me to get out of there, as men had threatened to hang and shoot me as well as Uncle John Smith and the teamster that was with us."

A soldier beckoned to John Smith to come outside. He took the old man by the arm and led him away.

"I am sorry to tell you, but they are going to kill your son Jack."

Smith knew it was hopeless. "I can't help it," he said. He went up to Chivington, who was standing near a campfire. "When I got to within a few feet of him," Smith said, "I heard a gun fired, and saw a crowd run to my lodge, and they told me that Jack was dead."

Three days later, Major Anthony, in a letter to his brother, wrote, "We, of course, took no prisoners, except John Smith's son, and he was taken seriously ill in the night, and died before morning."

Lauderback reported that it was a "damn shame" the way Jack Smith had been killed. "No matter what a man had done, they ought to give him a show for his life."

The Indian survivors of Sand Creek made their way northeast toward Smoky Hill. After the soldiers withdrew from the sand pits on the bank of the creek, the Cheyenne worked their way up the creek bed, dragging their wounded. After a few miles, they met some of the braves who had fled at the onset of the attack to try to save the horses. They managed to catch a few horses, and some of the wounded Indians were put across their backs.

One old man made his way back down the creek bed to search for his wife, who had been shot in the melee at the trenches. He found her alive; she had sustained nine wounds. She told her husband that the soldiers kept shooting at her as she lay in the sand. The old man hoisted her on his back and carried her away from the camp. He met up with an Indian on horseback who took them both to Smoky Hill. The woman survived. Her husband, Black Kettle, had saved her life. He was the only chief from Sand Creek left alive.

The main party of survivors made camp in a ravine ten miles from the battle. "It was very dark and bitterly cold," George Bent recalled. "Very few of us had warm clothing, for we had been driven out of our beds and had had no time to dress. The wounded suffered greatly. There was no wood to be had, but the unwounded men and women collected grass and made fires. The wounded were placed near the fires and covered with grass to keep them from freezing."

The Indians sat up through the night howling, to let other survivors know where they were. In the morning, they traveled only a short distance before they were met by patrols from the Smoky Hill settlement, bringing horses, food, and blankets, alerted to the disaster by braves who had caught horses after the attack began and had ridden straight to the camp. Most of the Sand Creek Indians had friends and relatives at Smoky Hill, and as they came within sight of the lodges, the entire village rushed out to greet them, "wailing and mourning in a manner that I have never heard equalled," said George Bent.

Before long, the wailing and mourning would become war cries. Sand Creek would be avenged.

11

All This Country Is Ruined

C hivington led his men away from Sand Creek on the morning of December 1. Despite his bold declaration to General Curtis that he would march to Smoky Hill, where large numbers of Cheyenne were camped, he headed in the opposite direction. The men rode back toward the Arkansas River, where Little Raven and a small band of Arapaho were reported to be stopping. The troops spent several days in pursuit but found no Indians.

By December 5, Chivington had grown discouraged. He called a meeting of his officers to discuss their course of action. The officers told him that the horses were worn out and the men were complaining about the constant, fruitless marching and the limited rations of hardtack. Smoky Hill was now impossible—if, indeed, it had ever been seriously contemplated—given the condition of the horses and the troops. Also, it would be unlikely that Chivington could surprise the Indians there, as he had at Sand Creek. He concluded that it was pointless to continue to chase after small bands of Indians, who managed to disappear whenever the soldiers approached, and so he decided to return to Denver.

They rode by way of Fort Lyon, where they left Robert Bent, who had guided them to Sand Creek, and his three sisters and their children, who had been in the Cheyenne lodge with John Smith. Three other Indian children were taken along to Denver, together with a number of other battle trophies.

Chivington rode ahead of the column, wanting to be the first to reach Denver, the first to reap the glory he knew was now his. William Byers had been trumpeting the victory in the *Rocky Mountain News.* On December 7, the residents of Denver learned for the first time of what Byers called the "big Indian fight."

"The First and Third Regiments have had a battle with the Indians on Sand Creek. Five hundred Indians are reported killed and 600 horses captured. *Bully for the Colorado boys!"*

The following day, Byers published Chivington's report, written on the day of the battle, along with a glowing editorial suggesting that the Indians' defeat at Sand Creek would bring an end to their reign of terror.

> This noted, needed whipping of the redskins by our First Indian Expedition was the chief subject of comment and glorification through town today. The [men] who collectively cleaned out the confederated savages on Sand Creek have won for themselves and their commanders, from colonel down to corporal, the eternal gratitude of dwellers of these plains. This brave beginning will bring down the *hauteur* of the treacherous tribes, all around, so that, should there not be even another similar defeat acted on them through this season, our people may rest easy in the belief that outrages by small bands are at an end, on routes where troops are stationed. Having tasted of the bitter end, the supremacy of our power will be seriously considered, and a surrender or a suing for peace be perhaps very soon proclaimed.

Byers apparently had forgotten or chose to ignore the fact that revenge was not practiced only by whites. He, and all the people of Colorado and the adjacent territories, would soon be reminded that violence begets violence. On one point, however, Byers was correct. Outrages perpetrated by small bands of Indians did cease, although they would eventually be replaced by outrages on a much grander scale.

Chivington reached Denver on December 16 and set to work preparing a lengthy report on the Sand Creek battle for General Curtis. He suggested that if he had more soldiers under his command, he could rid the country between the Platte and the Arkansas rivers of Indians for all time. He indicated that he had killed all the Cheyenne and Arapaho chiefs, some 500–600 Indians, and had taken no prisoners. Also, his men had found a white man's scalp that was no more than two or three days old. Chivington went on to berate Captain Silas Soule for conduct that was "ill-advised, [Soule] saying that he thanked God that he had killed no Indians, and like expressions, proving him more in sympathy with those Indians than with the whites."

Byers's next editorial was another stirring defense of Chivington and the Colorado regiments.

Among the brilliant feats of arms in Indian warfare, the recent campaign of our Colorado volunteers will stand in history with few rivals, and none to exceed it in final results.

Whether viewed as a march or as a battle, the exploit has few, if any, parallels. A march of 260 miles in but a fraction more than five days, with deep snow, scanty forage, and no road, is a remarkable feat, whilst the utter surprise of a large Indian village is unprecedented. In no single battle in North America, we believe, have so many Indians been slain.

A thousand incidents of individual daring and the passing events of the day might be told, but space forbids. We leave the task for eyewitnesses to chronicle. All acquitted themselves well, and Colorado soldiers have once again covered themselves with glory.

A simpler statement by Captain Cree, one of the Third's officers, was more prophetic. "All I can say for officers and men is that they all behaved well, and won for themselves a name that will be remembered for ages to come."

The now aptly named Bloody Third Regiment arrived in Denver on December 22 to a tumultuous welcome and a victory parade through streets lined with cheering crowds. The parade was, according to Byers, "a most imposing procession. As the 'bold sojer boys' passed along, the sidewalks and corner stands were thronged with citizens saluting their old friends." Chivington led the march, brandishing overhead on a pole a live eagle flapping its wings.

The "sojer boys" carried their celebration from one saloon to another, cadging drinks, recounting tales of valor, and displaying bloody scalps. There seemed to be hundreds of scalps, Byers reported. "Cheyenne scalps are getting as thick here now as toads in Egypt. Everybody has got one, and is anxious to get another to send east." Curiously, no one displayed the white man's scalp Chivington claimed to have discovered in the Cheyenne camp. Over the next days and weeks, the number of white scalps found grew in the telling. Nobody in town actually saw one, but everybody believed they knew someone who claimed he or she had.

The three captured Cheyenne children—two girls and a boy—were put on public display. For several nights, between acts at the Denver Theatre, they were lined up on stage in front of a rope from which dangled a hundred Indian scalps. The *Rocky Mountain News* printed posters and hung them around town to announce the appearance of the Indian captives along with "Seignor Franco, the great stone-eater, and Monsieur Malakoff, the celebrated sword swallower."

Three days after Christmas, the men of the Bloody Third were mustered out of the service. Their one hundred days were up and everyone agreed that they had more than done their duty.

On December 30, the war pipe was lit at Smoky Hill. Some two thousand warriors had assembled there and they vowed revenge for the massacre at Sand Creek. Almost all of the Southern Cheyenne were in the camp, including the Dog Soldier band, as well as many Sioux and Northern Arapaho. Only Little Raven's Arapaho braves refused to participate in another war. For the Cheyenne, Black Kettle was in disgrace and deposed as chief, replaced by Leg-in-the-Water and Little Robe, whose father died at Sand Creek. The Indians taunted Black Kettle for placing so much faith in the white man, and for betraying his own people by leading them to believe they were safe at Sand Creek. They threatened his life and demanded to know why he had not stayed with his village and died honorably as White Antelope had.

Jim Beckwourth, the black scout, visited the camp to urge the Indians not to wage war.

Leg-in-the-Water addressed him by his Indian name. "Medicine Calf," he said, "what have you come here for? Have you fetched the white man to finish killing our families again?"

Beckwourth replied that he wanted to talk and he asked the chief to summon the ruling council. When they had assembled, Beckwourth said he had come to persuade them to make peace. There were too many whites, he told them. They were "as numerous as the leaves of the trees."

"We know it," one chief said. "But what do we want to live for? The white man has taken our country, killed all our game; was not satisfied with that, but killed our wives and children. Now no peace. We want to go and meet our families in the spirit land. We loved the whites until we found out they had lied to us, and robbed us of what we had. We have raised the battle-axe until death."

The chiefs asked Beckwourth why he had accompanied the soldiers to Sand Creek. Beckwourth answered that if he had not agreed to go, the white chief would have hanged him.

"Go and stay with your white brothers," the chiefs told the black scout. "We are going to fight till death."

The Indians planned their war with great care, laying in a stock of food for the women, children, and old people so they would have enough to eat while the warriors were away. There would be no independent raids by small parties, no spontaneous actions by groups operating on their own. The soldier societies, particularly the Dog Soldiers, took charge and they exercised a degree of control not often found among the Indian nations. They forbade all minor raiding parties. When they attacked this time, it would be as a combined, united force. The huge encampment headed northwest for the South Platte River and a tiny settlement called Julesburg, near Fort Rankin. No white man saw them pass over the plains, for they moved as stealthfully as had Chivington to Sand Creek.

On the day the war pipe was lit at Smoky Hill, the residents of Denver read a report from Washington, which Byers published in the *Rocky Mountain News*. They were outraged. The article described mounting pressure from eastern newspapers for a congressional investigation into the killing of friendly Indians at Sand Creek. The charges were allegedly based on information provided by certain unnamed "high officials" in Colorado. Byers commented on the report in an editorial.

> Indignation was loudly and unequivocally expressed, and some less considerate of the boys were very persistent in their inquiries as to who those "high officials" were, with a wild intimation that they had half a mind to go for them. This talk about "friendly Indians" and a "surrendered" village will do to tell to Marines, but to us out here it is all bosh.
> The *confessed* murderers of the Hungate family were friendly Indians, we suppose, in the eyes of those "high officials." *They* fell in the Sand Creek battle. The confessed participants in a score of other murders of peaceful settlers and inoffensive travelers must have been *friendly,* or else the "high officials" wouldn't say so.

Possibly those scalps of white men, women, and children, *one of them fresh,* not three days taken, found drying in their lodges, were taken in a *friendly,* playful manner; or possibly those Indian saddle blankets trimmed with the scalps of white women, and with braids and fringes of their hair, were kept simply as mementoes of their owners' high affection for the paleface. At any rate, these delicate and tasteful ornaments could not have been taken from the heads of the wives, sisters, or daughters of those "high officials."

The saloons echoed with angry and bitter talk. Irate citizens muttered about the Indian-lovers back east who never had to worry about losing their scalps, having their wives raped, or their neighbors murdered. And everybody speculated about the identity of the high officials, the traitors who were spreading lies about Sand Creek.

One of them was Benjamin Hall, the chief justice of Colorado Territory, and the other was the Indian agent Sam Colley. Two days before the Bloody Third Colorado Regiment returned in triumph to Denver, Colley wrote to U.S. Senator James R. Doolittle of Wisconsin, who was a member of the Joint Congressional Committee on the Conduct of the [Civil] War. Colley said in his letter that the Indians at Sand Creek had been under the protection of his Indian agency and of Fort Lyon. "All the chiefs and their families were in camp and doing all they could to protect the whites and keep the peace when Colonel Chivington marched from Denver, surprised the village, killed one half of them, all the women and children, and then returned to Denver."

Insinuations, recriminations, and investigations multiplied rapidly, fueled by a wave of revulsion that spread through the eastern states over what the newspapers now deemed to be a "massacre of friendly Indians." On January 10, 1865, the U.S. House of Representatives directed the Committee on the Conduct of the War to hold hearings on the Sand Creek affair. At the same time, General Curtis requested and received Chivington's immediate resignation in the hope of preventing an army inquiry into the matter.

Curtis was too late. The amount of publicity was overwhelming and the pressure on the army to take some action had to be relieved. On January 11, General Halleck, army chief of staff, ordered Curtis to open an investigation. "Statements from respectable sources have been received here that the conduct of Colonel Chivington's command toward the friendly Indians has been a series of outrages calculated to make them all hostile."

Curtis replied that an inquiry would proceed. In what may have been an effort to distance himself from any forthcoming retribution for the events at Sand Creek, Curtis noted to Halleck that Chivington "may have transgressed my field orders concerning Indian warfare (a copy of which is here enclosed), and otherwise acted very much against my views of propriety in his assault at Sand Creek; still it is not true, as Indian agents and Indian traders are representing, that such extra severity is increasing Indian war. On the contrary, it tends to reduce their numbers, and bring them to terms."

Curtis was wrong, and, indeed, in the same message to Halleck, he asked for additional troops to deal with the Indians. They were hardly being brought to terms. He went on to lend support to the charge that the Sand Creek Indians were living under assurances of safety.

"I fear that Colonel Chivington's assault at Sand Creek was upon Indians who had received some encouragement to camp in that vicinity under some erroneous supposition of the commanding officer at Lyon that he could make a sort of 'city of refuge' at such a point. However wrong that may have been, it should have been respected, and any violation of known arrangements of that sort should be severely rebuked."

On the same day, Curtis wrote to Governor Evans, who was still in Washington, to condemn Chivington's actions. "I abominate the extermination of women and children." Curtis admitted, however, that the "popular cry of settlers and soldiers on the frontier favors an indiscriminate slaughter, which is very difficult to restrain. I abhor the style, but so it goes from Minnesota to Texas."

Trying to cover himself on several fronts, Curtis also ordered Major Edward Wynkoop to reassume command of Fort Lyon. He directed Wynkoop to conduct a thorough investigation of "recent actions" against the Indians and to submit a full report as soon as possible.

Wynkoop had learned why General Curtis had relieved him of his command. It had not been because of the course he had adopted with regard to the Indians—attempting to initiate peace by going to Smoky Hill—but because he had left his district without orders to escort the chiefs to Governor Evans in Denver instead of to Curtis. Wynkoop admitted his mistake but justified the action by saying that he thought at the time that the governor, as Superintendent of Indian Affairs, was the proper person for the chiefs to see.

When Curtis heard Wynkoop's explanation and read the letters from the Fort Lyon officers and the settlers in the area praising his actions, he removed the censure he had placed against Wynkoop. But by then,

Chivington had marched on Sand Creek. Wynkoop, stunned by the news, believed that his honor and good name would be forever tarnished by the attack. He also may have felt partly responsible because it was on the basis of his guarantee that Black Kettle and the Cheyenne and Arapaho had camped there to await word about a peace treaty.

Wynkoop returned to Fort Lyon on January 14 to begin compiling testimony about the battle. Within twenty-four hours of his arrival at the post, he dispatched to Curtis a scathing indictment of Chivington. Affidavits from John Smith, Sam Colley, David Lauderback, Watson Clark, and four officers from Fort Lyon were unanimous in denouncing the attack. Wynkoop referred to Chivington as an "inhuman monster" and described the attack as an "unprecedented atrocity."

Reciting a catalogue of the killings and mutilations, Wynkoop stated that Chivington was "all the time inciting his troops to these diabolical outrages. Previous to the slaughter commencing he addressed his command, arousing in them, by his language, all their worst passions, urging them on to the work of committing all these atrocities. Knowing himself all the circumstances of these Indians resting on the assurances of protection from the government, given them by myself and Major Scott J. Anthony, he kept his command in entire ignorance of the same."

Wynkoop pointed out that two thirds of those killed were women and children, and that Chivington was well aware that Indians never go to war with women and children along. He also said that Chivington lied in claiming the Indians numbered one thousand and that he had killed as many as six hundred, "the sworn evidence being that there were but 500 souls in the village, two thirds of whom being women and children, and that there were but from 60 to 70 killed, the major portion of whom were women and children."

And if the deed were not repulsive enough, Wynkoop continued, the consequences made it all the more horrendous. The unified Indian tribes had already struck, loosing terror among the whites on the plains.

"Since the last horrible murder by Colonel Chivington, this country presents a scene of desolation. All communication is cut off with the States except by sending large bodies of troops, and already over 100 whites have fallen as victims to the fearful vengeance of these betrayed Indians. All this country is ruined. There can be no such thing as peace in the future but by the total annihilation of all the Indians on the plains. It will take many more troops to give security to travelers and settlers in this country."

The renewed Indian menace was so severe that Wynkoop placed Fort

Lyon on alert. He had earthen breastworks and a stone wall built around the Bent building, which was used as a commissary. The urgency was so great that Wynkoop himself, dressed in a blue flannel shirt, worked with pick and shovel alongside his soldiers. If the Indians chose to attack in force, they could exterminate his whole command. They had already demonstrated the power of their need for revenge.

On January 6, a week before Wynkoop returned to Fort Lyon, more than one thousand warriors, accompanied by George Bent, attacked the settlement at Julesburg, 190 miles northeast of Denver. It wasn't much of a town—a stagecoach station, a store, and a warehouse, guarded by the soldiers of Fort Rankin, a small garrison a half mile away. Ten warriors chased a stagecoach into the fort. As the Indians expected, the post commander rode out with forty cavalrymen to pursue the Indians. The group of ten braves led the troopers into an ambush and fourteen of them were killed. The bulk of the Indians then encircled the fort, yelling and firing their guns, but they had no intention of assaulting the military enclosure with its two howitzers.

Instead, they raided Julesburg, whose inhabitants had taken refuge in the fort. They ransacked the shop and the warehouse, uncovering a huge assortment of food and provisions, including such delicacies as canned oysters. They also found a strongbox full of cash, hastily abandoned by the army paymaster. The warriors chopped up the bundles of green paper and tossed them into the wind. George Bent stuffed as much as he could into his pockets. The soldiers and civilians at the fort watched the destruction but could do nothing to stop it. In their frustration, the troopers fired the howitzers, but the Indians were too far away to be bothered by the exploding canisters.

War parties up to five hundred strong torched every ranch and coach station as far as eighty miles west of Julesburg, killing eight people and capturing fifteen hundred cattle and two wagon trains. Denver took the news of the uprising as proof that Chivington had been correct. The only way to deal with Indians was to kill them all. The new depredations increased public hostility toward the inquiries being made by the Indian-lovers back east. On the day after Julesburg, Byers expressed these sentiments in the *Rocky Mountain News*.

Since it is a settled fact that the friendly—peaceable—surrendered—high-toned—gentle-minded—inoffensive savages are again at it down the Platte, we respectfully suggest that a small select battalion of "high officials" be permitted to go down instanter to pacify the devils, receive their arms, and negotiate a treaty by which they will bind themselves not to massacre any but the outside settlements this winter, and also to let an occasional train come through with bread and meat. We have no doubt that the gentlemen are ready, willing, and waiting to enter upon the pleasant duty of proceeding under the protection of a white flag, with olive branches in their hands, to the country residences of Messrs. Black Kettle, White Antelope & Co., where it will be their pleasure to fix things up to suit them.

A week later, the chiefs held a council and decided to leave their lands between the Platte and Arkansas rivers and join forces with the Northern Sioux and Cheyenne on the Powder River in Wyoming. First, however, they planned to lay waste to the entire South Platte valley. Black Kettle protested, arguing again for peace with the whites. Unsuccessful, he left the camp and went to join Little Raven and the Southern Arapaho south of the Arkansas River. Eighty families chose to go with him.

Along a path stretching 150 miles in the South Platte valley, no whites were safe. Everything was burned or destroyed, even the telegraph poles. On February 2, a party of one thousand warriors returned to Julesburg. As they hoped, the warehouse had been restocked. The Indians carted off all the provisions and burned the building to the ground. That night they held a victory dance in view of the soldiers at Fort Rankin, who did not dare to leave the stockade. By the light of the fallen telegraph poles set ablaze, and intoxicated by the liquor supply originally destined for Denver, the warriors celebrated for many hours.

The Fort Rankin soldiers watched warily. "About one o'clock the orgy seemed to reach its height," recalled Captain Eugene Ware of the Seventh Iowa Cavalry. "The yells were the most bloodcurdling and frantic I ever heard, and although we were a long distance off, perhaps a half mile, we could hear them all upon the midnight air quite plainly. And we discussed among ourselves whether or not the bottled liquors would not get them finally worked up to a point that would lead them to besiege us. Suddenly the fire began to grow brighter, and greater, and the Indians circling around it seemed to form a larger ring."

The fire spread to the prairie grass, but there was no wind and so it burned slowly. It consumed an acre, then three or four, until it seemed to light up the whole territory. The shouting, cavorting forms of the

Indians danced around the perimeter of the flames. The circle widened, the Indians appeared to be more numerous, and by dawn the dense smoke completely surrounded the fort. When it cleared, the Indians were gone.

"The victories and plunder eased the stinging memory of Sand Creek. Fresh meat from the whites' cattle herds fed the [Indian] camps; the people ate flour, corn meal, hams, bacon, dried fruit, and molasses from Julesburg; and the warriors dressed themselves and their families from the clothing and materials taken from the freighting station and the captured trains." Many an unsuspecting farmer, stagecoach passenger, freight wagoner, and cavalryman paid a terrible price that winter for Chivington's fleeting moment of glory.

The residents of Denver also paid a price. The winter weather of 1864–1865 was severe, and the Indian uprising was much worse than the troubles of the previous spring and summer. Major Anthony wrote that the roads and settlements north of Fort Lyon were in great peril. Denver was isolated. For more than a month, not one stagecoach, freight wagon, or telegraph message reached the city from the east. To the west, the telegraph line to Salt Lake City had been uprooted for a distance of ten miles.

Ranches and coach stations lay in smoking ruins, some fifty whites were killed and others captured, six hundred tons of government hay burned, and uncounted quantities of food and supplies stolen. The city was threatened with famine as food supplies dwindled. Flour now cost twenty-seven dollars per hundred pounds, and bacon and sugar soared to an astounding fifty cents a pound. Samuel H. Elbert, the acting governor while Evans was in Washington, sent an urgent appeal to the federal government. "We must have 5,000 troops to clean out these savages or the people of this territory will be compelled to leave it. Everything is already at starvation prices. The general government must help us or give up the territory to the Indians."

Not only Colorado was affected by the latest Indian uprising. The burning and looting and violence spread from the Missouri River in Kansas to Salt Lake City in Utah. "It seemed as if an army of fiends had been turned loose to work their utmost cruelty upon mankind," one Colorado resident wrote. In Kansas, the legislature passed a resolution imploring the Secretary of War to provide sufficient troops to protect the Kansas frontier and to keep open the Overland and Santa Fe trails.

In Denver, Colonel Thomas Moonlight, the commandant of the Military District appointed to replace Chivington, found himself in a precarious position. He had only 200 troops available to patrol the Overland Trail and 250 for the Arkansas River valley, an area encompassing several thousand square miles. He fired off a series of entreaties to his superior officer, Major General Granville Dodge, who had replaced General Curtis at Fort Leavenworth. Moonlight noted: "we are in every respect the superior of the Indians, and can afford to wage a war of their own choosing, even to extermination."

Along with such bravado, however, he offered warnings of disaster if massive reinforcements were not received immediately. "As matters now stand in this district, having in a manner no troops, there is great danger of being overrun by the Indians." To Acting Governor Elbert, Moonlight wrote, "the blood of the innocent and unoffending martyrs cries aloud for vengeance, and starvation stares in the face of the living."

Moonlight placed the blame for the reign of terror on his predecessor, Colonel Chivington, and offered his opinion on what would soon be the subject of official inquiry. The Third Regiment had been mustered out, he told General Dodge, "thus denuding the district of troops, and at a time, too, when the Indians had suffered an overwhelming defeat, or been subjected to a wholesale massacre at the hands of Colonel Chivington, then commanding district; (I give you these distinctions, as the people here are divided on the question); at a time when the Indians were burning for revenge on the white men, women, and children, in retaliation for the killed by Colonel Chivington, commanding, for it is useless to deny this fact; at a time when the severity of the winter prevented the making of a campaign with any hope of success on our side, even had the troops been at my command. In view of these facts, and knowing, as he did, that the territory would be exposed to Indian assaults and depredations, while denuded of troops, I question much the policy and propriety of the Sand Creek battle fought by Colonel Chivington."

Despite the requests from Moonlight and Elbert, no troops could be spared from the war in the east. They attempted to raise a new regiment of hundred dazers to punish the savages, but this time there were no takers. "The denunciations heaped upon Sand Creek, and the disgrace pronounced upon that enterprise, prevented voluntary response. The companies were not furnished, nor did there appear to be any disposition among the people to meet this new phase of affairs."

Even the threats of starvation, rising prices, and reports of Indians on the outskirts of the city—all gloomy reminders of the previous year's depredations—failed to stimulate enlistments. In desperation, Colonel Moonlight proclaimed martial law in Denver on February 8, and closed down every business until 360 men were drafted into the service. The men of the Colorado Territory were not eager to go to war again.

12

A Foul and Dastardly Massacre

QUESTION: You say these Indians were of a remarkably friendly disposition?

ANSWER: Yes, sir.

QUESTION: And inoffensive toward our people?

ANSWER: There were never two bands of Indians more friendly to the whites than Black Kettle's band and White Antelope's band, and One-Eye, who was also killed in the massacre.

It was March 13, 1865, the first day of the congressional hearings held in Washington, D.C., by the Committee on the Conduct of the War. The witness, Colonel Jesse Leavenworth, was commanding officer of the Second Colorado Regiment in western Kansas. He had not been present at Sand Creek, but he had cultivated a long-term relationship with the Cheyenne and had predicted that Chivington's policies would lead to disaster. He testified that he had written to the Commissioner of Indian Affairs the year before stating that if "Colonel Chivington was not stopped in his course of sending Lieutenant Eayre after these Indians we should get into a general war on the frontier." He reported to the committee that a regular army officer had told him the same thing, namely, "If Colonel Chivington was not stopped in the course of hunting down these Indians it would get us into a war that would cost us millions of dollars."

John Smith was the next witness. He graphically described the battle scene, the killing and mutilating, and something of the background of the Indians camped at Sand Creek, noting the assurances of safety they had received from Major Wynkoop and Major Anthony. Smith told the committee that the village of approximately five hundred people included no more than seventy armed warriors at the time of the attack. The number of dead amounted to no more than seventy, so far as he could determine, and not the five hundred Chivington claimed.

Toward the end of his lengthy testimony, Smith was asked about the reason for the Sand Creek attack.

"I do not know any exact reason," he said. "I have heard a great many reasons given. I have heard that the whole Indian war had been brought on for selfish purposes. Colonel Chivington was running for Congress in Colorado and I understand he had this Indian war in view to retain himself and his troops in that country, and to carry out his electioneering purposes."

The third witness, and the only one friendly to Chivington, was Captain S. M. Robbins, one of the colonel's staff officers. He had been in Denver at the time of the raid. At the conclusion of his uninformative testimony, he offered another possible reason for Chivington's actions, one that was considerably less damaging.

"For the information of the committee," Robbins said, "I should like to say a friendly word under the circumstances, in the Chivington interest. For a year and a half past there has been a state of war existing between the Indians and the whites, as far as the opinion of the Indians was concerned; whether by the authority of the head chiefs or not we cannot tell. At all events, the interruption of communication on the Arkansas route and on the Platte route raised the price of everything consumed by the people out here. And the people emphatically demanded that something should be done. The point I wish to make is, that perhaps Colonel Chivington might have been forced into this by the sentiment of the people."

Could the sentiment of the people lead a man to attack Indians who were known to be friendly and who had tried to avert hostilities? "I should say it would," Robbins replied. "They wanted some Indians killed; whether friendly or not they did not stop long to inquire."

D. D. Colley, a trader and son of Indian agent Sam Colley, was called to the stand next. Both Colleys were criticized for illegal dealings with the Indians, including trading them their own annuities for goods. Both father and son made a great deal of money as a result of the elder

Colley's position as Indian agent, but formal charges against them were never filed.

Young Colley had nothing to say on Chivington's behalf. Because he, too, had not been at Sand Creek, he had little to offer beyond his opinion. "I have thought for more than a year," he said, "that [Chivington] was determined to have a war with these Indians. That has been the general belief of men in our part of the country. I was acquainted with all the chiefs who were there, and I know they had all tried hard to keep peace. All the chiefs who were killed by Colonel Chivington have labored as hard as men could to keep peace between the whites and Indians."

Thus ended the first day of the hearings.

The second day opened with the testimony of an important figure involved in the fighting, Major Scott Anthony. He was questioned at length about his participation, from the time he assumed command of Fort Lyon to the period immediately following the battle. Some of his answers were as damaging to himself as to Chivington. He admitted that he had, in effect, continued Major Wynkoop's policy by telling the Indians they could stay at Sand Creek until instructions were received from General Curtis. He had agreed to inform the Indians as soon as such orders came from department headquarters.

Anthony added what he deemed to be a major qualification. "I did not state to them that I would give them notice in case we intended to attack them. They went away with that understanding, that in case I received instructions from department headquarters I was to let them know it. But before I did receive any such instructions Colonel Chivington arrived there, and this affair on Sand Creek took place."

The committee noted that Anthony had "made haste" to accompany Chivington, even though the colonel had no authority over him. They considered his testimony to be sufficient evidence of how "unprovoked and unwarranted was this massacre."

Anthony was sharply critical of Chivington for letting so many Indians get away. The committee expressed its surprise to him that a command of seven hundred mounted troopers had allowed 500 Indians to escape on foot. When they asked why the fleeing Indians had not been pursued, Anthony said, "I do not know; that was the fault I found with Colonel Chivington at the time." (Statements taken from those present at the battle do not support Anthony's suggestion that he protested to Chivington about the failure to pursue the Indians. If Anthony had found fault with Chivington, he kept it to himself until his appearance before the committee.)

Anthony testified that he voiced his objections to the attack to Chivington, but no one else present recorded or remembered his doing so. Asked if he felt the attack ought not to have been made, Anthony answered, "I did. I made a great many harsh remarks in regard to it." He explained, however, that his objections were based on concern for the security of the white community, not because the Indians had been led to believe that Sand Creek was a place of refuge. He "did not so much object to the killing of Indians, as a matter of principle, merely as a matter of policy. I considered it a very bad policy, as it would open up the war in that whole country again."

When asked if he thought the attack on the Indians was impolitic, he said, "I do, very much so. I think it was the occasion of what has occurred on the Platte since that time. I stated [to Chivington] that the Indians were encamped at this point; that I had a force with me sufficiently strong to go out and fight them; but I did not think it policy to do so, for I was not strong enough to fight the main band [at Smoky Hill]. If I fought this band, the main band would immediately strike the settlements. But so soon as the party would be strong enough to fight the main band, I should be in favor of making the war general against the Indians. I did not believe we could fight one band without fighting them all."

Anthony admitted that he saw the soldiers committing many acts of mutilation but he noted that these were no worse than what Indians had done to whites. "The only way to fight Indians," he said, "is to fight them as they fight us; if they scalp and mutilate the bodies we must do the same. It is the general impression of the people of that country that the only way to fight them is to fight as they fight; kill the women and children." Then he added a curious afterthought: "At the same time, of course, we consider it a barbarous practice."

He disputed Chivington's claim that a white person's scalp, freshly taken, had been found at Sand Creek, as Chivington had noted in his initial report to General Curtis. "I did not hear anything about that," Anthony said, "until after Colonel Chivington had reached Denver. I was with him for 10 days after the fight, and never heard a word about a white scalp being found in the camp until afterward."

Sam Colley, the Indian agent, was the day's last witness. No, he had not been at Sand Creek, but he told the committee that he had no reason to believe that Black Kettle or Left Hand were hostile toward whites. Colley testified that Left Hand had told him: "My boys were mad, and I could not control them. But as for me, I will not fight the whites, and you cannot make me do it. You may imprison me or kill me; but I will not fight the whites."

At the third and last day of the hearings, the lead witness was Governor Evans, who spoke at length but said little. The committee members frequently prodded him with questions to try to extract information. He was evasive about everything, even something so simple as the distance between Denver and Fort Lyon. He refused to offer a definitive statement on any topic. Slipping and sliding, Evans tried to convey the impression that he knew nothing about anything even remotely connected with Indians. He pretended difficulty in recalling the names of the chiefs with whom he had spoken at Camp Weld.

As to the attack at Sand Creek, he was ignorant of the details. He had been in Washington at the time. He admitted knowledge of a planned expedition to be carried out against some Indians somewhere at some time, but he did not know where the troops were going.

After he recounted all the depredations committed by Indians during the previous spring and summer, Evans was asked whether he thought those actions afforded "any justification for the attack made by Colonel Chivington on these friendly Indians, under the circumstances under which it was made?"

"As a matter of course," Evans said, "no one could justify an attack on Indians while under protection of the flag. If those Indians were there under protection of the flag, it would be a question that would be scarcely worth asking because nobody could say anything in favor of the attack. I have heard, however—that is only a report—that there was a statement on the part of Colonel Chivington and his friends that these Indians had assumed a hostile attitude before he attacked them. I do not know whether this is so or not. I have said all I have to do with them. I suppose they were being treated as prisoners-of-war in some way or other."

The question was repeated. "But from all the circumstances which you know, all the facts in relation to that matter, do you deem that Colonel Chivington had any justification for the attack?"

Evans still refused to commit himself. "So far as giving an opinion is concerned, I would say this. That the reports that have been made here, a great many have come through persons whom I know to be personal enemies of Colonel Chivington for a long time. And I would rather not give an opinion on the subject until I have heard the other side of the question."

"I did not ask for an opinion," the committee counsel said. "Do you know of any circumstances which would justify the attack?"

The governor's reply dissolved into a rambling, waffling account of previous Indian attacks. The questioners gave up and dismissed Governor Evans as a witness. He hoped that his testimony would protect him from any personal culpability for the attack, but in the end, the events at Sand Creek aborted his political career for a time, as effectively as if he had lifted a scalp or two himself.

The final witness to appear before the committee was A. C. Hunt, the United States marshal for the District of Colorado and a longtime political foe of Chivington's. He had not been present at Sand Creek, and his remarks were based solely on what he had been told by some of the men of the Bloody Third after they returned to Denver. They had described their mutilations of the Indians. "They made no secret of telling what had been done," Hunt said, "but made no boast of it all. They said they were heartily ashamed of it."

Hunt also testified that after the massacre, Chivington had been "wroth" with anyone who maintained that Black Kettle and White Antelope had been friendly to the whites or who disputed his policy toward the Indians.

"What was his policy?"

"To exterminate the Indians."

"To kill them all?"

"Yes, sir, I should judge so; and that seemed to be quite a popular notion, too. That feeling prevails in all new countries where the Indians have committed any depredations. And most especially will people fly off the handle in that way when you exhibit the corpse of someone who has been murdered by the Indians. When they come to their sober senses they reflect that the Indians have feelings as well as we have, and are entitled to certain rights; which, by the way, they never get."

When asked if he knew why Chivington had planned the attack, Hunt said, "I was entirely satisfied that his motive was not a good and virtuous one. We regarded those Indians on the reservation as safe, and ought not to be attacked."

Pressed further about Chivington's motives, he added, "I think it was hope of promotion. He had read of Kit Carson, General Harney, and others who had become famous for their Indian fighting."

The key figure in the investigation, Colonel John M. Chivington, did not appear before the committee. It is not known whether he had not been invited—an omission that would have been most strange—or whether he refused to come. In Denver, he gave his version of events in a lengthy affidavit, responding to questions submitted in writing by the congressional committee. Some of his statements differed from his earlier reports. He placed the number of Indians in the Sand Creek village at between 1,100 and 1,200, of whom 700 were warriors. Previously, he had estimated the number at between 900 and 1,000 warriors. He changed the number of Indians killed, from 400–500 to 500–600.

Asked about the murders of women and children, Chivington swore there had been few, "no more than would certainly fall in an attack upon a camp in which they were. I myself passed over some portion of the field after the fight, and I saw but one woman who had been killed, and one who had hanged herself; I saw no dead children. From all I could learn, I arrived at the conclusion that but few women and children had been slain."

And his reason for making the attack? The colonel said that he believed the Indians at Sand Creek were hostile to whites. He catalogued the Indian atrocities of the previous months and stated that he found nineteen white scalps in the village, proof that they had been killing whites.

Chivington was asked whether he had any reason to believe that Black Kettle and his band were at peace at the time of the attack. No, he replied, because he had been told by Major Anthony that they were hostile, and that Anthony said he would have attacked them himself if he'd had enough men. "Indians had been killing and burning for months," Chivington added. "I had every reason to believe that these Indians were either directly or indirectly concerned in the outrages which had been committed upon the whites. I had no means of ascertaining what were the names of the Indians who had committed these outrages other than the declarations of the Indians themselves; and the character of Indians in the western country for truth and veracity, like their respect for the chastity of women who may become prisoners in their hands, is not of that order which is calculated to inspire confidence in what they may say."

In summary, then, it was, to Chivington, the Indian raids of the previous months, Major Anthony's statement about the Cheyennes' hostility, plus the "positive orders from Major General Curtis, commanding the department, to punish these Indians [that] decided my course, and resulted in the battle of Sand Creek, which has created such a sensation in Congress through the lying reports of interested and malicious parties."

Chivington demanded "as an act of justice to myself and the brave men whom I have had the honor to command in one of the hardest campaigns ever made in this country, whether against white men or red, that we be allowed that right guaranteed to every American citizen, of introducing evidence in our behalf to sustain us in what we believe to have been an act of duty to ourselves and to civilization. We simply ask to introduce as witnesses men that were present during the campaign and know all the facts."

Chivington's request was granted in two subsequent hearings. Men who participated in the Sand Creek campaign did testify, but that did not change history's final judgment.

Chivington had reason to feel aggrieved at the initial hearings in Washington. Of the eight witnesses who testified in person, only two had been with him at Sand Creek—Major Anthony and John Smith. The others provided hearsay evidence and their personal speculations about Chivington's motives, testimony susceptible to bias because of their own feelings about him. It is difficult to ascertain why so many people who were not directly involved in the event were asked to make the expensive and difficult trip to Washington, whereas hundreds of eyewitnesses—the soldiers who took part in the battle—were not invited to the committee hearings.

Also, the congressmen on the committee did not appear to take their responsibilities seriously. On the first day of the hearings, only three of the nine members were present. By the third and final day, only one was in attendance. The chairman, the senator from Ohio, Benjamin "Honest Ben" Wade, later admitted that he had not gone to any of the hearings. The committee counsels did all the work, questioning the witnesses and writing the final report.

They judged the attack at Sand Creek to be an atrocity of the highest order, perpetrated against a band of Indians who were friendly to whites and who had been led to believe that they would be treated as such. In stark and melodramatic terms, the report described the carnage.

> And then the scene of murder and barbarity began—men, women,
> and children were indiscriminately slaughtered. In a few minutes all the

Indians were flying over the plain in terror and confusion. A few who endeavored to hide themselves under the bank of the creek were surrounded and shot down in cold blood, offering but feeble resistance. From the suckling babe to the old warrior, all who were overtaken were deliberately murdered. Not content with killing women and children, who were incapable of offering any resistance, the soldiers indulged in acts of barbarity of the most revolting character; such, it is to be hoped, as never before disgraced the acts of men claiming to be civilized. No attempt was made by the officers to restrain the savage cruelty of the men under their command, but they stood by and witnessed these acts without one word of reproof, if they did not incite their commission. For more than two hours the work of murder and barbarity was continued, until more than 100 dead bodies, three fourths of them women and children, lay on the plain as evidence of the fiendish malignity and cruelty of the officers who had so sedulously and carefully plotted the massacre, and of the soldiers who had so faithfully acted out the spirit of their officers.

It is difficult to believe that beings in the form of men, and disgracing the uniform of United States soldiers and officers, could commit or countenance the commission of such acts of cruelty and barbarity.

Major Anthony was chastised for his role, but greater blame was attached to Governor Evans. The report stated that Evans's testimony was "characterized by such prevarication and shuffling as has been shown by no witness they have examined during the four years they have been engaged in their investigations [on the conduct of the war]; and for the evident purpose of avoiding the admission that he was fully aware that the Indians massacred so brutally at Sand Creek, were then, and had been, actuated by the most friendly feelings toward the whites, and had done all in their power to restrain those less friendly disposed."

A little more than a month after the committee report was released, Governor Evans received a blunt message from Secretary of State William H. Seward.

Sir: I am directed by the President to inform you that your resignation of the office of Governor of Colorado Territory would be acceptable. Circumstances connected with the public interest make it desirable that the resignation should reach here without delay.

Two weeks later, Evans sent an equally brief note to President Andrew Johnson, tendering his resignation. His dream of national political power had come to an end.

The committee's supreme wrath and scorn were reserved for Chivington.

> As to Colonel Chivington, your committee can hardly find fitting terms to describe his conduct. Wearing the uniform of the United States, which should be the emblem of justice and humanity; holding the important position of commander of a military district, and therefore having the honor of the government to that extent in his keeping, he deliberately planned and executed a foul and dastardly massacre which would have disgraced the veriest savage among those who were the victims of his cruelty. Having full knowledge of their friendly character, having himself been instrumental to some extent in placing them in their position of fancied security, he took advantage of their inapprehension and defenseless condition to gratify the worst passions that ever cursed the heart of man. [He] surprised and murdered, in cold blood, the unsuspecting men, women, and children on Sand Creek, who had every reason to believe they were under the protection of the United States authorities, and then returned to Denver and boasted of the brave deeds he and the men under his command had performed.

Chivington's dreams of glory were also finished.

Two other investigations into Sand Creek were also under way.* On March 7, 1865, a joint special committee of the U.S. Senate and the U.S. House of Representatives began collecting testimony from a number of people in several locations. From Washington, D.C., to forts Riley, Larned, and Lyon, from Santa Fe to Denver, the committee questioned eyewitnesses as well as others, such as Kit Carson, who were well informed about relations between Indians and whites in the west. This committee concluded that Chivington's men had perpetrated a massacre of Indians at Sand Creek who believed they were under the protection of the American flag.

The third hearing, presided over by a three-man military commission, opened in Denver on February 9, 1865, and met for seventy-six

---

* All three investigations inquired into the plunder allegedly taken from the Indian village at Sand Creek. Evidence indicated that several hundred horses, ponies, mules, and buffalo robes—of great value in the aggregate—had been taken by the soldiers as spoils of war. This aspect of the affair is not discussed here because, relative to the atrocities, it seems of lesser importance.

days. This was Chivington's forum. It provided an arena in which he could confront his opponents, and it led to a tragedy on the streets of Denver. The atmosphere in the city was tense throughout the lengthy proceedings and tempers were short not only in the hearing room but also among the public. Although the hearings were conducted in secret, word leaked out, and much of each day's testimony was known all over town by nightfall. In addition, Chivington wrote his own synopsis of the day's proceedings, which Byers obligingly published in the *Rocky Mountain News.*

The military inquiry was neither a trial nor a court-martial. Chivington had resigned from the service and was beyond the reach of the military judicial system. The purpose of the investigation was to determine whether he had behaved in accordance with the recognized rules of civilized warfare, whether the Indians had been under government protection at the time of the attack, and whether Chivington had taken steps to prevent "unnatural outrages" by his men during and following the attack. The officers on the panel—chosen by Colonel Moonlight, Chivington's successor—were Lieutenant Colonel Samuel F. Tappan, Captain Edward A. Jacobs, and Captain George H. Stilwell. All were in the Colorado First. None had been at Sand Creek.

Chivington went on the offensive from the first, as soon as the formal charge was read to the panel. He asked that the hearings be made public and that reporters be admitted. He objected on the grounds of prejudice to Colonel Tappan's appointment as chairman of the commission. Tappan had been second in command of the Colorado troops at Glorietta Pass and had been in line to replace Colonel Slough when he resigned. Tappan had stepped aside, however, when the men of the regiment demanded that Chivington be their new commander. Because of that, Chivington said, Tappan had developed great animosity toward him.

Chivington further charged that Tappan had "repeatedly expressed himself very much prejudiced against the killing of the Indians near Fort Lyon and has said that it was a disgrace to every officer connected with it." Therefore, Chivington added, Tappan could not "divest himself of his prejudices sufficiently to render an impartial verdict."

Tappan admitted to having described the attack at Sand Creek as the "greatest military blunder of the age, and fatal in its consequences," but he ruled that any personal hostility he held toward Chivington would not influence the performance of his duty. He would continue as chairman of the panel. He also ruled that the hearings would remain closed to the public and to reporters—a blow to Chivington, who expected to pack the hearing room with vocal supporters.

Pro-Chivington feelings in Denver were intense as the hearings got under way. It was considered unwise for anyone to speak against the fighting parson, particularly to veterans of the Bloody Third. Angry crowds milled about the saloons and along the sidewalks as the first witness, Captain Silas Soule, took the stand.

Captain Soule, who had protested against undertaking the attack, and who ordered his men to refrain from taking part in it, was questioned by the commission and rigorously cross-examined by Chivington for a total of seven days. It was Soule's fate to turn much public sentiment against Chivington, but not by his words in the hearing room.

Stocky, twenty-six years old, and of average height, with dark hair, a mustache, and a close-cropped beard, Soule was a jovial fellow and much liked by the men of his company of the First Colorado Regiment. In the 1850s, he and his father had helped establish the first station on the underground railroad in Kansas, used by slaves escaping from the plantations of the south. Because of his active abolitionist stance, he was asked to join the rescue attempt of John Brown from his jail cell at Harpers Ferry, where he was condemned to hang. Brown and seventeen of his followers had seized the federal arsenal at Harpers Ferry as the first step in a planned revolt of the slaves. He was captured by a force of U.S. Marines led by an army officer, Colonel Robert E. Lee.

Adopting a thick Irish brogue he had picked up from working with Irish laborers as a boy, Soule appeared drunk on the streets of Charles Town and was promptly arrested, just as he had planned. Incarcerated in the Harpers Ferry jail, he soon became a favorite of the jailer and his family because of his quick Irish wit, carefree manner, and endless supply of funny songs and stories. He was allowed free run of the facilities and spoke to John Brown in his cell to tell him of the escape plan. The fanatical Brown declined his help, however, saying that he could do more to bring about the abolition of slavery by dying than by living.

After Soule's release, he went to Philadelphia to continue his work with the abolitionists, including the poet Walt Whitman. When Soule returned to Kansas, the Colorado gold rush had begun, and off he went to Pikes Peak. He failed to strike it rich, and when the Civil War began, he enlisted as a private in Kit Carson's scouts in New Mexico, working his way up through the ranks and transferring to the First Colorado as a captain. He fought valiantly at Glorietta Pass and was one of the regiment's most popular officers.

Never one to flinch in the face of danger, Soule volunteered to testify against Chivington, despite warnings from his friends that his life would be in jeopardy. Threats were made against him and several shots were fired at him, but that only increased his determination to speak against what he considered to be a moral outrage.

The commission began its intensive examination of Captain Soule with Major Wynkoop's expedition to Smoky Hill, proceeding to the Camp Weld council, and finally to the battle itself. The captain spoke of his protestations to Major Anthony that the Sand Creek Indians were under the flag of protection, and also about the mutilations he saw committed. Neither Chivington nor Anthony had made any effort to prevent them. Soule also described the absence of any semblance of military organization, once the attack was under way, and how the troops fired on one another as a result.

In Chivington's cross-questioning, he tried, without success, to depict Wynkoop's expedition as a foolhardy venture in which the major had exposed his men to unnecessary risk by his own ineptitude and by the drunkenness of his officers. Soule remained calm and articulate throughout the long and grueling session. His testimony, and that of subsequent witnesses, was highly damaging to Chivington, despite the colonel's efforts to discredit it.

The hearings were labored and tedious. Over the next forty-eight days, sixteen additional witnesses were called, fifteen of whom had been at Sand Creek. They included Major Wynkoop; lieutenants Cannon, Minton, and Cossitt; Jim Beckwourth; John Prowers (Chief One-Eye's son-in-law); and enlisted men including David Lauderback. All of the officers and men were from the First Colorado, and all testified to seeing atrocities and mutilations committed, acts Chivington made no attempt to stop. The officers spoke of trying to prevent the attack by objecting to Chivington that Black Kettle and his band were encamped under government protection.

Chivington badgered the witnesses, cast doubt on their probity, and suggested other causes for the mutilations. He depicted Wynkoop as foolish for going to Smoky Hill and recklessly endangering his command, and he charged that Wynkoop had given whiskey to the Indians. None of the allegations held up. Chivington tried, again without success, to suggest that the witnesses were hostile to him and had been told what to say by Colonel Tappan.

He then implied that Captain Soule was responsible for mutilating the Indian bodies when he returned to the site a few days after the battle.

"On your second visit to Sand Creek, with Captain Soule," Chivington asked Naman Snyder, one of Soule's men, "did not Captain Soule send a number of his men ahead of his command to Sand Creek, with instructions to mutilate the dead?"

"No," Snyder said.

With another enlisted man of the First Colorado Regiment, James Adams, Chivington suggested that dogs had done it.

"Do we understand that you state positively that all the Indians you saw were scalped, and that the Indians you saw mutilated were really scalped? Might they not have been so mutilated by dogs, wolves, or other animals?"

"I don't hardly think that dogs or wolves would chew the scalp off and leave the body alone," Adams said.

A few minutes later, Chivington remarked to Adams that any mutilations were probably the result of souvenir hunters.

"Did not the men who were cutting the fingers off the dead Indians for rings tell you that they were simply obtaining trophies, to preserve as reminiscences, to bequeath to their children, of the glorious field of Sand Creek?"

"No, sir," Adams said.

And so it went, day after day, for page after page of devastating testimony, until an event outside the hearing room hurt Chivington more than anything that had been said so far.

On the night of April 23, in Denver, a drunken brawl erupted at the corner of Lawrence and G streets. Several shots were fired. A few blocks away, Captain Soule and his bride of less than a month were walking home from the theater. On hearing the gunfire, Soule ran toward the sound; maintaining public order was part of his job as provost marshal. When he reached the corner, Charles Squiers, a soldier in the Second Colorado, was waiting for him, gun in hand. Soule drew his own weapon and both men fired. Squiers was hit in the right arm but his bullet entered Soule's cheek and lodged in the brain, killing him instantly. Squiers vanished into the darkness.

The next morning in the hearing room, Colonel Tappan, tugging nervously on his drooping mustache, stared at Chivington and read a brief statement in cold, clipped tones. He described Soule's death not as a shooting, or even as a murder, but as an assassination, with all the premeditation, malice, and revenge the ugly word suggests.

The clerk recorded the proceedings:

> Captain Silas S. Soule, veteran battalion First Colorado cavalry, having—while in the performance of his duty as provost marshal—been assassinated in the streets of this city, the commission, in respect to the memory of the deceased, adjourned until 9 A.M. tomorrow morning, April 25, 1865.

All of Denver was shocked. A few people said that Soule had it coming to him, but the majority—including staunch Chivington supporters—were sobered to the point of reconsidering their judgment about the fighting parson. Some suggested that Chivington had arranged the murder. No proof of this was ever uncovered, but subsequent events added to the suspicion.

Crowds flocked to the funeral service, though few of the mourners were close friends. Many came to show where their sympathies lay. The *Rocky Mountain News* reported that the funeral was "attended by an unusually large and respectable procession, with his mother and his young widowed bride, who has thus been draped in weeds before the orange blossoms scarce had time to wither."

The service was conducted by the Reverend H. H. Hitchins, who spoke of Captain Soule as a man who had no fear of danger or of death. "Did he not in the darkness of the night, almost at the midnight hour, go out to discharge his duty? Did he not go when he had every reason to believe that the alarm which called him out was only to decoy him into danger? Did he not go when he knew positively that his life was threatened, and that weeks ago five shots had been sent at him with deadly intent? Did he not go, feeling so certain that his doom was sealed, that he took farewell of his young wife, telling her what she must do in case he returned no more alive?

"Yes; and there is the spirit of the soldier and the good soldier, too; he did his duty in the midst of danger, did his duty in the face of death, and fell by the assassin's hand."

There was one conspicuous absence among Denver's leading citizenry. In defiance of military custom, Christian charity, and common decency, Colonel Chivington did not attend, and that cost him more support than all the damaging testimony taken together. It would have been a noble gesture, a savvy exercise in public relations, had he paid his respects to the deceased. Further, it was expected that a man of Chivington's standing in the community and his stature as a preacher would publicly condemn the crime and offer sympathy and comfort to the dead man's family. But Chivington said nothing.

Soule had been widely regarded as a man of the highest character and integrity. It was a reprehensible as well as stupid move on Chivington's part to attempt to blacken his reputation, particularly on the day after he was laid to rest.

The military commission resumed its hearings and Chivington introduced an affidavit, taken two and a half weeks earlier from Lipman Meyer, a freighter from Leavenworth, Kansas. Meyer's statement had no bearing on Sand Creek. It was intended for the sole purpose of defaming Captain Soule. Meyer called Soule a coward, a drunkard, and a thief. He described meeting Soule about a week after the Sand Creek battle, when the captain was leading a detachment in search of Indians. They spotted smoke in the distance, but, Meyer said, Soule was too afraid—and too drunk—to investigate. Meyer's testimony continued in this vein and, as a final insult, he stated that either Soule or Lieutenant Cannon (who had also testified against Chivington) had stolen two pairs of blankets from him.

Colonel Tappan was irate. He immediately filed a written protest objecting to the admission of Meyer's testimony into evidence. Tappan stated that he had known Soule for several years and had never been given any reason to suspect him of drunkenness, theft, cowardice, or neglect of duty. He introduced a statement taken from Captain George F. Price, an army district inspector in Denver, saying that the month before, Soule had told Price that he "fully expected to be killed on account of that testimony; that he was also fully satisfied, after they had killed him, his character would be assailed, and an attempt made to destroy his testimony." The three-man military panel rejected Meyer's testimony.

Undaunted by this failure to blacken Soule's name and thus reduce the effect of his testimony, Chivington introduced sixteen witnesses on his behalf to vindicate his conduct at Sand Creek. Most of them were officers of the Third, his own regiment. Some of them testified that there had been no American flag or white flag flying over the Indian village at Sand Creek before the attack. Also, they said, the Indians had opened fire first. Earlier witnesses had agreed that they had seen both flags and that the soldiers had fired the first shots.

Other witnesses Chivington called attempted to establish that Indian agent Sam Colley and interpreter John Smith were engaged in a conspiracy against the colonel to avenge the financial losses they suffered at Sand

Creek. Major Presley Talbot of the Third stated in an affidavit that while at Fort Lyon recovering from a wound, he had discussed the battle with Colley and Smith. Both men had complained, Talbot said, that they had experienced great financial hardship and had filed a claim against the government for six thousand dollars to compensate them for 105 buffalo robes, two ponies, and a wagonload of goods lost at Sand Creek. Smith also reportedly told Talbot that before they were finished, they hoped to collect $25,000 from the government. Further, "they would do anything to damn Colonel John M. Chivington."

Additional defense witnesses charged that Fort Lyon officers loyal to Major Wynkoop were out to get Chivington. Captain T. G. Cree of the Third Colorado reported a conversation with Lieutenant Joseph Cramer, who had been a witness against Chivington. Cramer allegedly said that all Chivington was "working for was a brigadier general's commission, and that he did not care how many lives he lost in getting it." According to Captain Cree, Cramer also vowed that he and other Fort Lyon officers would do their best to bring Chivington down. Cramer said that he "thought they could make a massacre out of the Sand Creek affair and crush him."

A soldier in the First Colorado Regiment testified that Major Wynkoop had been drinking heavily when he took his men to Smoky Hill, thus endangering their lives. "There was some talk that there was more whiskey aboard than necessary. Some said that they had full confidence in Major Wynkoop when sober, but that they did not like to trust themselves with him among the Indians when he had been drinking."

And another witness stated that the Sand Creek Indians had committed numerous depredations against whites, as evidenced by the scalps found in the camp. Sergeant Stephen Decatur of the Third reported seeing many white scalps as well as women's clothing, cosmetics, and a powder puff. He counted 450 dead warriors on the field of battle, a figure more than twice that reported by anyone else, except Chivington.

The regimental surgeon of the Third Colorado, Caleb Burdsal, testified that he was shown scalps which he judged, after a "casual look," to be those of white persons. Except for some scalping, however, he did not see any mutilations on the bodies of the Indians.

The most telling argument against the existence of white scalps was Chivington's own initial report after the battle in which he mentioned finding only one scalp. And according to Major Anthony's testimony, in the ten days following the battle, Chivington did not once talk to him about finding any white scalps.

Finally, some of Chivington's witnesses swore that the Indians had prepared extensive fortifications—deep pits and well-designed trenches—before the battle occurred. That was taken as proof of their hostile intentions toward whites. None of the other witnesses, however, mentioned such trenches, testifying instead about the crude shallow holes the Indians hastily scooped out of the earth with their hands while under fire from Chivington's troops.

The last witness was called on May 24, 1865. Six days later the committee adjourned. In accordance with their charter, they were acting only in a fact-finding capacity. They issued no conclusions, no judgments of guilt or innocence. Their 228-page record of testimony was not printed for two years, and then it was filed in government archives, where it can be found today. With the dissolution of the panel, nearly five months of investigations came to an end, leaving only a paper trail of murder, deceit, and treachery, and the name of an obscure creek in Colorado to become a monument, in Cheyenne memories, to perfidy.

13

The Deliberate Judgment
of History

S and Creek exacted one more death in Denver. Six weeks after the
military hearings ended, Charles Squiers, the man who had shot
Captain Soule, was spotted in New Mexico. Lieutenant James Cannon—
the officer accused by Lipman Meyer of stealing blankets and who testified against Chivington—was sent to escort Squiers back to Denver.
Cannon and his prisoner arrived in town on July 12, and Squiers was
turned over to the military authorities for court-martial.

Two days later, Lieutenant Cannon was found dead in his hotel
room. He had been in excellent health, and there were no marks of
violence on his body. The cause of death was not determined, although it
was suspected that he had been poisoned. A few days after that, Squiers
escaped from the army jail, found a horse waiting nearby, and rode out
of town. The matter was never investigated, and whoever assisted
Squiers in his escape went unpunished. Squiers himself was never recap-
tured.

There were those who said that Chivington must have had a hand in
Cannon's death, or if not him directly, then some of his boys from the
Bloody Third. But there was no proof. Chivington had probably left the
area by that time, anyway. He departed Denver shortly after the military
hearings concluded—the exact date is not known—to build a new life
elsewhere.

Chivington's career as a soldier was over, and so was his vocation as a
preacher. He had been temporarily suspended from the ministry when he

joined the military, and there are two versions of why he did not return to the Church.

According to one version, Chivington was bitter about the public attack on his conduct at Sand Creek. "Accordingly, he felt himself incapable of preaching forbearance and brotherly love to others. Further, he had no desire to plunge the church into the controversy which was raging between the different factions relative to the Sand Creek engagement." In a second and less sympathetic version, the Methodist Church refused to reinstate him because he had become too controversial and notorious.

As for his decision to leave Denver, this may be seen as a bit surprising. Although it was undeniable that the Sand Creek affair and the Soule assassination turned many people against him, he retained a number of loyal friends and supporters, including the influential newspaper publisher William Byers. It is likely, however, that Chivington felt more strongly the need to escape the scene of his lost glory.

He moved his family to Nebraska, where he invested his small savings in a freight-hauling business, but it became no more than a limited success. It is ironic that one of the reasons his business venture did poorly was because of the frequent Indian raids on freight trains, a continuing legacy of the Sand Creek tragedy. When his wife died and his son drowned while crossing the North Platte River in a freight wagon, Chivington sold his business and moved to California for a short time. Soon he returned to Warren County, Ohio—where he had lived as a child—to operate a farm. In 1873, at the age of fifty-two, he married the forty-year-old widow of a soldier. He bought a newspaper in Blanchester, Ohio, and in 1883 was nominated by the Republican Party as a candidate for the state legislature. When his opponent resurrected the image of Sand Creek, Chivington was forced to withdraw from the race. Even the passage of nearly twenty years had not dimmed the savage memories.

During the campaign, he received an invitation to address a meeting of the Colorado Pioneers on the occasion of the twenty-fifth anniversary of the founding of Denver. He accepted gladly, seeing it as a welcome opportunity to get away from the embarrassing controversy over his past that was then raging in Ohio. Several distinguished speakers from Denver's early days were presented to the assembled crowd that September 13. All were received with enthusiasm, but none more so than Colonel John M. Chivington.

"We all remember the Indian wars of 1864 and '65," said the chairman of the proceedings in his introductory remarks, "and with what joy we received the news that some of them at least had met the reward due their treachery and cruelty. The man who can tell you all about those wars, who can tell you all you want to know of those Indians, and who can give you the true story of Sand Creek is here. I have the honor, ladies and gentlemen, to introduce Colonel Chivington."

Now sixty-two years old, Chivington had lost none of his power and magic as a speaker, and the crowd listened breathlessly to his account of those far-off days. Once again, the fighting parson boomed righteously from his pulpit.

"Were not these Indians peaceable?" he thundered. "Oh, yes, peaceable! Well, a few hundred of them have been peaceable for almost 19 years, and none of them has been so troublesome as they were before Sand Creek. What of the trains captured from Walnut Creek to Sand Creek on the Arkansas route and from the Little Blue to the Kiowa on the Platte route? Of supplies and wagons burned and carried off and of men killed? Aye, what of the scalps of white men, women, and children, several of which they had not had time to dry and tan since taking? These, all these, and more were taken from the belts of dead warriors on the battlefield at Sand Creek, and from their tepees which fell into our hands on the 29th of November, 1864. What of the Indian blanket that was captured fringed with white women's scalps? What says the sleeping dust of the 208 men, women, and children, ranchers, emigrants, herders, and soldiers, who lost their lives at the hand of these Indians? Peaceable!"

The audience sat spellbound, transfixed by the passion of the legendary figure before them as he proclaimed, "I say here, as I said in my home town in a speech one night last week: 'I stand by Sand Creek.'"

The *Rocky Mountain News* also praised him. Byers wrote, "Colonel Chivington's speech was received with an applause from every pioneer, which indicated that they, to a man, heartily approved the course of the colonel 20 years ago, in the famous affair in which many of them took part, and the man who applied the scalpel to the ulcer which bid fair to destroy the life of the new colony, in those critical times, was beyond doubt the hero of the hour."

Back at home in Ohio, Chivington was being castigated for Sand Creek, but in Denver, he was hailed as a hero and he soon decided to return. He never regained his former political stature, but over the next several years he held minor public offices, including the post of deputy sheriff. He demonstrated that age had not diminished his fiery temper or his fighting spirit. When charged with bringing in a desperate fugitive by the name of Newt Vorse, who was wanted for murder, Chivington did not hesitate. Vorse had barricaded himself in a cabin in a clearing and threatened to shoot anyone who approached him.

"Come out with your hands up, Vorse," Chivington roared, "or I will throw this charge of dynamite and blow you and your cabin to atoms."

Vorse surrendered immediately. He knew from Chivington's reputation that he would do precisely as he said.

Over the next ten years, there were occasional awkward reminders that not everyone in Colorado held Chivington in high esteem. Mary Prowers, the granddaughter of Chief One-Eye, remembered the time when her mother was attending an Eastern Star meeting in Denver. Someone brought the colonel over to meet her.

"'Mrs. Prowers, do you know Colonel Chivington?'

"My mother drew herself up with that stately dignity peculiar to her people," Mary recalled, "and ignoring the outstretched hand, remarked in perfect English, audible to all in the room, 'Know Colonel Chivington? I should. He was my father's murderer.'"

The fighting parson died on October 4, 1894, unable to conquer the cancer that left him semiconscious for the last several weeks of his life. His funeral was held in his old church, Trinity Methodist, which was filled to overflowing. People came from all over Colorado, including many who had served with him at Glorietta Pass and Sand Creek. There were six hundred of his fellow Masons in the processional. Former Governor Evans attended, and Major Anthony was one of the pallbearers.

The Reverend Robert McIntyre, one of Chivington's oldest friends, conducted the service and told the congregation that the colonel had fought the good fight for a good cause.

"When Colorado lifts aloft the scroll of honor, the name of Colonel John M. Chivington will be emblazoned near the top."

The Reverend McIntyre was not exaggerating. Many Coloradans, and many others throughout the west, viewed Chivington as a hero and Sand Creek as a victory. The passage of time, however, has dimmed that perception as historians continue to debate Chivington's position. For a majority of the pioneers who settled the west, criticisms of Chivington and Sand Creek reflected the attitudes of Indian-loving easterners who had nothing to fear from the Indians. "The farther from them a citizen lived, the better he liked them." A soldier in the Third Colorado Regiment, Irving Howbert, wrote in 1925 that the condemnation heaped upon Sand Creek was only one of the "many acts of injustice experienced by the frontier settlers [who] in addition to defending themselves from savages, always had to contend with the sentimental feeling in favor of the Indians that prevailed in many sections of the East. The people of the East had forgotten, or had never read of, the atrocities perpetrated on their ancestors by the savages, and resting securely in the safety of their own homes, they could not realize the privations and dangers that those who were opening up the frontier regions of the West had to endure."

Howbert accused the federal government's Indian department of being dominated by sentimentalists who had "neither sympathy for the frontier settler, nor any conception of a just and proper method of dealing with the Indians."

Another Colorado historian, writing in 1924, noted: "He who condemns the Colorado pioneers because of Sand Creek, must likewise condemn the colonists of New England, New York, Pennsylvania, Florida, and the Middle Western states because of their extermination of Indian tribes."

The belief that the western attitude toward the Indians was not understood in the east led many settlers to oppose any hint of gentle treatment urged by the Bureau of Indian Affairs. As Indian agent Sam Colley testified at the Sand Creek hearings, most people in the Colorado Territory were opposed to making peace and believed that the only solution to the Indian problem was to kill them all. He described the feeling as a "natural antipathy" toward Indians, which was strengthened by the continuing raids and depredations.

When Colonel Chivington led the impatient men of the Third out to find Indians, he knew that the people of Colorado would support him wholeheartedly no matter how many Indians he killed or to which tribe they belonged. It did not matter, so long as some were killed.

And what of the Indians attacked at Sand Creek? The verbatim proceedings of the Camp Weld council show that Governor Evans, as ex officio Superintendent of Indian Affairs, did not offer immunity or peace terms to the chiefs. He stated clearly that because the Indians—or at least some of them—had been at war with the United States, he did not have the authority to make peace. "Whatever peace you make must be with the soldiers and not with me," he had told them.

Chivington, in his capacity as commandant of the Military District of Colorado, also refused to offer peace or immunity at Camp Weld. All he said was that the Indians could go to Major Wynkoop at Fort Lyon when they were ready, but he promised them nothing even if they did go to the fort.

Chivington's superior officer, General Curtis, had telegraphed him on the day of the Camp Weld conference to say that no peace terms would be offered until the Indians had suffered more, until, that is, they were properly punished for their past actions. Had Chivington offered peace terms, or even a temporary amnesty, he would have been in violation of his orders.

It was well known at Camp Weld that at least some Cheyenne and Arapaho had been making war on the whites since the previous spring. Black Kettle and other chiefs admitted this. It was because of those raids, and the settlers' "natural antipathy" to the Indians, that there existed such a strong sentiment against making peace until a measure of vengeance against the Indians had been taken.

Another Sand Creek soldier, Frank Hall, wrote thirty-one years after the battle that "when a body of outlaws raid our settlements, kill the settlers, carry off their women and children, and rob them of their property; attack and destroy lines of communication, and make themselves a terror to all the country round about, they should be pursued and punished, not permitted to come in after their devilish work is done, and by simply saying, 'We confess everything, but want peace,' have it immediately granted with immeasurable gratitude for the offer. This is just what Wynkoop, Smith, Colley, and the rest who declaimed most vehemently against the attack at Sand Creek, demanded of authorities."

Such was the popular feeling. Any peace terms offered by Governor Evans would have been unpopular with most of his constituents.

Another factor mitigating against peace was the existence of the Third Regiment of Colorado Volunteers, for which Evans had long pleaded. How embarrassing it would have been for him to admit that the Third Colorado was not needed! "But what shall I do with the Third?" Evans had asked Wynkoop. There was only one possible answer: Kill Indians. There was no other reason for the regiment's existence.

But if the Third was going into action, it had to be soon. Enlistments were due to expire shortly after Christmas. Once the regiment disbanded, Colorado Territory would be defenseless. If the troops struck right away, a major defeat of the Indians might discourage others from going on the warpath. No peace could be considered until the Third had done its duty.

Governor Evans shared the responsibility for the events at Sand Creek, but it was Chivington who led the men there. It was Chivington who decided that Black Kettle's band—relatively small, lightly armed, encamped with their women and children, believing themselves to be in a place of safety—would be the ones to bear the brunt of the need for retribution, and perhaps also the brunt of his own personal need for a victory.

Glorietta Pass was a fading memory. A successful battle with the Indians could be a stepping-stone to a seat in Congress. A military triumph would restore his heroic stature. Colorado veteran Frank Hall wrote, "No doubt the gigantic colonel felt, as he surveyed the gory field strewn with dead savages, that he had won a brilliant victory which would cover his name with imperishable renown, and perhaps embellish his uniform with the coveted stars of a brigadier."

Whatever Chivington's motivation may have been, he deliberately attacked Indians whom he knew had received at least temporary assurances of safety from a fellow officer, Major Wynkoop at Fort Lyon. Chivington was also aware that Black Kettle and his people had been given reason to feel secure at Sand Creek because Wynkoop had told them they could camp there unharmed until General Curtis reached a decision about a peace treaty. Wynkoop may have exceeded his authority in offering that guarantee, but he did offer it. The Indians had received the word of a United States Army officer. That Chivington refused to honor Wynkoop's pledge was the Indians' misfortune, and, ultimately, his own.

It was the manner in which the attack was carried out that proved to be Chivington's undoing. Some of the chiefs—Black Kettle, Left Hand, White Antelope, One-Eye, among others—had tried to restrain their warriors and had never personally committed any crimes against whites. Even Major Anthony, as eager as he was to attack Indians, urged Chivington to surround the camp and let Black Kettle and some of the others escape before attacking.

Chivington had no interest in attempting to discriminate between friendly and hostile Indians, and he attacked with orders to take no prisoners. He could not have avoided seeing the atrocities his troops committed on both living and dead victims, yet there was no indication that he made the slightest effort to stop them. He had often made his feelings about the Indians known.

By expressing such sentiments and by tacitly countenancing the mutilations, he allowed what history might have judged a victory for the settlers to become a hideous and infamous massacre. It was the unrestrained atrocities more than the killings that disturbed so many people and instigated the three investigations. By the act of mutilating the Indians, the soldiers became savages themselves in the eyes of many people and brought history's wrath down upon them.

Yet, in fairness to Colonel Chivington, it has to be said that even if he had tried to stop the horrors, he might not have succeeded. The unruly mob of troopers had gone berserk. The men of the volunteer regiments had always been fiercely independent and undisciplined, and showed no hesitation in defying orders. Once the attack at Sand Creek was under way, the officers may have had little control over their troops. Inflamed by past Indian raids, by the editorial campaign in the *Rocky Mountain News,* and by Chivington's own speeches, the soldiers ran amok as soon as they were released on their enemies.

"When the encampment was first observed," Major Anthony wrote, the troops "plunged at once into the fray with the single purpose of destroying these reputed fiends."

In the judgment of a Colorado historian one hundred years after the event, "What Chivington ordered and his men effected at Sand Creek violated all the rules of civilized warfare, all the tenets of Christianity, and the spirit of an enlightened democratic nation. Had Chivington or his soldiers made the slightest effort to spare women and children, had they forgone the brute pleasures of scalping and mutilating and the boastful show of their clotted trophies, they might have gotten away with their 'glorious battle' for a while, because there were few people in Colorado who did not firmly believe in the hostility of Black Kettle's village and the propriety of Chivington's attack upon it."

That view agrees with the opinion of the soldier Frank Hall, who was at Sand Creek that cold morning in the Month of the Freezing Moon. The warrant for the atrocities, he believed, was Chivington's order that no prisoners be taken.

"Whether the battle of Sand Creek was right or wrong, these fiendish acts can never be palliated, nor can there ever be in this world or the next any pardon for the men who were responsible for them. It was this more than any other stain attaching to this historic tragedy which brought the condemnation of mankind upon the leaders of that terrible day, and which, strive as we may to efface it, will remain as the deliberate judgment of history."

14

The Buffalo Will Not
Last Forever

"My shame is as big as the earth," Black Kettle said. It was October 14, 1865, eleven months after Sand Creek. The Cheyenne chief had aged. He looked worn and beaten as he addressed the delegation of whites who were offering yet another treaty to the Cheyenne and other Indian tribes. They were meeting at Bluff Creek, a tributary of the Salt Fork of the Arkansas River. The federal government, trying to atone for Chivington's raid, had sent an influential commission to talk with the chiefs. The Superintendent of Indian Affairs was present, along with General William S. Harney and Major General John B. Sanborn. There were also friends of the Indians on hand, men the chiefs felt they could trust, including Jesse Leavenworth, Kit Carson, and William Bent.

"I once thought that I was the only man that persevered to be the friend of the white man," Black Kettle continued, "but since they have come and cleaned out our lodges, horses, and everything else, it is hard for me to believe the white man any more." He described Colonel Chivington and his men as a "fool-band" of soldiers that killed women and children. He said that other Indians were afraid to meet with whites anymore for fear of being betrayed, as he had been. He remained unafraid of the whites, and he still wanted to take them by the hand, but he was afraid of the soldiers.

"Your young soldiers," Black Kettle told the delegation, "I don't think they listen to you. You bring presents, and when I come to get them I am afraid they will strike me before I get away. When I come in to receive presents I take them up crying."

General Sanborn opened the talks with the Cheyenne and Arapaho by conceding that some of the Indian bands had been forced to go on the warpath by the actions of Colonel Chivington at Sand Creek. He announced that the Great White Father in Washington wanted to make restitution to the Sand Creek survivors for the property lost there. He described the attack as a gross and wanton outrage perpetrated against the Indians and was prepared to offer 160 acres of land to each woman who lost a husband at Sand Creek and each child who lost a parent. Black Kettle accepted the offer for the Cheyenne and Little Raven for the Arapaho.

The terms of a new peace treaty were discussed. Both tribes were to relinquish all land granted them in earlier treaties and move to a new reservation. No whites, except for traders and Indian agents, would be allowed on this land. Each Indian brave would be paid forty dollars a year. The Indians had to agree to stop raiding white settlements and to stay away from major travel routes such as the Smoky Hill and Platte River trails.

Black Kettle and Little Raven questioned the wisdom of signing a treaty that involved ceding so much land when so few of their people were present to be consulted about the terms. Black Kettle pointed out that only eighty lodges of Cheyenne were with him. More than two hundred lodges, including the Dog Soldier bands, were away to the north. Although he might consent to the treaty, that would not bind those who were absent.

The government spokesmen assured Black Kettle that only the signers would be bound by the treaty. Other bands could agree to abide by it at any time over the coming months.

Encouraged by the presence of William Bent, who had a reputation for dealing fairly with the Indians, Black Kettle, Little Raven, and several other chiefs affixed their *X*'s to the document, which became known as the Treaty of the Little Arkansas. Black Kettle seemed pleased with the new paper. Perhaps now, after so much deceit and bloodshed on both sides, they could finally live in peace.

Peace, however, remained a distant dream. Black Kettle and Little Raven adhered to the terms of the treaty, as they had done with previous treaties, but some of the Dog Soldiers had not been informed of the agreement and continued to make sporadic raids. Wagon trains, settlements, and stagecoach stations came under siege. Whites fell victim to the arrow and the scalping knife, and the territory resounded with cries for help and, of course, for revenge.

The attacks continued into the new year, 1866, when a new Indian agent was appointed for the Cheyenne and Arapaho. It was Major Edward Wynkoop. In mid-February, he set out with a company of cavalry to find the Cheyenne bands that had not yet signed the treaty. On February 25, he met with Black Kettle and several chiefs who had not signed, including the war chief of the Dog Soldiers, Medicine Arrows. After much talk, they did sign the treaty, although they protested the clause that excluded them from the Smoky Hill country, their favorite hunting ground.

In March, Wynkoop met with four hundred Cheyenne, Sioux, and Arapaho warriors and obtained their reluctant consent to the treaty. His powers of persuasion were impressive and Black Kettle vouched for his trustworthiness. For several months, through the spring and early summer of 1866, no Indian raids were reported. By midsummer, however, some of the Indians had reconsidered the situation. William Bent, John Smith, and Edmond Guerrier received word from the Cheyenne Dog Soldiers that although they agreed not to attack travelers along the Platte River and Santa Fe trails, they would never give up the Smoky Hill country.

In Washington, D.C., the U.S. Senate had not ratified the Treaty of the Little Arkansas, now eight months old. William Bent journeyed to the capital to urge speedy ratification with no amendments and to warn the legislators that failure to approve it would lead to the bloodiest Indian war of all time. The senators continued to argue and stall. At the same time, Black Kettle was forced by his warriors to repudiate that portion of the document requiring them to leave the Smoky Hill lands.

Wynkoop was ordered by his immediate superior, former Indian agent and now commissioner Sam Colley, to distribute one thousand dollars' worth of annuity goods to the Cheyenne and Arapaho. He was also to deliver a warning: "If the government is obliged to open war upon them, *all* the people will suffer terribly, and such chastisement will be made that there will be nobody left to make war."

On August 14, Wynkoop met with Black Kettle and seven other chiefs, including some of the Dog Soldiers. He persuaded them to relinquish their last hunting ground, the Smoky Hill area. The Indians even offered to kill any of their own people who attacked whites, if that was the only way to achieve peace.

In return, they wanted six hundred ponies purchased for them with the money the government pledged as reparations for Sand Creek. The Indians also demanded the return of the Cheyenne children captured by Chivington's men. One was in Denver, another on exhibit in a traveling sideshow, and a third had been adopted by Colonel Tappan.

In October, the chiefs of the warrior bands wrested power from the peace chiefs. They forced Black Kettle and the others to renounce the Treaty of the Little Arkansas and they took to the warpath. A stagecoach station on the Smoky Hill road was burned, two of its inhabitants murdered, and the stock was stolen. When news of the killings—the first in some months—reached Major General Winfield Scott Hancock of the Department of the Missouri, who had jurisdiction over Smoky Hill, he began to organize the largest army expedition ever mounted against Indians in that part of the country. The Civil War was over and lots of soldiers were available for duty in the west. Hancock was determined to punish the Cheyenne and subdue them once and for all.

While Hancock was preparing his punitive expedition, his superior, the dour and demanding William Tecumseh Sherman, was making an inspection tour of the troubled frontier. Sherman had been named for the great Shawnee chief Tecumseh; the name William was given him by a priest when the boy was baptized at the age of ten.

At first, General Sherman did not believe there was much danger of an Indian war—unless the whites started it. He felt that the ranchers and farmers were exploiting and exaggerating the reported raids so that army forces would be sent to the territory, to become customers for their grain and cattle. When his tour was complete, Sherman recommended that the control of the Indians be taken away from the civilian Bureau of Indian Affairs and turned over to the army. He also suggested that the Cheyenne and the other tribes be moved out of the area between the Platte and the Arkansas rivers. That land, which contained the two major travel routes and the new railroad line under construction, should be reserved for whites. The Cheyenne should be settled near more civilized tribes in the hope that they would turn to farming.

However, when Sherman learned of depredations committed by the Sioux, and was convinced by Hancock that the Cheyenne had been responsible for killing two stage-line employees, he concluded that a war was inevitable. "They must be exterminated," he wrote, "for they cannot and will not settle down, and our people will force us to do it."

Major Wynkoop tried to defend the Cheyenne, denying that they had committed any recent acts of violence. "I have been among them constantly," he said, "and never knew them to feel better satisfied or exhibit such a pacific feeling." He was correct about the Indians who followed Black Kettle and the other peace chiefs, but the Dog Soldiers continued to harass the whites throughout the early months of 1867.

They ran off some stock belonging to a group of buffalo hunters and forced a rancher to cook a meal for them, then threatened to kill him because he had no sugar. They stole mules and horses from a wagon train and took goods from a trader while holding target practice with new rifles and revolvers, bragging about how much ammunition they had.

In March, General Hancock told Wynkoop that the purpose of the planned expedition was to show the Indians that the government now had the men and resources necessary to punish any band that caused trouble. He asked Wynkoop to notify the Indians that if they stopped harassing whites, they would not be punished, but that if they wanted war, they would have it. Sherman wrote to his old friend General U. S. Grant that "Our troops must get among them, and must kill enough of them to inspire fear, and then must conduct the remainder to places where Indian agents can and will reside among them, and be held responsible for their conduct."

Hancock assembled a force of 1,400 troops, including six companies of infantry, a battery of artillery, 15 Delaware Indians to serve as scouts, three white scouts including James Butler "Wild Bill" Hickock, and the newly commissioned Seventh Cavalry under the command of the dashing and impulsive Lieutenant Colonel George Armstrong Custer. It was a formidable army and Hancock was eager to use it. "We shall have war," he told his men, "if the Indians are not well disposed toward us."

In response to requests from Wynkoop, fourteen Cheyenne chiefs came to Fort Larned on April 12 to meet with General Hancock. Black Kettle was not among them; he was too far away when the message reached him. The council took place at night around a bonfire with the officers arrayed in all their finery—full dress uniforms with gold epaulets, tall hats glittering with gold, and shiny swords. They sat on one side of the fire facing Wynkoop and the chiefs. A twenty-six-year-old reporter for the *St. Louis Missouri-Democrat*, Henry Morton Stanley, described for his readers the appearance of the chiefs.

The Indians were dressed in various styles, many of them with the orthodox army overcoat, some with gorgeous red blankets, while their

faces were painted and their bodies bedizened in all the glory of the
Indian toilette. To the hideous slits in their ears were hanging large
rings of brass; they wore armlets of silver, wrist-rings of copper, and
[President] Johnson silver medals, and their scalp-locks were adorned
with a long string of thin silver discs.

General Hancock rose, removed his overcoat, and started to speak in a
gruff voice, pausing periodically to allow Edmond Guerrier to translate.
He was disappointed to see so few chiefs there, he said. The next day, he
would lead his men to the Indian camp so that he could address all the
chiefs together. Then he produced the Indian boy who had been taken at
Sand Creek and said he would be returned to his people, along with a
girl who was now being brought to Fort Larned.

"You see the boy has not been injured," Hancock said, gesturing to
the child, and "the girl will be delivered by us also uninjured. Look out
that any captives in your hands be restored to us equally unharmed.
Now, I have a great many soldiers, more than all the tribes put together.
The innocent, and those who are truly our friends, we shall treat as
brothers. If we find hereafter that any of you have lied to us, we will
strike you. I have heard that a great many Indians want to fight; very
well, we are here, and are come prepared for war. If you are for peace,
you know the conditions; if you are for war, look out for its consequences."

He told them that the Indian agent Wynkoop was their friend, but
that he would not be able to protect them if they chose war. The soldiers
had orders to remain on Indian land to see that both the white man and
the red man abided by the treaty, and to protect the railroad. The "steam
car" must run, he said, and the wagon trains must be allowed to pass
along the trails, for both would carry gifts for the Indians.

"You know very well if you go to war with the white man, you
would lose. The Great Father has many more warriors. It is true you
might kill some soldiers and surprise some small detachments, but you
would lose men, and you know that you have not a great many to lose.
You cannot replace warriors lost; we can. I have no more to say. I
will await the end of this council, to see whether you want war or
peace."

The chiefs listened in silence, except when Hancock vowed to punish
any whites who mistreated Indians, at which point the Indians groaned
and muttered in disbelief. When the general sat down, everyone remained quiet until one of the chiefs lit a pipe, took three puffs, and

handed it around. After the last man had smoked, Tall Bull, a Cheyenne chief, rose and gravely shook hands with each officer.

Tall Bull directed brief and noncommittal remarks to General Hancock, saying nothing about not interfering with passage on the railroad and the trails. He warned the general not to bring his soldiers to their camp the next day, telling him that he would have no more to say there than here. Hancock interrupted Tall Bull in a loud voice.

"I am going, however, to your camp tomorrow," he said.

The council ended on that acrimonious note. Tall Bull asked Wynkoop to urge the general to refrain from bringing troops to the village. The memories of Sand Creek were too fresh. If the women and children saw the soldiers approaching, they would flee in terror. Wynkoop tried to dissuade Hancock but to no avail, and the command left Fort Larned on the morning of April 13. As the long column made its way majestically over the plains, small bands of Indians collected at a safe distance to watch its progress.

The troops suddenly came upon a chilling sight: a line of Cheyenne and Sioux warriors that stretched for more than a mile. Custer described it as one of the most impressive military displays he had ever seen. The newspaper reporter Stanley remembered that every brave held arrows in his hand and had his bow drawn. Although the Indians were outnumbered four to one, they held their ground as the troops advanced, prepared to die to protect their women and children.

Wynkoop urged his horse forward and rode out to the Indian line. The Indians let him come on unmolested. Roman Nose received him and Wynkoop assured the Cheyenne chief that the soldiers would not attack the village. Bearing a white flag, Wynkoop led Roman Nose and a few other chiefs back toward General Hancock, who met them halfway. Roman Nose, who was over six feet tall, sat proud and erect on his pony facing the burly general. A carbine hung at the Indian's side, four revolvers were stuffed in his belt, and he carried a strung bow and several arrows in his left hand. Hancock was blunt. Did the Indians want peace or war?

"We don't want war," Roman Nose said. "If we did, we would not come so close to your big guns."

Hancock said that he had come to talk to all the chiefs together. He wanted them to come to see him in his tent as soon as the soldiers made camp. Roman Nose said nothing. He turned and rode back to his battle line, which broke abruptly and headed off to the village.

At two o'clock that afternoon, the troops reached a point within sight of the Indian village and bivouacked close by its 250 lodges. The chiefs did not come all that afternoon and Hancock grew increasingly angry. Finally, at dusk, four Indians rode out to the army camp to report that all the women and children had fled in fear. Hancock demanded that they be brought back, and he gave the Indians fresh horses so they could catch them.

During the night, nothing further was heard from the chiefs. Hancock ordered Custer to surround the village and train the howitzers on it, to keep the chiefs and the warriors inside. By the time Custer had his men in place, the village was empty. All the Indians had vanished. An enraged Hancock sent Custer out after them.

That night, Major Wynkoop pleaded with Hancock to spare the Indian camp. The general had threatened to destroy the village, and Wynkoop argued that the action would only make the Indians more antagonistic, and make it more difficult to arrange councils with other Indian tribes in the future. Colonel Andrews, one of Hancock's senior officers, supported Wynkoop, but the general would not commit himself. He might burn the village or he might not. It would depend on what the Indians chose to do.

In the morning, Hancock placed guards around the deserted village, but they could not keep out the determined souvenir hunters among the soldiers. "In spite of the strict guard kept," wrote the newspaper reporter Stanley, "the 'boys in blue' are continually carrying away mementoes of their bloodless victory, such as stiff buffalo robes, dog skins, calumets [ceremonial pipes], tomahawks, war clubs, beadwork, moccasins, and we saw one officer of the artillery carrying off a picininny Indian pup which looked very forlorn. Arrows and knives are picked up by the dozens, and also little dolls, which had been the gratification of the papooses."

Custer led his men for miles across the prairie in pursuit of Indians who not only knew the territory better but who also could travel faster, unencumbered by supply wagons. The weather was so pleasant that Custer galloped far ahead of his troops, mounted on his thoroughbred horse, Custis Lee, with his five fine hunting dogs trailing behind. Custer knew it was foolhardy to ride alone in Indian country, but he always believed in his own luck, which had never yet failed him. Besides, it was such a glorious day for hunting.

He was several miles out in front and had just decided to turn back when he spotted a magnificent buffalo as large as his horse. He immediately gave chase. After about three miles, he caught up with the bull and trotted alongside. He pulled out his rifle and took aim. The bull swung toward him, making his horse shy away. Custer reflexively squeezed the trigger, the gun roared, and Custis Lee fell dead with a bullet in its head. Custer tumbled to the ground in the buffalo's path. For a moment, he was too stunned to move. The man and the bull eyed each other, then the great beast shook its head and lumbered away.

> Custer got up, and with a pair of field glasses slung around his neck, trailed by the dogs, he started walking back in what he hoped was the right direction. If he did not meet the column he could look forward to a wandering band of hostiles or death by starvation. [He] may have walked for an hour before noticing a dust cloud, which necessarily meant buffalo, Indians, or the Seventh. He provided at least three versions of his rescue. *Turf, Field & Farm* is the least dramatic. Here he simply recognizes the cavalry, sits down, and waits. In a letter to his wife he spoke of seeing the wagons. But for the admiration of his public in *My Life on the Plains*—which Captain Benteen chose to call *My Lie on the Plains*—he describes hiding in a gully with the dogs nestled around him until at last, through field glasses, he is able to make out a guidon with the Stars and Stripes fluttering above the riders. Hurrah! Once again he had been lucky.

He was not so lucky in finding the Indians. On April 16, Custer reached the Smoky Hill road without having seen a single warrior, but the following day, employees at a stagecoach stop told him that they had seen Indians heading north for the last twenty-four hours. They also described depredations committed along the road since the previous day. Custer dispatched a rider to General Hancock with the news. Two days later, Custer reached a stagecoach station that had come under heavy attack. The buildings had been burned to the ground, the stock run off, and three bodies left so horribly burned that they were scarcely recognizable.

Custer sent a second message to Hancock, describing the scene, but he was careful to note that neither he nor his Delaware scouts had found any evidence to tell which tribe had done the deed. He did not want to blame the Cheyenne without proof.

Hancock was less interested in such a fine point. Indians were Indians, and he calculated that the Cheyenne could have reached the Smoky Hill trail in time to make the attack. That was his explanation for the action he had taken on the previous day; as soon as he had received Custer's first message, he had put the torch to the Cheyenne village.

Wynkoop was disappointed and angry. He wrote to the Commissioner of Indian Affairs: "I know of no overt act that the Cheyenne had committed to cause them to be thus punished, not even since their flight." The Cheyenne had been forced into war, he contended, a position supported by Jesse Leavenworth, who said that the situation would be much better if Hancock had never come. After hearing from Leavenworth, the Superintendent of Indian Affairs concluded that the Cheyenne and the Sioux had been peaceful before Hancock entered their country. The general's hasty actions were predicted to have serious consequences for the frontier settlements.

Black Kettle doggedly tried to make peace again, offering to meet Hancock at Fort Larned for a council. Hancock could not get there in time but he offered to protect and feed Black Kettle and his group at any army post. Nothing came of it, perhaps because it sounded too similar to the promises made prior to Sand Creek, and within a month, the serious consequences foretold by the Superintendent of Indian Affairs began. This time there was no question about who was doing the killing. The Cheyenne were bent on revenge.

They paid particular attention to what General Hancock had called the steam car, the Union Pacific railroad line snaking its way across Indian land north of the Smoky Hill trail. For a month, from late May to late June, construction on the line was brought almost to a halt. Stagecoach employees were attacked in their outposts and every station over a distance of 170 miles along the Smoky Hill road was raided at least four times. Coaches and freight trains were kept off the road and for several weeks nothing passed over it except Indians.

Newspapers from Denver to Boston were full of stories of the bloody Indian raids. According to Henry Morton Stanley, "Between Bishop's ranch and Junction cutoff, 80 miles from Denver, there are no less than 93 graves, 27 of which contain the bodies of settlers killed within the last six weeks. Dead bodies have been seen floating down the Platte. The Indians, indistinguishable from the earth they lie on, continue to watch patiently from behind the hills, or from the sagebrush that screens them from view. As soon as they perceive a chance to get scalps or plunder they dart down and the deed is done."

Soldiers did not dare to venture far from the forts, and those who did were frequently attacked, sometimes within sight of the post. One lieutenant and ten troopers were ambushed by a band of Cheyenne and Sioux, who killed them all, then hacked and disfigured the bodies.

General Sherman declared that contrary to the provisions of the Treaty of the Little Arkansas, the Indians should be removed completely from the lands between the Platte and the Arkansas rivers. After he had toured that area, he had written to Secretary of War Stanton that "if 50 Indians are allowed to remain between the Arkansas and Platte we will have to guard every stage station, every train, and all railroad working parties. Rather get them out as soon as possible and it makes little difference whether they be coaxed out by Indian commissioners or killed."

In a letter to General Grant, however, Sherman was more sympathetic. "The Indians are poor and proud. They are tempted beyond the power of resistance to steal of the herds and flocks they see grazing so peacefully in this valley. To steal they sometimes kill. We in turn cannot discriminate—all look alike and to get the rascals, we are forced to include all."

Sherman knew that the people of the western territories saw only one solution to the Indian problem: extermination. He hoped to prevent that because he believed it would be a national disgrace, but he told friends that unless the army took steps to stop it, that would be the result. And as Sherman was building up his forces to take the offensive, the fighting and killing in the west continued over the rest of the summer. Before Sherman was ready to take to the field, however, Congress established an Indian peace commission, which was scheduled to come to the Plains in the fall. Until then, the army was restricted to defensive operations, patrolling the roads and maintaining the garrisons.

Sherman was pessimistic about this latest attempt to make peace, certain that the commission, like earlier groups, would be unable to meet with the younger warriors who were causing the trouble, but only with the older peace chiefs like Black Kettle, who no longer held any power. "And to talk with the old ones," Sherman told Grant, "is the same old senseless twaddle."

The charter of the Indian peace commission was ambitious, nothing less than a permanent peace with the hostile tribes and the removal of all Indians to reservations far from roads and railroads. Congress appropriated fifty thousand dollars to bring about this final solution to the Indian problem and appointed three military leaders to head it: Sherman and two old-west hands, General Alfred Terry and General William S. Harney.

Messengers were sent to those Cheyenne, Arapaho, and Kiowa-Apache known to be friendly, asking them to come to Fort Larned where they would be given food and shelter until the council convened in October. On September 2, Little Raven and a small band of Arapaho arrived at the fort. They appeared destitute but said they had no peace to make because they had not been at war. It was the Cheyenne who had been on the warpath all summer, they claimed.

The next day, Black Kettle arrived with seven other Cheyenne. They were well dressed, well fed, and rode strong ponies. They were not, however, very friendly. Black Kettle seemed sullen and morose, and he shook hands with the post commander reluctantly.

Perhaps he was glum because he had lost his standing among the Cheyenne. George Bent told Wynkoop that Black Kettle no longer had any influence beyond his own small band and that the young warriors had ridiculed him for his peace overtures. Neither Black Kettle nor the other peace chiefs had been able to persuade the Cheyenne braves to stop their raids. Despite their inability to control the Indians who were committing the depredations, Black Kettle and the chiefs expected to meet with the new peace commission from Washington.

Little Raven suggested that the talks be held at Medicine Lodge Creek, a favorite campsite of the Indians located sixty miles south of Fort Larned. Many tribes, Little Raven said, were afraid to come closer to an army post because the troops usually fired on them, whether they were friendly or hostile. Superintendent of Indian Affairs Murphy agreed to the site, and on September 17, he and Major Wynkoop left Fort Larned with a large wagon train of provisions. Forty warriors—Arapaho, Kiowa-Apache, and a few Cheyenne among them—accompanied the party as guards against hostile bands.

When they reached Medicine Lodge Creek three days later, they found 1,400 Arapaho encamped. A village of Kiowa and Comanche was only twenty miles away. Murphy and Wynkoop were visited by six Cheyenne who said that a camp of hostile Cheyenne under Tall Bull, Roman Nose, and other war chiefs was three days' ride to the west. The six Cheyenne agreed to take Edmond Guerrier to that village with a letter from Murphy inviting the war chiefs to the council. Guerrier returned on September 27 with Roman Nose, Gray Beard, and several others.

Murphy told the Indians that he wanted to take the Cheyenne by the hand and make a good road to peace and happiness for them. Gray Beard was skeptical—the Indians had heard the same words too often—but he admitted that he was encouraged by the fact that Murphy had come to see them without soldiers. He explained that the only reason they had gone to war was because General Hancock had burned their village. "We are only revenging that one thing," he said.

Murphy told him that the burning of the camp had not been authorized or approved by the government, and that the man who had ordered the destruction had been sent back to Kansas, away from the Indian country. Gray Beard and Roman Nose agreed to return to their camp to convey Murphy's invitation to the other war chiefs. Some, but not all, agreed to come.

The superintendent returned to Fort Larned to meet the Indian peace commission and escort them to the Medicine Lodge Creek campsite. On October 13, a train of sixty-five wagons left the fort. It was a formidable procession, including seven peace commissioners, one of whom was Sam Tappan, who had presided over Chivington's military hearing. The governor, lieutenant governor, and senator from Kansas came along, together with eleven reporters, a photographer, five hundred men of the Seventh Cavalry, and a battery of Gatling guns. When they arrived at Medicine Lodge Creek, they found more than five thousand Indians gathered.

The council was a colorful affair on both sides, decorated with bizarre costumes and behavior. One writer described the participants' "roguish individuality."

> Commissioner John "Black Whiskers" Sanborn, for instance, resplendent in a purple suit; or the Cheyenne interpreter Margaret Adams, of Arapaho and French-Canadian parentage, thrice married, an ostrich feather adorning her chapeau and a scarlet satin dress provocatively visible beneath the hem of her cloak. She is said to have attended every meeting drunk.
>
> General "White Whiskers" Harney, the ranking officer, physically huge and ceremoniously erect, would have made quite a show by himself. With a great masculine head topped by an epicene little cap of the sort college sophomores used to wear, he could be mistaken for a gingerbread general. [And] there was fastidious General Terry, described in one account as "calmly dumb," in another as "intrepid."

One wonders what the Indians thought of these people, or of Sam Tappan, who sat through the proceedings whittling on a stick. General Sanborn picked his teeth and laughed frequently while General Harney peered intently at one Indian face after another. General Terry amused himself by printing the letters of the alphabet in sequence, as though preparing a schoolroom exercise. Jesse Leavenworth watched his children romp nearby and exchanged knowing signals with Santanta, the oldest chief of the Kiowa. Another child played beneath the table.

The chiefs dressed themselves in their most lavish finery and painted their faces in red ocher and multicolored designs. After Senator Henderson of Missouri completed his obligatory, and probably dreaded, embraces with the chiefs, reporters noticed that "his nose was yellow, one cheek retained a red streak, and the other cheek had several green tattoos. No color photos exist, but a black-and-white picture reveals a middle-aged man with a grizzled beard, plenty of forehead, and frazzled hair. The pupils of his eyes are distinctly enlarged, giving him a dazed look, as though he could not believe it."

A number of the chiefs, recognizing the importance of the occasion, had taken the colorful blankets they usually draped around themselves and spread them over anthills. The ants swarmed over the blankets, picking them clean of lice. A vigorous shake of the blanket got rid of the ants, an effective cleaning method indeed.

Black Kettle was dressed in a long blue robe and a dragoon's hat. Santanta, the Kiowa chief, wore a brass bugle around his neck on a rawhide thong; he liked to toot the instrument at mealtimes. His face was smeared with red paint. For war, he painted his whole body red, but for the council, his muscular frame was sedately covered by a blue U.S. Army officer's jacket with epaulets. Tiny brass bells were attached to his leggings.

Other Indians sported brass medallions and silver crosses, feathered bonnets, moccasins decorated with bright beads, and pieces of military uniforms, often taken from the bodies of dead soldiers, or so the Indians liked to boast, but army uniforms were also prized gifts from the Great Father in Washington.

As the council opened, the Indians eyed the heavily laden wagons, wondering what gifts they would receive this time. The presents were put on display in three huge piles: one for the Kiowa and Comanche, one for the Arapaho and Apache, and the third for the Cheyenne. The array was dazzling—bushel baskets of glass beads, knives, and trinkets of every imaginable shape and color, and of the most questionable taste. The Indians were allowed to look at the gifts but they could not touch them or claim them until after they had signed a treaty. It was a powerful incentive: no treaty, no gifts.

Surplus items from the Civil War were stacked up in abundance: 2,000 blankets, complete uniforms from boots to hats, 3,423 bugles. There was more food than most Indians saw in a year, more than they could consume during the council, more than they could load on their ponies and carry away. Since the government's system of purchasing, accounting, and inventory had no provisions for returning anything from where the forms said it should be delivered, much of that food would be left to rot in the fields.

The most valuable presents, not distributed until everything else would be disposed of, were the guns and the kegs of black powder, percussion caps, lead, and paper cartridges. Most of the warriors, when they received these gifts, attempted to fire the guns right away, and more than a few were disappointed when the revolvers exploded in their hands. These were cheap, shoddy weapons manufactured by a war profiteer, but there were also plenty of Colt revolvers. The Indians knew that Colts always worked.

Some of the civilian peace commissioners were concerned about putting guns in Indian hands, but the generals assured them that the Indians needed the weapons and ammunition for hunting. A reporter was heard to say that the Indians were low on ammunition because they had used so much of it to kill the white settlers, and that it was sportsmanlike of the government to give them more.

The chiefs spoke briefly in the opening days of the council. "I had a talk with the Great Father himself when I was at Washington," one good-natured elderly chief said. "I am willing to repeat it here. Since I have made peace with the white man I have received many presents, and my heart has been made glad. My young men look upon you with gladness. I have not much to say, except it be to say that we are willing to travel any road you lay out for us."

An Apache chief added, "When the grass was green I was on the Washita, and I heard that the commissioners wanted to see me. I am glad. I would like to get my annuity goods as soon as possible, as I understood they were here. I will wait four days for the talk. I have spoken."

Black Kettle petulantly blamed other tribes for the current troubles. "We were once friends with the whites, but you nudged us out of the way by your intrigues, and now when we are in council you keep nudging each other. Why don't you talk, and go straight, and let all be well?" Little Raven agreed, urging the other chiefs to "behave themselves and be good."

The commissioners spoke in turn of the government's friendship and concern for the Indians and how they wanted to protect and feed and house them. But the Indians would have to abandon their old way of life, which was dying with the buffalo. Senator Henderson warned them that they would have to change.

> What we say to you may at first be unpleasant, but if you follow our advice it will bring you good, and you will soon be happy. You say you do not like the medicine houses of the whites, but you prefer the buffalo and the chase, and express a wish to do as your fathers did. We say to you that the buffalo will not last forever. They are now becoming few, and you must know it. When that day comes, the Indian must change the road his father trod, or he must suffer, and probably die. We tell you that to change will make you better. We wish you to live, and we will now offer you the way.
>
> The whites are settling up all the good lands. They have come to the Arkansas River. If you oppose them, war must come. They are many, and you are few. You may kill some of them, but others will come to take their places. And finally, many of the red men will have been killed, and the rest will have no homes. We are your best friends, and now, before all the good lands are taken by whites, we wish to set aside a part of them for your exclusive home. On that home we will build you a house to hold the goods we sent you; and when you become hungry and naked, you can go there and be fed and clothed. To that home we will send a physician to live with you and heal your wounds, and take care of you when you are sick. There we will also send you a blacksmith to shoe your ponies, so that they will not get lame. We will send you a farmer to show your people how to grow corn and wheat, and we will send you a mill to make for you meal and flour.
>
> We propose to make that home on the Red River and around the Wichita Mountains, and we have prepared papers for that purpose. Tomorrow morning at nine o'clock we want your chiefs and head men to meet us at our camp and sign the papers.

All the Indians would need to do was give up all the desirable land ceded to them by the previous treaty and pledge not to interfere with the railroads under construction in the Platte and Smoky Hill valleys. They must never again attack a wagon train or settlement, or kill or scalp a white person.

The Kiowa and Comanche signed the treaty immediately, but the Cheyenne took longer. Black Kettle had been called away by the Dog Soldiers, who threatened to kill his horses if he made peace. He mollified them and returned to the council, where, on October 28, he and Little Raven signed the treaty as representatives of the peace faction. Bull Bear and other chiefs of the soldier societies also signed, but some of the war chiefs refused even to attend the meetings.

After the signings, more than two thousand Cheyenne, including five hundred warriors, accepted presents from the commissioners. They loaded the goods on their ponies and filed slowly across the plains to winter camps on the Cimarron River south of Fort Dodge. The commissioners and the soldiers departed Medicine Lodge Creek shortly after, leaving piles of rotting food. Vultures and coyotes stood ready to devour the feast.

The Cheyenne lived in peace with the whites through the winter of 1867–1868. They did battle with old enemies—the Kaw and the Osage—and roamed the territories freely to hunt buffalo and trade the robes for food, trinkets, and whiskey. It was illegal to sell whiskey to Indians, but the profits were so enormous and the risk of being caught so slight that the practice continued unchecked, even within sight of army posts. Cheyenne braves, all the more truculent with a bellyful of liquor, harassed and frightened some whites, but no one died and no scalps were taken.

In February, Black Kettle, Little Raven, and the war chief Medicine Arrows brought their people to Wynkoop at Fort Larned for the food promised by the Medicine Lodge Creek Treaty. They carried away eighty tons of beef, sixty tons of flour, twenty tons of bacon, five tons of coffee, ten tons of sugar, and four and a half tons of salt. Wynkoop wrote to Superintendent Murphy that such a distribution of supplies would go a long way toward keeping the Cheyenne "content with their lot, and tend toward civilizing them by weaning them from their old habits."

Major Wynkoop was wrong. The Cheyenne and Arapaho were becoming increasingly discontent with their lot. Black Kettle and Little Raven told George Bent that they were unwilling to accept a reservation along the Red River. They did not wish to live there and hoped to move their people farther west into the Rocky Mountains to avoid all contact with the whites.

Peace lasted until the summer months. In May, after losing a fight with the Kaw, Cheyenne braves stole some cattle and scared a few settlers away from their ranches in western Kansas. When Murphy learned of the battle and its aftermath, he told Wynkoop to withhold the guns and ammunition due the Cheyenne in July as part of their annual distribution. When the Indians arrived at the fort to receive their goods, they were sullen and refused to accept any of the other supplies until they got their weapons.

When the Indian commissioner, Taylor, was informed that the Cheyenne were angry, he told Wynkoop to distribi .e the arms as long as he thought they were necessary to maintain peace, with the understanding that the Cheyenne would not use them against whites. On August 9, the whole of the Southern Cheyenne nation appeared at the fort. They obtained 160 revolvers, 8 rifles, 12 kegs of powder, 1½ kegs of lead, and 15,000 percussion caps. Wynkoop was convinced that they would use the guns only for their fall hunting, and that most of them were still peaceably inclined.

Some were not, however, and within a week two hundred Cheyenne braves and a few Arapaho and Sioux went on a rampage, killing more than a dozen settlers, kidnapping several children, burning homes and barns, stealing cattle, and forcing hundreds of whites to abandon their homes. Each tribe and each band within a tribe made its own arrows, which provided as distinctive a signature as a fingerprint. The arrows found in the dead settlers came from the camps of Black Kettle, Bull Bear, and Medicine Arrows. One of the leaders of the war party was a brother of White Antelope, killed by the soldiers at Sand Creek.

Superintendent of Indian Affairs Murphy felt betrayed when he learned of the killings. "I can no longer have confidence in what they say or promise," he wrote. "War is surely upon us."

In September, the Cheyenne committed more depredations against settlers and attacked a small detachment of troops. Major Wynkoop defended them as best he could. Although he did not deny that some Cheyenne had committed violent acts, he thought they had done so because of food shortages in the villages. If Congress had appropriated just a few thousand dollars more for supplies, Wynkoop said, there would have been no outbreak of violence. He was wrong again.

Murphy disagreed with Wynkoop and demanded that the Cheyenne and Arapaho be held accountable for the recent outrages. He contended that the government had fulfilled its part of the Medicine Lodge Creek Treaty obligations and had given the tribes all the goods they were due. The Indians, he said, had broken their pledge not to attack whites. Disillusioned, he urged that the army deal with the Indians until they sued for peace.

Wynkoop, frustrated by his and the peace chiefs' inability to control the warriors, and by Murphy's stance, applied for a leave of absence. He went home to Philadelphia, where, on October 17, 1868, he submitted his resignation as Indian agent. He had faithfully served the Cheyenne and Arapaho for four years, ever since he led his troops to Smoky Hill on the daring and dangerous mission to meet Black Kettle.

His resignation was an admission of failure. There was nothing more he could do, and thus this well-intentioned man disappeared from the history of the west, leaving the Cheyenne without an influential friend in high places. Now it was the army's job to deal with the Indians. The last time they had tried, General Hancock had destroyed a Cheyenne village, provoking renewed violence. The time before, Chivington had attacked Sand Creek, setting off a war. History was soon to repeat itself yet again.

The raids and murders continued throughout the fall. Wagon trains, ranches, stagecoach stations, army detachments all became targets. Men were cut down by bullet and arrow and lance, and women were borne into the long night of captivity from which few emerged. War parties two hundred strong besieged far larger army units, in one case for days before reinforcements raised a trail of dust in the distance. That was the most welcome sight a man could hope for when he was down to his last bite of hardtack, his canteen was dry, and he could hold all his bullets in one clenched fist. Indians died, too, Roman Nose among them, but more appeared on the horizon each day, and they had plenty of weapons and ammunition.

A new general was sent after the Cheyenne, Alfred Sully, with nine companies of the Seventh Cavalry and one of the Third Infantry, guided by John Smith. Even this massive force was not safe from attack. Three days after leaving Fort Dodge, Cheyenne Dog Soldiers ambushed it and fought it to a standstill for three days until Sully retreated to the fort to await reinforcements. Cheyenne braves followed the troops all the way back, thumbing their noses and slapping their buttocks, a traditional gesture of scorn. General Sully was astonished by the precision with which the war chiefs controlled their braves, signaling their commands with bugle calls. It is not recorded whether Sully realized where the Indians got so many bugles.

General Sherman refused to acknowledge defeat. He was determined to punish the Indians. "All the Cheyenne and Arapaho are now at war," he wrote. "Admitting that some of them have not done acts of murder, rape, et cetera, still they have not restrained those who have, nor have they on demand given up the criminals as they agreed to do." The Indians had only one choice to make, according to Sherman: either extermination or survival. He urged that food and clothing be made available at Fort Cobb for those Indians who might be left after the army's next campaign, but he made it plain that he did not expect there would be many survivors.

To Sherman, the issue was clear and the solution straightforward. It was now a matter of national pride. Either the Indians had to be subdued or the whites would have to give up all the land west of the Missouri River. The latter could not be tolerated; it would be an admission that the United States government had been beaten by a few thousand savages.

Sherman wrote to Colonel Tappan that he had approved of the peace-making policies of the Indian department in the past, but now it was too late to talk of peace. "They laugh at our credulity, rape our women, burn whole trains with their drivers to cinders, and send word that they never intended to keep their treaties. We must submit," he added, "or we must fight them."

The campaign against the Cheyenne was mounted and another officer chosen to lead it, Philip Sheridan, newly appointed to command the Department of the Missouri. The bandy-legged, obstinate Sheridan, a man given to quick rages, allowed as how the only good Indians he ever saw were dead. It was a sentiment that rapidly caught the national consciousness, rephrased as "the only good Indian is a dead Indian."

Sheridan's war against the Indians was to be without mercy, without pity. Sherman had made that clear to him in a message that seemed to sanction any action, so long as it led to victory.

As soldiers, Sherman wrote, they must "accept the war begun by our enemies, and hereby resolve to make its end final. If it results in the utter annihilation of these Indians, it is but the result of what they have been warned again and again, and for which they seem fully prepared. I will say nothing and do nothing to restrain our troops from doing what they deem proper on the spot, and will allow no mere vague general charges of cruelty and inhumanity to tie their hands, but will use all the powers confided to me to the end that these Indians, the enemies of our race and of our civilization, shall not again be able to begin and carry on their barbarous warfare on any kind of pretext that they may choose to allege. You may now go ahead in your own way and I will back you with my whole authority, and stand between you and any efforts that may be attempted in your rear to restrain your purpose or check your troops."

It was a more genteel and polished version of what Chivington had said to his men before he set them loose on Sand Creek.

On November 20, 1868, while Sheridan was organizing his expedition, Black Kettle, Little Raven, and two other chiefs went to Fort Cobb to meet with one of Sherman's subordinates, Major General William B. Hazen. Black Kettle told Hazen that he and his camp of 180 lodges located on the Washita River wanted to make peace. He said he had no control over any other Cheyenne and should not be held accountable for them. General Hazen told him that he was not authorized to make peace—just what Governor Evans had told Black Kettle at the Camp Weld council four years before. This time, however, there would be no haven while a decision was reached on the issue. Hazen told Black Kettle that he could not stay under the protection of Fort Cobb. He would have to take his chances in his own encampment.

Black Kettle and the other chiefs left the fort and made their way home to await an uncertain fate. This time, Black Kettle had no assurances of safety. This time, he knew that flying the American flag over the Cheyenne lodges would offer no more protection than it had last time in this same Month of the Freezing Moon. This time, perhaps, he knew that the Cheyenne had no places of refuge left.

The soldiers of the Seventh Cavalry surrounded Black Kettle's village in the early morning hours of November 27. The weather was bitterly cold and snow lay on the ground. The men waited for the first light of dawn to attack. Custer, dressed in fringed buckskins and mounted on a black stallion, ordered his troopers to maintain absolute silence—no talking, no moving around, no stamping their feet to get warm. He had brought his column of eleven companies, Osage scouts, and the regimental band— Custer liked his music—over the barren plains on a four-day march undetected. He had led them to within sight of the Indian village, and he was not about to be found out now by a stray cough or a boot accidentally snapping a twig on the ground.

He had even ordered the dogs killed during the night. Several strays had attached themselves to the command during the march, living on handouts from the cavalrymen. Concerned that a single bark could reveal their presence, Custer had the dogs muzzled with ropes. Some were then strangled, the rest stabbed. Two of his own hunting dogs were put to death but he spared his favorite staghound, Blucher.

Shortly before dawn, the troopers were startled to see what looked like a rocket rise out of the ground fog and ascend into the cold night air, appearing larger and more brilliant as it climbed. Indians often signaled one another with burning arrows, and the men were certain they had been discovered. It was only a morning star, however, and the village remained silent in sleep. No one had seen the seven hundred soldiers.

Slowly the contours of the land and the riverbanks and the lodges in the tall timber took vague form with the first hint of dawn. Custer signaled the regimental band to strike up the cavalry favorite *Garry Owen*. At last, wrote one of the Seventh's officers in melodramatic fashion, "the inspiring strains of this rollicking tune broke forth, filling the morning air with joyous music. On rushed these surging cavalcades from all directions, a mass of Uncle Sam's cavalry thirsty for glory."

With gunfire and horns and shouts and pounding hooves, the cavalry charged from all directions, firing and slashing their way through the Indian camp. The women and children, confused and half-asleep, raced for the river, looking for a place to hide. The warriors stood their ground and fought back with whatever weapons they found at hand. Riding at the head of his company, twenty-four-year-old Captain Louis Hamilton, the youngest captain in the U.S. Army and the grandson of Alexander Hamilton, fell with a bullet in his heart.

Other soldiers were hit. Captain Benteen—who had never been one of Custer's admirers and who would survive him at the Little Big Horn—felt a bullet whiz past his ear. An instant later, his horse was killed. Benteen tumbled over in the snow but managed to kill the brave who had fired at him. Major Elliott led fifteen soldiers along the riverbank after some of the families, but he went too far and was ambushed. His entire detachment was slaughtered and their bodies were mutilated. Custer lost twenty-one men killed and four wounded, but in no more than ten minutes, the Indian village was his, along with eight hundred horses and mules and fifty-three women and children prisoners.

He would later claim that he had killed 103 warriors, a great victory, indeed, but it turned out that no more than twenty of the dead were warriors. The remaining bodies were those of women, children, and old men. In all his years in the west, this was Custer's only victory over the Indians.

Custer had, however, made a miscalculation that could have cost him the lives of the Seventh Cavalry. When during the night he had come upon Black Kettle's village, he decided to attack without first scouting the area to see whether any other Indians were nearby. As a result, he did not know that as many as six thousand Cheyenne, Arapaho, Kiowa, and Kiowa-Apache were camped along the river in a string of villages, all within the sound of his guns. He had made the same mistake during the Civil War, attacking a rebel division without being aware—because he had failed to scout properly—that another Confederate division was nearby. Despite his fabled luck, he did not learn from his mistakes.

By mid-afternoon, he had extracted his companies without additional casualties and rode them hard for six hours until he judged they were out of danger. He had ordered the Indian ponies and mules killed. Everything else was burned.

On December 1, the Seventh Cavalry returned to its camp. Phil Sheridan was waiting for them, and Custer put on a show as he marched in. The band played *Garry Owen,* and the fifty-three Indian widows and orphans were paraded past, slumped on their ponies as though they expected to be killed. The troopers posed and swaggered, and the Osage scouts dangled bloody Cheyenne scalps from their lances. One scout, Koom-la-Manche, was particularly proud of his trophy. He boasted that it came from the head of Black Kettle.

That story was a lie. Black Kettle had been killed but not scalped. Survivors of the village found his body the next morning, along with that of his wife, whom he had saved at Sand Creek. They were lying face down in the river. Black Kettle was carried to the top of a sandy knoll and buried, so that soldiers would not find his grave and dishonor it.

Almost seventy years later, on July 13, 1934, workers extending a bridge over the Washita River uncovered a skeleton wearing jewelry identified as belonging to the Cheyenne chief. The bones were given to a local newspaper, the *Cheyenne Star,* which put them on display in its window.

Epilogue: You and Your Whole Command Will Be Killed

O n March 15, 1869, Custer and the Seventh Cavalry came upon 160 Cheyenne lodges on the Sweetwater River in what later became Oklahoma Territory. Sheridan had sent him out to try to persuade the Indians to surrender. Many bands had already done so at Fort Cobb over the winter, coming in on foot because their ponies were too weak to carry them. They had begged Sheridan for food and for peace on whatever terms he wished. "It is for you to say what we have to do," one chief told him.

Throughout the territory, bands of destitute Cheyenne and Arapaho were making their way to the fort, and Custer and his men were out looking for the main band of Dog Soldiers. Now he had found them.

Eight braves from the village came out to invite him to the camp to meet with their chief, Medicine Arrows. Ordering his men to surround the village, Custer, with blind faith in his phenomenal luck, rode into the camp, accompanied only by his adjutant and an interpreter. The Indians were decorated for war and were well armed, but they appeared poorly fed and their ponies looked weak. The warriors stared at the soldiers with hostility but let them pass unharmed.

Custer, alone, was ushered into the lodge of Medicine Arrows, who gestured for him to sit at his right, beneath four sacred medicine arrows that were hanging from a forked stick. To sit there was to be dishonored, but Custer did not know that. The chief lit his pipe, puffed on it, and passed it to Custer, who, although he did not smoke, forced himself to partake of the ritual. Using sign language, he told Medicine Arrows that he had not come to make war on the Cheyenne.

Speaking in his native tongue, which Custer could not understand, the chief told him that he was not a good man; he remembered what Custer had done on the Washita. He warned Custer that if he ever made war on the Cheyenne again, "You and your whole command will be killed."

Medicine Arrows turned his pipe upside down and tapped the ashes out onto Custer's boots, the Cheyenne way of wishing a man bad luck. Custer did not understand the gesture.

Cheyenne were among the Indians Custer and the Seventh Cavalry attacked at the Little Big Horn on June 25, 1876, the day his luck turned bad. After the battle, two Cheyenne squaws wandering over the field came upon Custer's body. They had seen him before, in Indian territory, when he had visited Medicine Arrows in his lodge.

They kneeled down and punctured his eardrums with sewing needles. They did it to improve his hearing, they said, because obviously he had not heard Medicine Arrows's warning about making war on the Cheyenne.

Chapter Notes

1. A GLORIOUS VICTORY

"Were there any acts": *Massacre of Cheyenne Indians* (Joint Committee on the Conduct of the War, 1865), p. 9. "They killed everything": ibid., p. 45. "I did not see a body": ibid., p. 88. "I believe that was part": ibid., p. 45. "This village were friendly": ibid., Appendix, p. 54. "In the last ten days": ibid., Appendix, p. 91. "How many warriors": ibid., pp. 11–12. "I am satisfied": ibid., p. 22. "He thought he had done": ibid., Appendix, p. 74. "I have not time": ibid., Appendix, p. 92. "Statements from respectable sources": ibid., p. 74. "You refer to a conversation": *Sand Creek Massacre* (Report of the Secretary of War, 1867), p. 105. "Did you hear any plans": ibid., p. 25. "The white man has taken": ibid., pp. 73–74. Description of Chivington: Utley, *Frontiersmen in Blue*, p. 285. "Among the brilliant feats": Gardiner, *Great Betrayal*, p. 149. "Had you been living": Harvey, *Colorado Magazine*, pp. 144–149. "Perhaps the honorable": Werstein, *Massacre at Sand Creek*, pp. 134–135. Smoking the war pipe: Grinnell, *Cheyenne Indians*, Vol. I., pp. 74–75.

2. YOU WILL ALL DIE OFF

Sweet Medicine: Grinnell, *Cheyenne Indians*, Vol. II, pp. 345–381. "Their fighting spirit": Grinnell, *Fighting Cheyennes*, p. 12. Counting coup on one's enemies: Grinnell, *Cheyenne Indians*, Vol. II, pp. 32–34. "We cut off his hands": Marquis, *Wooden Leg*, p. 12. "Scalp and torture the wounded": Longstreet, *War Cries on Horseback*, p. 56. "Before there were whites": Conard, *Uncle Dick Wootton*, p. 102. "Some day I will come back": Grinnell, *Cheyenne Indians*, Vol. I, p. 33. "By his fair and open dealings": Grinnell, *Pawnee, Blackfoot and Cheyenne*, p. 245. "They also stated":

Grinnell, *Cheyenne Indians*, Vol. I, p. 46. "If I could see this thing": Grinnell, ibid., Vol. II, pp. 164–165. "It was a daring experiment," "Creeping up the North Platte," and "If the traders occasionally": Smith, *Moon of Popping Trees*, pp. 10–11. "It is wrong to tear loose": Marquis, op. cit., p. 374. "I have seen the plains": Conard, op. cit., pp. 68, 69. "A smothered passion": Lavender, *Bent's Fort*, p. 343. "Manifest destiny": Longstreet, op. cit., p. 24. "Neither Christian nor white": ibid., p. 204. "The chiefs who had come": Smith, op. cit., p. 13. "Old Sumner": Utley, *Frontiersmen in Blue*, p. 121. "The enemy is at last": Berthrong, *Southern Cheyennes*, p. 139. "Colonel Sumner has worked": Utley, op. cit., p. 125. "Before 1861": Tebbel and Jennison, *American Indian Wars*, p. 238. "Scrupulously maintain": Grinnell, *Fighting Cheyennes*, p. 125. "It was freedom of movement": Marshall, *Crimsoned Prairie*, pp. 14–15. "God damn a potato!": Smith, op. cit., p. 60.

3. A UNIVERSAL TRIUMPH

"New gold discovery": Abbott, *Colorado*, p. 53. "We are bound to have a territory": ibid., p. 54. "I have never seen men eat": Berthrong, *Southern Cheyennes*, p. 145. "We were surprised": Abbott, op. cit., p. 54. "Gold exists": Young and Young: *Pikes Peak*, p. 32. "We seem to have reached": Abbott, op. cit., p. 7. "Oh, Ann," and "We met one thousand": Perkin, *First Hundred Years*, pp. 90, 91. "On one side": ibid., p. 117. "Gentlemen, I have washed": Young and Young, op. cit., p. 42. "Denver was a strange medley": ibid., p. 36. "There was the man": Hafen, *Colorado and Its People*, p. 237. "More brawls": Young and Young, op. cit., p. 48. "Almost every day": Perkin, op. cit., p. 52. "We never hanged": ibid., p. 176. "That coarseness and strength": Turner, *Significance of the Frontier*, p. 235. "I run all over town": Abbott, op. cit., p. 71. "Lofty buildings": Hafen, op. cit., p. 197. "We have as sharp": Abbott, op. cit., p. 61. "A through ticket": ibid., p. 75. "Many a time," and "I saw a band of Indians": Ashley, *Colorado Magazine*, pp. 222–223. "A civilized and enlightened people": Perkin, op. cit., p. 261.

4. A SOLDIER IN GOD'S WAR

"Until the national authority" and "I am a man": Mumey, *Roundup*, p. 6. Southern sympathizer story: Craig, *Fighting Parson*, pp. 19, 53–54. "As near as I can": Chivington, First Colorado Regiment, p. 1. "She could read and write," "I do not propose," and "Take your foot off that step": Craig, op. cit., pp. 26–27, 32. "By the grace of God": Speer, interview with Mrs. Chivington. "The authority of": Craig, op. cit., p. 45. "On that first Sunday": Noel, *The City and the Saloon*, p. 13. "Less frequently now": Utley, *Frontiersmen in Blue*, p. 217. "If they were not willing": Chivington, First Colorado Regiment, p. 2. "They did not like": Craig, op. cit., p. 70. "They deserted at will": Perkin, *First Hundred Years*, pp. 240–242. "Walking whiskey keg": Robbins, *The New York Times,* Nov. 29, 1987. "You shoot Kerber," "A very hard fate," and "Some of them fared badly": Chivington, *Denver Republican,* Apr. 20, 1890. "You can take 'em," "Our first business," "My men didn't come," "Crazy preacher," and "Their commander": Mumey, op. cit., pp. 7–9. Chivington's description of the Glorietta Pass action: Chivington, First Colorado Regiment, pp. 4–5. "It is only a question": Craig, op. cit., pp. 140–141. "I would rather command" and "It is only necessary": Chivington, *Denver Republican,* May 4, 1890.

5. THE FOUL CONSPIRACY

"The white men are like locusts": Marshall, *Crimsoned Prairie,* p. 25. "Dispatched with a savagery": Utley, *Frontiersmen in Blue,* p. 265. "We passed the winter": Chivington, First Colorado Regiment, p. 6. "The feminine phalanx" and "Such outrages": Perkin, *First Hundred Years,* pp. 260–263. "Showing that they intended": Bent, *Frontier.* Bull Bear story: MacMechen, *Life of Governor Evans,* p. 118. "Moved systematically," "I saw the principal chiefs," "Each step of progress," and "While citizens and soldiers": Berthrong, *Southern Cheyennes,* pp. 169–174. "Three years have elapsed": Grinnell, *Fighting Cheyennes,* p. 149. "I hope you will use all diligence": Hall, *History of the State of Colorado,* p. 331.

6. THE INDIANS ARE COMING!

Dunn expedition: *Sand Creek Massacre* (Report of the Secretary of War, 1867), p. 181. Chivington takes hard line against Indians: Berthrong, *Southern Cheyennes,* p. 180. Downing expedition: Grinnell, *Fighting Cheyennes,* p. 143; *Massacre of Cheyenne Indians* (Joint Committee on the Conduct of the War, 1865), Appendix, pp. 69–70. Wolf Chief quotations: Grinnell, op. cit., pp. 145–146. "An extensive Indian war": Berthrong, op. cit., p. 193. McKenney report: Grinnell, op. cit., p. 147. Goldrick article: Young and Young, *Pikes Peak or Bust,* pp. 63–64. "By the light of bonfires": Sanford, *Colorado Magazine,* 1927, pp. 103–104. Curtis telegrams to Chivington: *Sand Creek Massacre* (Report of the Secretary of War, 1867), p. 172. Evans messages to Curtis and Stanton: Hoig, *Sand Creek Massacre,* p. 60; Berthrong, op. cit., p. 5. Evans proclamation to the friendly Indians of the Plains: *Sand Creek Massacre* (Report of the Secretary of War, 1867), pp. 167–168.

7. KILL AND SCALP ALL

"Dead cattle": Hafen, *Colorado and Its People,* p. 311. "A little powder": Berthrong, *Southern Cheyennes,* p. 197. "Neglect of this military concealment" and "Have honor to report": *Sand Creek Massacre* (Report of the Secretary of War, 1867), pp. 170–171. "A group of leading businessmen" and "Indian

Murders": Perkin, *First Hundred Years*, pp. 266, 268. "Scalp dances": Grinnell, *Fighting Cheyennes*, p. 155. "Authorizing all citizens": *Massacre of Cheyenne Indians* (Joint Committee on the Conduct of the War, 1865), p. 47, and Perkin, op. cit., p. 265. "A few months": Berthrong, op. cit., p. 201. "Extensive Indian depredations" and "Pray give positive orders": *Massacre of Cheyenne Indians* (Joint Committee on the Conduct of the War, 1865), pp. 65, 72. "The guns given us" and "I wish to emphasize": Howbert, *Memories of a Lifetime*, pp. 119–120, 135, 156. "Recruited from the dregs": Utley, *Frontiersmen in Blue*, p. 293. "They looked upon": Werstein, *Massacre at Sand Creek*, pp. 39–40. "Chicken and melon stealing": Perkin, op. cit., pp. 269–270. "Kill and scalp all": *Massacre of Cheyenne Indians* (Joint Committee on the Conduct of the War, 1865), Appendix, p. 71. "Now, if these red rebels": Berthrong, op. cit., p. 203. "They died for want of breath": *Sand Creek Massacre* (Report of the Secretary of War, 1867), p. 191. "The statements given": Hall, *History of the State of Colorado*, p. 316. "Bound with ropes": Conard, *Uncle Dick Wootton*, pp. 393–394. "The whole five were butchered": Hoig, *Sand Creek Massacre*, pp. 72–73. "I assure you": *Rebellion Records*, Series I, Vol. XLI, Part II, pp. 613–614. "It looks lonely here": Sanford, *Colorado Magazine*, 1930, p. 135. "The major": *Massacre of Cheyenne Indians* (Joint Committee on the Conduct of the War, 1865), p. 14. "We received a letter from Bent": Bent, *Frontier*.

8. WHAT SHALL I DO WITH THE *THIRD?*

"Appeared to be perfectly satisfied": *Sand Creek Massacre* (Report of the Secretary of War, 1867), p. 84. "I was bewildered": Hoig, *Sand Creek Massacre*, p. 99. "The substance of Wynkoop's letter": *Massacre of Cheyenne Indians* (Joint Committee on the Conduct of the War, 1865), Appendix, p. 66. "They lined up": Bent, *Frontier*. "Putting on as bold a front": Report of Major Wynkoop in *Annual Report* of the Commissioner of Indian Affairs, 1864, p. 234. "Major Wynkoop stated": *Massacre of Cheyenne Indians* (Joint Committee on the Conduct of the War, 1865), Appendix, p. 49. "He also went on to state": ibid., Appendix, p. 50. "I said it would be strange": ibid., Appendix, p. 77. "They had been raised": ibid., Appendix, p. 77. "What shall I do with the *Third*": ibid., Appendix, p. 77. "I told him that I had not the power": *Sand Creek Massacre* (Report of the Secretary of War, 1867), p. 85. "I have now got to talk": ibid., p. 56. "He was ashamed": ibid., p. 31. "He was glad to hear": ibid., p. 31. "Would have to stop it": ibid., pp. 55–56. "Gone out and fought them": ibid., p. 90. "I shall require the bad Indians": ibid., p. 173. "Everything was all right": Grinnell, *Fighting Cheyennes*, p. 160. "We are opposed": Perkin, *First Hundred Years*, p. 268.

9. ASSURANCES OF SAFETY

Camp Weld Conference: *Massacre of Cheyenne Indians* (Joint Committee on the Conduct of the War, 1865), Appendix, pp. 87–89. "The chiefs brought in": ibid., Appendix, p. 82. "He preferred to have them": ibid., p. 87. "By what authority": ibid., p. 70. "Could make but a feeble fight": ibid., p. 70. "Pretend that they want peace": ibid., p. 71. Camp Weld Conference: *Sand Creek Massacre* (Report of the Secretary of War, 1867), p. 213. "Earnest in their desire for peace": ibid., p. 168. "I told them that they could consider themselves": ibid., p. 91. "After learning all the circumstances": ibid., p. 87. "I told them how I was situated": ibid., pp. 102, 103. "They said they were perfectly satisfied": ibid., pp. 105–106. "Productive of more good": ibid., p. 93. "Had it not been for the course": ibid., p. 94. "To hold yourself in readiness": Berthrong, *Southern Cheyennes*, p. 212. "That was the last any of us saw": Hudnall, *Colorado Magazine*, p. 237. "Can we get a fight": Grinnell, *Fighting Cheyennes*, p. 167. "A definite threat": Carey, *Colorado Magazine*, p. 293. Chivington-Connor conversation: Chivington, *Denver Republican*, May 18, 1890.

10. TAKE NO PRISONERS

"As I was aware": *Massacre of Cheyenne Indians* (Joint Committee on the Conduct of the War, 1865), Appendix, p. 57. "Indians were recognized": ibid., Appendix, p. 54. "I saw one man dismount": ibid., p. 27. "I saw five squaws," ibid., Appendix, p. 96. "I saw a little boy": ibid., Appendix, pp. 74–75. "During the massacre": ibid., Appendix, p. 61. "Colonel Chivington": ibid., Appendix, p. 74. "To the best of my knowledge": ibid., Appendix, p. 74. "But unless you give your men": ibid., pp. 22–23. "I can't help it": ibid., p. 10. "We, of course, took no prisoners": ibid., Appendix, p. 92. "They don't expect me": *Sand Creek Massacre* (Report of the Secretary of War, 1867), p. 116. "Oh! You must be mistaken": ibid., p. 116. "Scalps are what we are after": ibid., p. 117. "Well, I long": ibid., p. 117. "Hereafter, no officer": ibid., p. 165. "He was in for killing": ibid., p. 13. "I was perfectly willing": ibid., p. 47. "Black Kettle would not be killed": ibid., p. 47. "Off with your coats": ibid., pp. 68–69. "After that I could see no order": ibid., p. 13. "A great many started": ibid., pp. 50–51. "A son-of-a-bitch": ibid., p. 136. "Let him go to rest": ibid., p. 71. "I thought it was a damn shame": ibid., p. 136. "Chivington takes command": Perrigo, *Colorado Magazine*, p. 54. "Cursed the maggoty hardtack": Perkin, *First Hundred Years*, p. 269. "My recommendation" and "Has been engaged in bloody war": Craig, *Fighting Parson*, pp. 183–184. "On expedition against Indians": Hoig, *Sand Creek Massacre*, p. 142. "Insist on peace" and "At the proper time": Berthrong, *Southern Cheyennes*, pp. 215–216. "I feel that you are" and "The Cheyenne nation": Craig, op. cit., pp. 186–187. "Damn any man": Hoig, op. cit., p. 143. "Wolf, he howl" and "I haven't had an Indian to eat": Grinnell, *Fighting Cheyennes*, pp. 169–170. "Nothing lives long" and "We fought back": Grinnell, ibid., pp. 177–178. "Shoot the old," "Run here, Uncle John," and "One old squaw": Perkin, op. cit., pp. 273–274. "Never saw more bravery": Grinnell, op. cit., p. 172. "I was so utterly exhausted" and "We rushed out":

Howbert, *Memories of a Lifetime*, pp. 129–130. "It was very dark" and "Wailing and mourning": Grinnell, op. cit., pp. 179–180.

11. ALL THIS COUNTRY IS RUINED

"The First and Third Regiments," "This noted, needed whipping," "Among the brilliant feats," "Cheyenne scalps," "Seignor Franco," "Indignation was loudly," and "Since it is a settled fact": Perkin, *First Hundred Years*, pp. 275–279. "Ill-advised, saying he thanked God," and "A most imposing procession": Hoig, *Sand Creek Massacre*, p. 161. "All the chiefs": Craig, *Fighting Parson*, p. 209. "I abominate the extermination": Berthrong, *Southern Cheyennes*, p. 221. "About one o'clock": Ware, *Indian War of 1864*, p. 374. "The victories and plunder": Berthrong, op. cit., p. 228. "We must have five thousand troops": Hafen, *Colorado and Its People*, p. 317. "It seemed as if an army of fiends," and "The denunciations heaped upon Sand Creek": Hall, *History of the State of Colorado*, pp. 359–360. Beckwourth statements: *Sand Creek Massacre* (Report of the Secretary of War, 1867), pp. 73–74. "All I can say": *Massacre of Cheyenne Indians* (Joint Committee on the Conduct of the War, 1865), p. 53. "Statements from respectable sources": ibid., p. 74. "I fear that Colonel Chivington's assault": ibid., p. 75. "All the time inciting": ibid., p. 83. "The sworn evidence": ibid., pp. 83–84. "Since the last horrible murder": ibid., pp. 83, 84. "We are in every respect": ibid., pp. 95, 97, 98. "Thus denuding the district of troops": ibid., p. 96.

12. A FOUL AND DASTARDLY MASSACRE

"You say these Indians": *Massacre of Cheyenne Indians* (Joint Committee on the Conduct of the War, 1865), p. 4. "Colonel Chivington was not stopped": ibid., pp. 3, 4. "I do not know any exact reason": ibid., p. 14. "For the information of the committee": ibid., pp. 14–15. "I have thought for more than a year": ibid., p. 15. "I did not state to them": ibid., p. 20. "Unprovoked and unwarranted": ibid., p. iv. "I do not know; that was the fault": ibid., p. 22. "Did not so much object": ibid., p. 28. "The only way to fight Indians": ibid., p. 26. "I did not hear anything": ibid., p. 26. "My boys were mad": ibid., p. 31. "As a matter of course": ibid., pp. 42–43. "They made no secret": ibid., p. 44. "What was his policy?": ibid., pp. 45–46. "I was entirely satisfied": ibid., p. 46. "No more than would certainly fall": ibid., p. 103. "Indians had been killing": ibid., p. 104. "Positive orders": ibid., p. 108. "As an act of justice": ibid., p. 108. "And then the scene": ibid., pp. iii–iv. "Characterized by such prevarication": ibid., p. iv. "As to Colonel Chivington": ibid., p. v. "Had repeatedly expressed himself": *Sand Creek Massacre* (Report of the Secretary of War, 1867), p. 5. "Greatest military blunder": ibid., p. 8. "On your second visit to Sand Creek": ibid., p. 79. "Do we understand": ibid., pp. 151, 152. "Captain Silas S. Soule": ibid., p. 159. "He did not know which way":

ibid., p. 186. "Fully expected to be killed": ibid., p. 189. "They would do anything": ibid., p. 208. "He thought they could make a massacre": ibid., p. 190. "There was some talk": ibid., p. 206. "Sir: I am directed": MacMechen: *Life of Governor Evans*, pp. 140–141. "Was attended by an unusually large": Gardiner, *Great Betrayal*, p. 243. "Did he not in the darkness": Prentice, *Colorado Magazine*, pp. 227–228.

13. THE DELIBERATE JUDGMENT OF HISTORY

"Accordingly, he felt," "We all remember," "Were not these Indians peaceable?," "Colonel Chivington's speech," "Come out with your hands up," and "When Colorado lifts aloft": Craig, *Fighting Parson*, pp. 232–238. "Mrs. Prowers": Hudnall, *Colorado Magazine*, p. 238. Debate on Chivington's position in history: Carey, *Colorado Magazine*, pp. 279–298; Lecompte, *Colorado Magazine*, pp. 315–335; Sievers, *Colorado Magazine*, pp. 116–142; and Unrau, *Colorado Magazine*, pp. 299–313. "The farther from them": Connell, *Son of the Morning Star*, p. 159. "Many acts of injustice": Howbert, *Memories of a Lifetime*, pp. 158–159. "He who condemns": MacMechen, *Life of Governor Evans*, p. 136. "When a body of outlaws," "No doubt the gigantic colonel," and "Whether the battle of Sand Creek": Hall, *History of the State of Colorado*, pp. 347–354. "What Chivington ordered": Lecompte, op. cit., p. 335.

14. THE BUFFALO WILL NOT LAST FOREVER

"My shame is as big": Hoig, *Sand Creek Massacre*, p. 174. "Your young soldiers": Berthrong, *Southern Cheyennes*, p. 242. "If the government is obliged": ibid., p. 261. "They must be exterminated": ibid., p. 268. "I have been among them": ibid., p. 270. "Our troops": ibid., p. 272. "We shall have war": ibid., p. 273. "The Indians were dressed": Stanley, *My Early Travels*, p. 29. "You see the boy": ibid., pp. 32–33. "I am going": ibid., pp. 34–35. "We don't want war": ibid., p. 38. "In spite of the strict guard": ibid., p. 39. "Custer got up": Connell, *Son of the Morning Star*, pp. 142–143. "I know of no overt act": Berthrong, op. cit., p. 279. "Between Bishop's Ranch": Stanley, op. cit., p. 129. "If fifty Indians": Berthrong, op. cit., p. 284. "And to talk with the old ones": ibid., p. 288. "We are only revenging": ibid., p. 294. "Commissioner John," and "His nose was yellow": Connell, op. cit., pp. 144–146. "I had a talk": Stanley, op. cit., pp. 233–235. "What we say to you": ibid., p. 256. "Content with their lot": Berthrong, op. cit., p. 301. "I can no longer have confidence": ibid., p. 307. "All the Cheyenne": ibid., p.

309. "When they laugh": ibid., p. 320. "Accept the war": Connell, op. cit., p. 180. "The inspiring strains": ibid., p. 183.

EPILOGUE: YOU AND YOUR WHOLE COMMAND WILL BE KILLED

"It is for you to say": Berthrong, *Southern Cheyennes,* p. 333. "You and your whole command": ibid., p. 337.

Bibliography

Abbott, C. *Colorado: A History of the Centennial State.* Boulder: Colorado Associated University Press, 1976.

Ashley, S. R. Reminiscences of Colorado in the Early 'Sixties. *The Colorado Magazine*, November 1936, pp. 219–230.

Bent, G. Forty Years with the Cheyennes. *The Frontier: A Magazine of the West,* October 1905–March 1906 [6 parts].

Berthrong, D. J. *The Southern Cheyennes.* Norman: University of Oklahoma Press, 1963.

Brown, D. *The Galvanized Yankees.* Springfield: University of Illinois Press, 1963.

Brown, D. *Bury My Heart at Wounded Knee: An Indian History of the American West.* New York: Holt, Rinehart & Winston, 1970.

Burkey, E. R. The Site of the Murder of the Hungate Family by Indians in 1864. *The Colorado Magazine,* July 1935, pp. 139–142.

Carey, R. G. The Puzzle of Sand Creek. *The Colorado Magazine,* 1964, 41(4), 279–298.

Catton, B. *The Army of the Potomac: Glory Road.* Garden City, New York: Doubleday, 1952.

Chivington, J. M. The First Colorado Regiment. Manuscript Collection, State Historical Society of Colorado, Denver, October 18, 1884.

Chivington, J. M. The Pet Lambs. *Denver Republican,* April 20, 1890–May 18, 1890 [5 parts].

Conard, H. L. *Uncle Dick Wootton: The Pioneer Frontiersman of the Rocky Mountain Region.* Chicago: R. R. Donnelley & Sons.

Congressional Globe, 38th Congress, 2nd Session. Washington, D.C.: Congressional Globe Office, 1865.

Connell, E. S. *Son of the Morning Star: Custer and the Little Bighorn.* San Francisco: North Point Press, 1984.

Craig, R. S. *The Fighting Parson: The Biography of Colonel John M. Chivington.* Los Angeles: Westernlore Press, 1959.

Dunn, J. P., Jr. *Massacres of the Mountains.* New York: Archer House, 1958.

Edmunds, R. D., Ed. *American Indian Leaders: Studies in Diversity.* Lincoln: University of Nebraska Press, 1980.

Ellis, E. Colorado's First Fight for Statehood, 1865–1868. *The Colorado Magazine,* January 1931, pp. 24–30.

Gardiner, D. *The Great Betrayal.* Garden City, New York: Doubleday, 1949.

Grinnell, G. B. *The Fighting Cheyennes.* New York: Scribner, 1915.

Grinnell, G. B. *The Cheyenne Indians: The History and Ways of Life.* New Haven: Yale University Press, 1923 [reprint, University of Nebraska Press, 1972, 2 vols.].

Grinnell, G. B. *Pawnee, Blackfoot and Cheyenne.* New York: Scribner, 1961.

Hafen, L. R., Ed. *Colorado and Its People.* New York: Lewis Historical Publishing Co., 1948 [vol. I].

Hall, F. *History of the State of Colorado.* Chicago: Blakely Printing Co., 1889 [vol. I].

Harvey, J. R. Pioneer Experiences in Colorado: Interview with Elizabeth J. Tallman. *The Colorado Magazine,* July 1936, pp. 144–149.

Hill, A. P. *Tales of the Colorado Pioneers.* Denver: Pierson & Gardner, 1884.

Hill, A. P. *Colorado Pioneers in Picture and Story.* Denver, 1915.

Hoig, S. *The Sand Creek Massacre.* Norman: University of Oklahoma Press, 1961.

Hollister, O. J. *Boldly They Rode: A History of the First Colorado Regiment of Volunteers.* Lakewood, Colorado: Golden Press [originally published as "A History of the First Regiment of Colorado Volunteers," 1863].

Howbert, I. *Memories of a Lifetime in the Pikes Peak Region.* New York: Putnam, 1925.

Hudnall, M. P. Early History of Bent County. *The Colorado Magazine,* November 1945, pp. 233–247.

Jackson, H. H. *A Century of Dishonor.* New York: Harper and Row, 1965.

Lavender, D. *Bent's Fort.* Garden City, New York: Doubleday, 1954.

Lecompte, J. Sand Creek. *The Colorado Magazine,* 1964, 41 (4), 315–335.

Longstreet, S. *War Cries on Horseback: The Story of the Indian Wars of the Great Plains.* Garden City, New York: Doubleday, 1970.

MacMechen, E. C. *Life of Governor Evans, Second Territorial Governor of Colorado.* Denver: Wahlgreen Publishing Co., 1924.

Marquis, T. B. *Wooden Leg: A Warrior Who Fought Custer.* Lincoln: University of Nebraska Press, 1931.

Marshall, S. L. A. *Crimsoned Prairie: The Indian Wars.* New York: Scribner, 1972.

Miles, N. A. The Indian Problem. *North American Review*, March 1879, pp. 304–313.

Moore, J. H. *The Cheyenne Nation: A Social and Demographic History.* Lincoln: University of Nebraska Press, 1987.

Mumey, N. *History of the Early Settlements of Denver, 1859–1860.* Glendale, California: Arthur H. Clark Co., 1942.

Mumey, N. John Milton Chivington, the Misunderstood Man. [Denver Posse of Westerners] *Roundup*, November 1956, pp. 5–15.

Nankivell, J. H. *History of the Military Organizations of the State of Colorado, 1860–1935.* Denver: W. H. Kistler Stationery Co., 1935.

Noel, T. J. *The City and the Saloon: Denver, 1858–1916.* Lincoln: University of Nebraska Press, 1982.

Perkin, R. R. *The First Hundred Years: An Informal History of Denver and the* Rocky Mountain News. Garden City, New York: Doubleday, 1959.

Perrigo, L. I. Major Hal Sayr's Diary of the Sand Creek Campaign. *The Colorado Magazine*, March 1938, pp. 41–57.

Prentice, C. A. Captain Silas S. Soule, a Pioneer Martyr. *The Colorado Magazine*, November 1935, pp. 224–228.

Robbins, C. C. Texas and New Mexico Battle over Remains of Fallen Confederate Soldiers. *The New York Times*, November 29, 1987.

Rocky Mountain News [various issues].

Sanford, A. B. The "Big Flood" in Cherry Creek, 1864. *The Colorado Magazine*, May 1927, pp. 100–105.

Sanford, A. B., Ed. Life at Camp Weld and Fort Lyon in 1861–62: An Extract from the Diary of Mrs. Byron N. Sanford. *The Colorado Magazine*, July 1930, pp. 132–139.

Shaw, L. *True History of Some of the Pioneers of Colorado.* Hotchkiss, Colorado, 1909.

Shinn, C. H. *Mining Camps: A Study in American Frontier Government.* New York, 1884.

Sievers, M. A. Sands of Sand Creek Historiography. *The Colorado Magazine*, 1972, 49(2), 116–142.

Smiley, J. C. *History of Denver.* Denver, 1901.

Smiley, J. C. *Semi-Centennial History of the State of Colorado.* Chicago: Lewis Publishing Co. [2 vols.].

Smith, R. A. *Moon of Popping Trees.* Lincoln: University of Nebraska Press, 1975.

Speer, J. Report to George A. Martin of Interview with Mrs. John M. Chivington. John M. Chivington Miscellaneous Papers, Manuscript Division, Kansas State Historical Society, Topeka, March 11, 1902.

Stanley, H. M. *My Early Travels and Adventures in America.* Lincoln: University of Nebraska Press, 1982 [originally published, 1895].

Straight, M. *A Very Small Remnant.* New York: Alfred A. Knopf, 1963.

Tebbel, J., & Jennison, K. *The American Indian Wars.* New York: Harper and Row, 1960.

Thayer, W. *Marvels of the New West*. Norwich, Connecticut: Henry Bill Publishing Co., 1888.

Turner, F. J. *The Significance of the Frontier in American History*. New York: Holt, 1947.

U.S. Congress. *Massacre of Cheyenne Indians*. Report of the Joint Committee on the Conduct of the War, 38th Congress, 2nd Session [vol. 4, no. 142, part 3]. Washington, D.C.: Government Printing Office, 1865 [includes Appendix: *The Chivington Massacre*].

U.S. Congress. *Sand Creek Massacre*. Report of the Secretary of War, 39th Congress, 2nd Session [Senate Executive Document 26]. Washington, D.C.: Government Printing Office, 1867.

U.S. Congress. *Condition of the Indian Tribes*. Report of the Joint Special Committee, 39th Congress, 2nd Session [no. 156]. Washington, D.C.: Government Printing Office, 1867.

U.S. War Department. *The War of the Rebellion: A Compilation of the Official Records of the Union and Confederate Armies* [cited in Chapter Notes as *Rebellion Records*]. Washington, D.C.: Government Printing Office, 1880–1901 [series I, vols. 22, 34, 41, and 48].

Unrau, W. E. A Prelude to War. *The Colorado Magazine*, 1964, 41(4), 299–313.

Utley, R. M. *Frontiersmen in Blue: The United States Army and the Indian, 1848–1865*. New York: Macmillan, 1967.

Ware, E. F. *The Indian War of 1864*. New York: St. Martin's, 1960 [originally published, Crane & Co., Topeka, 1911].

Werstein, I. *Massacre at Sand Creek*. New York: Scribner, 1963.

Young, B., and Young, J. *Pikes Peak or Bust: The Story of the Colorado Settlement*. New York: Julian Messner, 1970.

Index

Abolitionist movement, 45–46,
    48–49, 168
Adams, James, 170
Adams, Margaret, 195
Agents for Indian affairs, *see* Indian
    agents
Albuquerque, 53
American Fur Company, 18
Andrews, Colonel, 190
Annuity payments, 23, 26, 28, 104,
    184, 185, 196–197, 199, 200
Anthony, Scott J., 67, 116–119, 122,
    123, 126–132, 134, 135, 137,
    140, 141, 150, 153, 158–160,
    163–165, 169, 173, 178, 181,
    182
Antobe, Charley, 112
Apache, 65, 88, 95, 194, 196, 205
Apache Canyon, 56
Arapaho, 8, 21–23, 26–28, 33, 39,
    42, 43, 51, 61–68, 76, 77, 81,
    84, 85, 88, 90, 95, 96, 99, 101,
    103–105, 112–116, 118, 122,
    129, 130, 133, 134, 143, 144,
    146, 150, 152, 180, 184, 185,
    194, 196, 199–202, 205, 207

Arkansas River, 19, 26, 39, 66, 68,
    77, 84, 88, 93, 115, 120, 122,
    125, 127, 143, 144, 152, 154,
    158, 177, 183, 186, 193, 198
Arrows, 17, 200
Ashley, Susan Riley, 43
Astor, John Jacob, 18
Auraria, 32, 33, 35
    See also Denver

Bannock, 120
Beckwourth, Jim (Medicine Calf),
    126, 133, 146–147, 169
Bennett, H. P., 67–68
Bent, Charles, 64, 66, 72
Bent, George, 75, 87, 98, 137,
    141–142, 151, 194, 199
Bent, Robert, 133, 143
Bent, William, 18–19, 22, 26, 27,
    64, 83, 95, 133, 183–185
Bent's Fort, 18, 26, 118, 151
Benteen, Frederick, 191, 204
Black Hills, 24
Black Kettle, 4, 51, 64, 76, 77,
    95–96, 106, 113–115, 117–120,
    122–123, 128, 130–135, 139,

Black Kettle (*cont.*)
  141, 146, 150, 152, 157,
  161–163, 169, 180–182,
  185–187, 199–201, 203, 205
  spokesman at peace councils, 28,
    98–104, 109–111, 183–184,
    192–194, 196, 197
Bloodless/Bloody Third, *see* Third
  Colorado Volunteer Regiment
Bluff Creek council, 183–184
Boone's ranch, 120, 121, 125
Boston *Journal,* 36, 38
Box Elder Creek, 80
Brown, John, 168
Browne, S. E., 92
Brulé Sioux, 22, 62, 80
Buffalo herds, 12, 20, 21, 27, 28, 67,
    68, 198
Bull Bear, 65, 100–101, 113, 199,
    200
Burdsal, Caleb, 173
Bureau of Indian Affairs, 63, 179, 186
  See also Commissioners of Indian
    Affairs; Indian agents;
    Superintendents of Indian Affairs
Byers, William, 5–7, 32–34, 38, 40,
    41, 44, 61–63, 73, 78, 85, 87,
    88, 92, 106, 137, 143–145, 147,
    151, 167, 176, 177

Camp Weld, 52, 79
Camp Weld council, 109–115, 122,
    161, 169, 179, 180, 203
Canadian River, 19
Canby, Edward R. S., 54, 55, 57
Cannon, James, 130, 169, 172, 175
Captives, Cheyenne, 143, 146, 186,
    188
  treatment of, 15–16
  white, 95–96, 100–105, 109
Carleton, James, 129
Carson, Kit, 71, 163, 166, 168, 183
Cavalry charge, 25–26
Cavalry regiments, 25, 187, 195,
    201–208

Cavalry regiments (*cont.*)
  See also Volunteer regiments
Cedar Canyon, 74–75, 79
Cherry Creek, 21, 31–35, 40, 41, 78
Cheyenne, 1–9, 39, 42, 43, 51,
    71–77, 79–85, 88, 90, 94–106,
    109–120, 122, 128–131, 133,
    134, 144–146, 150, 152, 157,
    163, 174, 180, 183–187,
    191–194, 199–203, 205
  beliefs and rituals, 1, 9, 11–13, 15,
    21, 25–26, 29, 64, 109, 146,
    188–189, 196, 207–208
  history, 11–29
  peaceful intentions of, 61–66, 68,
    94–96, 99–102, 109–118
  warriors, 13–16
Cheyenne Dog Soldiers, 14, 22, 72,
    100, 146, 147, 184, 185, 187,
    199, 201, 207
Cheyenne Star, 205
Chivington, John Milton, 3–8,
    68–69, 72–75, 79–81, 83, 86,
    88–94, 105, 106, 109, 113, 114,
    116, 119–123, 125–137,
    139–141, 143–145, 147–151,
    153, 154, 157–164, 166–184,
    195, 201, 203
  action against Confederates, 52–58
  death, 178
  early years, 45–50
  history's judgment of, 166,
    178–182
  political ambitions, 63, 73, 90,
    92–93, 181
Chivington, Martha Rollason, 47, 48,
    176
Cholera epidemic, 19–20
Cimarron River, 19, 199
Cincinnati *Times,* 36
Civil War, 45–46, 50–51, 53–57,
    120–121, 186
  See also Confederate Army
Clark, Watson, 123, 128, 134, 136,
    140, 150

Clark, William, 23
Colley, D. D., 158–159
Colley, Samuel G., 66, 68–69,
    83–85, 95, 96, 104, 113, 123,
    132, 148, 150, 158–161, 172,
    173, 179, 180, 185
Colorado Territory, 45
  statehood for, 63, 65, 73, 87, 90,
    92–93, 121
Colorado Volunteers, *see* Volunteer
    regiments
Colt revolvers, 197
Comanche, 62, 64, 65, 84, 88, 95,
    112, 115, 194, 196, 199
Combs, James, 125–126
Commissioners of Indian Affairs, 22,
    27, 66–68, 88, 113, 114, 157,
    185, 192, 200
Concord stagecoaches, 41
Conestoga wagons, 21, 42
Confederate Army, 3, 6, 45, 51,
    53–57, 64, 68, 74, 89, 91, 111
Connor, Patrick Edward, 120–121
Coronado, Francisco Vásquez, 16
Cossitt, C. M., 130, 132, 169
Councils, 64–65, 192
  Bluff Creek, 183–184
  Camp Weld, 109–115, 122, 161,
    169, 179, 180, 203
  Fort Cobb, 203
  Fort Cottonwood, 80
  Fort Laramie, 22
  Fort Larned, 187–189
  Fort Wise, 27–28
  Horse Creek, 23
  Medicine Lodge Creek, 193–201
  Smoky Hill, 99–103
Counting coup, tradition of, 14–15,
    24
Cramer, Joseph, 100, 103, 109,
    131–132, 135, 173
Cree, T. G., 91, 145, 173
Crow, 126
Curtis, Samuel R., 4, 7, 68, 69, 73,
    77, 79, 80, 82, 83, 86, 88, 89,

Curtis, Samuel R. (*cont.*)
    91–93, 106, 115–119, 122, 127,
    129–131, 143, 144, 148–150,
    154, 159, 160, 164, 180, 181
Custer, George Armstrong, 21, 187,
    189–192, 203–207

Davis, Jefferson, 24
de Soto, Hernando, 16
Decatur, Stephen, 173
Delaware, 25, 187, 191
Denver, 21, 32–44
  fire, 64
  flood, 78–79
  food shortages, 64, 79, 87–89, 153
  martial law, 82, 86, 155
  twenty-fifth anniversary, 176
Denver council, *see* Camp Weld
    council
Diseases, 19–20, 67
Dodge, Granville, 154
Dog Soldiers, 14, 22, 72, 100, 146,
    147, 184, 185, 187, 199, 201,
    207
Dole, H. P., 66
Doolittle, James R., 148
Douglas, Stephen A., 46
Downing, Jacob, 74–75, 79, 102
Dunn, Clark, 72–73, 102

Eayre, George S., 72, 74–76, 102,
    157
Elbert, Samuel H., 153, 154
Elliott, Joel, 204
Evans, John, 8, 62–69, 73, 79–85,
    87–89, 92, 93, 95, 102,
    104–106, 109–114, 121–122,
    129, 132, 137, 149, 153, 165,
    178–180, 203
  Sand Creek testimony, 161–162
Evans proclamation of refuge, 83–84,
    95–96, 102, 109, 111, 114

Farming, Indian attitudes toward,
    28–29, 59, 63, 186, 198

First Colorado Volunteer Regiment,
    52–58, 61, 63, 74, 79, 86, 90,
    94, 125, 129, 132, 134, 144,
    170, 173
Food shortages, 64, 79, 87–89, 153,
    200
Forest, Mountain Charley, 38
Fort Cobb, 202, 203, 207
Fort Cottonwood, 80
Fort Dodge, 199, 201
Fort Kearny, 23–25, 51
Fort Laramie, 22, 51, 73, 84
Fort Larned, 50, 64, 66, 67, 75, 76,
    83, 84, 101, 194, 195, 199
Fort Larned council, 187–189, 192
Fort Leavenworth, 4, 7, 53, 93, 154
Fort Lyon, 3, 6–8, 64, 66–68, 80,
    83, 91, 94, 96, 98, 100–102,
    104, 109, 111, 113–120, 122,
    125–127, 132, 143, 148–150,
    159, 173, 179, 181
    description, 93–94
Fort Rankin, 147, 151, 152
Fort Ridgely, 60
Fort Riley, 115, 116, 122
Fort Sumter, 45
Fort Union, 53–55, 57
Fort Wise, 51
Fort Wise Treaty, 27–28, 63, 65, 68
Forts, defenses against Indians, 85–86,
    116, 127–128, 150–151,
    192–193
Forty-niners, 21
    See also Gold
Freight trains, see Wagon trains
Frontier justice, 38

Gambling, 36, 37, 40, 49, 50
Gannt, John, 19
"Garry Owen," 204–205
Gatling guns, 195
Gerry, Elbridge, 65, 79, 88, 89
Gilpin, William, 52
Gilpin treasury drafts, 52, 74

Gilpin's "pet lambs," 52
    See also First Colorado Volunteer
        Regiment
Glorietta Pass, 56–57, 73, 93, 94,
    135, 167, 168, 181
Gold, quest for, 20–21, 23, 26, 27,
    31–37, 40, 45, 51, 53
Goldrick, O. J., 78
Government agents for Indian affairs,
    see Indian agents
Grant, Ulysses S., 187, 193
Gray, Issa, 54
Gray Beard, 194–195
Greeley, Horace, 34–38
Greenwood, A. B., 27–28, 134
Gregory Gulch, 36
Grinnell, George Bird, 11
Guerrier, Edmond, 95, 98, 185, 188,
    194

Hall, Benjamin, 148
Hall, Frank, 180–182
Halleck, Henry H., 7, 148, 149
Hamilton, Louis, 204
Hancock, Winfield Scott, 186–192,
    195, 201
Hardin, G. H., 103
Harney, William S., 163, 183,
    194–196
Harpers Ferry, 168
Hazen, William B., 203
Heap of Whips, 33
Henderson, Senator, 196, 198
Henning, B. S., 115–117, 129
Hickock, James Butler "Wild Bill,"
    187
Hitchins, H. H., 171
Horse Creek Treaty, 23, 24, 26–27
Horses, Indian attitudes toward,
    16–17, 24, 43–44, 67, 76
Howbert, Irving, 178–179
Howitzers, 72, 76, 97, 98, 103, 151
Hundred dazers, see Third Colorado
    Volunteer Regiment

Hungate family, 80–81, 106, 112, 134, 137, 147
Hunt, A. C., 162

Indian agents, 22, 24, 26, 66–69, 80, 83–85, 95, 104, 109, 113, 132, 148, 159, 160, 172, 179, 185, 201
Indian chiefs, 22, 23, 66
  peace versus war chiefs, 51, 77, 101, 146–147, 152, 184–187, 201
  Indian expeditions by United States forces, 24–26, 72–76, 102, 119, 125–139, 186–191, 201–204
  Indian raids, on Indians, 13–16, 23, 24, 51, 199–200
  on white settlements, 24, 59–62, 71–74, 76, 77, 80–81, 85–89, 146–147, 150–153, 184–187, 191–193, 200, 201
Indian reservations, 23, 26–28, 64, 184, 198, 199
Indian scouts, 25, 133, 187, 191, 203, 205
Indians, civilian versus military control over, 104, 111–114, 186
  extermination policy toward, 2, 63, 67, 73–75, 85, 90, 94, 104–107, 115, 119–121, 134, 158, 160, 162, 179, 180, 182, 186, 193, 202–203
  favorable attitudes toward, 18–19, 22, 27, 42–44, 67, 68, 77, 97–98, 147–148, 151, 179, 193
Infantry regiments, 50, 201
  See also Volunteer regiments
Irwin and Jackman & Co., 71

Jacobs, Edward A., 167
Johnson, Andrew, 165, 188
Jones, Jack (William McGaa), 82–83
Julesburg, 147, 151–153

Kansas City, 31, 41
Kaw, 199, 200
Kerber, Lieutenant, 54
Ketchum, H. T., 67
Kiowa, 19, 62, 64–66, 76, 77, 84, 95, 112, 115, 129, 194, 196, 199, 205
Knock Knee, 4
Koom-la-Manche, 205

Larimer, William, 32, 41
Lauderback, David, 123, 128, 134, 136, 140–141, 150, 169
Lawrence, 31
Lean Bear, 75–76, 79, 81, 100, 102, 113
Leavenworth, 31, 33
Leavenworth, Jesse, 157, 183, 192, 196
Lee, Robert E., 168
Left Hand, 76, 101–104, 126, 128, 130, 135, 161, 181
Leg-in-the-Water, 9, 146
Lewis, Meriwether, 23
Lincoln, Abraham, 45, 46, 58, 60, 62, 76, 111, 135
Little Arkansas Treaty, 184–186, 193
Little Big Horn, 21, 208
Little Crow, 59–61
Little Old Man, 19
Little Raven, 28, 32, 66, 101, 143, 146, 152, 184, 194, 198, 199, 203
Little Robe, 4, 146

Mail service, 41, 86, 87, 127
Manifest destiny, 22, 39
Mankato, 60
Martial law, 82, 86, 155
Maynard, Lieutenant, 132
McCannon, Captain, 134
McGaa, William (Jack Jones), 82–83
McIntyre, Robert, 178
McKenny, T. I., 77

Medals, presidential, 76, 111, 135, 188
Medicine Arrows, 185, 199, 200, 207–208
Medicine Calf (Jim Beckwourth), 126, 133, 146–147, 169
Medicine Lodge Creek Treaty, 193–201
Merrill, Moses, 19
Meyer, Lipman, 172, 175
Military expeditions against Indians, 24–26, 72–76, 102, 119, 125–139, 186–191, 201–204
Militia, see Volunteer regiments
Miller, Robert, 26
Min-im-mie, 95, 97
Minnesota uprising (Sioux), 59–62, 77, 83
Minton, W. P., 127, 130, 132, 169
Missouri River, 33–35, 61, 153, 202
Mitchell, Mister (Superintendent of Indian Affairs), 23
Mitchell, William (United States Army), 83
Month of the Freezing Moon, 1, 9, 182, 203
Moonlight, Thomas, 154–155, 167
Murphy, Mister, 194, 195, 199–201

Neva, 112, 113
New Ulm, 60
New York Morning News, 22
New York Tribune, 8, 34, 35
North, Robert, 65–66, 82, 83

Oglala Sioux, 22, 62, 80
Old Yellow Wolf, 17
Omaha, 31, 40, 41
One-Eye, 95–101, 119, 128, 130, 139, 157, 169, 178, 181
Oregon Trail, 20
Osage, 64, 199, 203, 205
O'Sullivan, John L., 22
Overland Trail, 120, 153, 154

Parmeter, Captain, 76, 101, 132
Pawnee, 16, 23, 24
Peace chiefs, see Indian chiefs
Peace pipe, 109
Philbrook, Sergeant, 54
Phillips, Charles, 100, 103
Pierce, George, 136
Pikes Peak, 33, 34
Pioneer spirit, 39
Pipe ceremonies, 9, 64, 109, 146, 188–189, 207–208
Platte River, 20, 24, 31, 32, 39, 72, 74, 77, 79, 80, 85–88, 119, 144, 147, 152, 158, 177, 184–186, 192, 193, 198
Powder River, 152
Price, George F., 172
Proclamation of refuge, 83–84, 95–96, 102, 109, 111, 114
Prowers, John Wesley, 118–119, 169
Prowers, Mary, 119, 126, 139, 178
Pueblo, 18

Railroad, transcontinental, 186, 188, 189, 192, 193
Red River, 198, 199
Refuge, proclamation of, 83–84, 95–96, 102, 109, 111, 114
Regular army, see United States Army
Remington, Frederic, 25
Reparations, 184, 186
Republican Party, 176
Reynolds, Jim, 91–92
Richardson, Albert, 36, 38
Richmond, Harry, 139
Ripley, Mister, 72
Robbins, S. M., 158
Rocky Mountain News, 5–7, 32, 40, 41, 44, 62, 78, 85, 87, 88, 92, 106, 144–148, 151–152, 167, 171, 177, 182
Rollason, Martha, see Martha Rollason Chivington

Roman Nose, 66, 112, 189, 194–195, 201
Roper, Laura, 103, 104
Rumors of Indian raids, 64–68, 81–83, 88–90
Russell, William Green, 31

Salt Lake City, 153
Sanborn, John B., 183, 184, 195–196
Sand Creek camp, 2, 23, 84, 118–119, 127–130
    protected by American flag, 5, 114, 121–122, 134, 148, 149, 161, 166, 169, 172, 203
    white scalp allegedly found at, 4, 6, 144, 145, 160, 173
Sand Creek massacre, 132–142
    analysis of, 178–182
    atrocities, 1, 2, 137–139, 150, 157–158, 160, 162, 164–167, 169–170, 181–182
    captives taken, 143, 146, 186, 188
    casualty figures, 4–5, 139, 144, 150, 158, 163, 173
    Congressional investigations, 1–8, 147, 148, 157–166
    military investigations, 7–8, 137–139, 148–150, 166–174
    opposition to, 130–132, 159–160, 169
    survivors, 2–3, 141–142, 184, 186
Sanford, Mrs. Byron, 79, 93–94
Sante Fe, 53, 55
Santa Fe Trail, 20, 153, 185
Santanta, 196
Santee Sioux, 59–61
Sayr, Hal, 125
Scalping, 2, 7, 15, 16, 24, 43, 85, 146, 192, 198
Scalps at Sand Creek camp, 4, 6, 144, 145, 160, 173
Scouts, 25, 133, 187, 191, 203, 205
Second Colorado Volunteer Regiment, 61, 88, 89, 157

Settlements, 20–22, 26, 33, 42–44, 77, 86–88, 151–152, 184, 198, 200
Seward, William H., 165
Sheridan, Philip, 202, 203, 205, 207
Sherman, William Tecumseh, 186–187, 193, 201–203
Shook, Denton, 61, 62
Shook, Peter, 61, 62
Shoshone, 62, 120
Shoup, George L., 89, 109, 121, 132, 133
Sibley, Henry H., 53–57
Sioux, 6, 9, 14, 22, 23, 59–62, 64–66, 68, 80, 84, 85, 95, 96, 110, 112, 113, 123, 152, 189, 193, 200
Sitting Bull, 29
Slavery, 45–46, 48–49, 168
Slough, John, 52, 54–57, 167
Smith, Jack, 134, 140–141
Smith, John, 66, 74, 99–102, 109, 112, 113, 115, 118, 123, 128, 130, 134, 136, 139–141, 143, 150, 157–158, 164, 172, 173, 180, 185
Smoky Hill camp, 3, 6, 9, 96, 128, 130–131, 141–143, 146, 147, 160
Smoky Hill council, 98–104, 107, 109, 115, 122, 169, 201
Smoky Hill River, 21, 35, 66, 184, 185, 191, 192, 198
Snyder, Naman, 170
Soldier societies (Cheyenne), 14, 22, 72, 100, 146, 147, 184, 185, 187, 199, 201, 207
Soule, Silas S., 100, 109, 127, 130–132, 135, 136, 144, 168–172, 175, 176
    assassination of, 169
Squiers, Charles, 170, 175
St. Joseph, 20
St. Louis, 18, 31

St. Louis Missouri-Democrat, 187
St. Paul, 60
Stagecoach routes, 21, 24, 40–42, 66,
    76, 120, 125, 127, 151, 153,
    184, 186, 191–193, 201
Stanley, Henry Morton, 187, 189,
    192
Stanton, Edwin M., 58, 66, 82, 88,
    89, 120, 193
Statehood for Colorado, 63, 65, 73,
    87, 90, 92–93, 121
Stilwell, George H., 167
Stuart, J. E. B., 26
Sully, Alfred, 201
Sumner, Edwin "Bull," 24–26
Superintendents of Indian Affairs, 23,
    63, 149, 179, 183, 192, 194,
    200
Sweet Medicine legend, 11–13,
    16–17, 19–21, 27, 29, 42
Sweetwater River, 207

Talbot, Presley, 173
Tall Bull, 189, 194
Tallman, Elizabeth, 7
Tappan, Samuel F., 52, 55, 57, 167,
    169–172, 186, 195, 202
Taylor, Mister, 200
Tecumseh, 186
Telegraph lines, 72, 152, 153
Teller, Henry, 92
Terry, Alfred, 194–196
Third Colorado Volunteer Regiment,
    6, 89–90, 93, 105–107, 111,
    119–121, 123, 125, 129,
    144–146, 154, 162, 173, 179,
    180
  at Sand Creek, 132–141
Traders, 17–20, 67, 123, 128,
    158–159
Treaty councils, *see* Councils
Treaty of Fort Wise, 27–28, 63, 65,
    68
Treaty of Horse Creek, 23, 24, 26–27

Treaty of the Little Arkansas,
    184–186, 193
Treaty of Medicine Lodge Creek,
    192–201
Turner, Frederick Jackson, 39
Twiss, Thomas, 24

Underground railroad, 168
Union Administration Party, 92
Union Pacific railroad line, 188, 192
United States Army, 50–51, 77
  First Cavalry, 25
  Second Dragoons, 25
  Second Infantry, 50
  Third Infantry, 201
  Seventh Cavalry, 187, 195,
      201–208
  See also Indian expeditions;
      Volunteer regiments
United States Mint, 40, 81
Ute, 43, 51, 62, 90

Victory parades, 6, 58, 145, 205
Villard, Henry, 36
Volunteer regiments, 51–53, 63–64,
    81, 82, 86–90, 106, 154–155
  First Colorado, 52–58, 61, 63, 74,
      79, 86, 90, 94, 125, 129, 132,
      134, 144, 170, 173
  Second Colorado, 61, 88, 89, 157
  Third Colorado, 6, 89–90, 93,
      105–107, 111, 119–121, 123,
      125, 129, 132–141, 144–146,
      154, 162, 173, 179, 180
Vorse, Newt, 178

Wade, Benjamin "Honest Ben," 164
Wagon trains, 18, 20–22, 66, 79, 85,
    89, 153, 177, 184, 192, 198,
    201
Wallen, H. D., 77
Walnut Creek, 76, 85, 177
War chiefs, *see* Indian chiefs

War Department, 24, 58, 66, 68, 82,
   87–89, 120, 153, 193
War pipe, 9, 64, 146
Ware, Eugene, 152
Warriors, 13–16
   See also Dog Soldiers
Washakie, 29
Washita River, 203, 205, 208
Whiskey, effects on Indians, 19, 44,
   51, 67, 68, 74, 152, 199
White Antelope, 4, 28, 111–112, 130,
   135, 146, 152, 157, 162, 181,
   200

Whitely, Simeon, 109
Wilson, Luther, 132, 134, 136
Wolf Chief, 75, 76
Wooden Leg, 21
Wootton, Richens Lacy "Uncle Dick,"
   16, 21, 34, 91
Wynkoop, Edward, 94–107,
   111–119, 126, 129–131,
   149–151, 158, 159, 173,
   179–181, 185–190, 192, 194,
   199–201
   Smoky Hill mission, 98–107, 109,
   115, 122–123, 169, 201